HAMILTON PARK

CREATING
THE NORTH AMERICAN
LANDSCAPE

Gregory Conniff, Bonnie Loyd,
Edward K. Muller, David Schuyler
Consulting Editors

George F. Thompson
Series Founder and Director

Published in cooperation
with the Center for American Places,
Harrisonburg, Virginia

HAMILTON PARK

*A Planned
Black Community
in Dallas*

William H. Wilson

The Johns Hopkins University Press
Baltimore and London

For my daughters, Kate and Meg

PENROSE MEMORIAL LIBRARY
WHITMAN COLLEGE
WALLA WALLA, WASHINGTON 99362

© 1998 The Johns Hopkins University Press
All rights reserved. First edition
Printed in the United States of America
on acid-free paper
9 8 7 6 5 4 3 2 1
The Johns Hopkins University Press
2715 North Charles Street
Baltimore, Maryland 21218-4319
The Johns Hopkins Press Ltd., London

Library of Congress Cataloging-in-Publication Data
will be found at the end of this book.
A catalog record for this book is available
from the British Library.

ISBN 0-8018-5766-X

CONTENTS

Preface and Acknowledgments   vii

1   Community and the History of Hamilton Park   1
2   Searching for a Black Subdivision   10
3   Organizing for Hamilton Park   33
4   A Transition in White and Black   54
5   The Early Community and Beyond   67
6   Organizing in Hamilton Park   92
7   School and Community   118
8   The School Transformed   138
9   Another Transition and the Buyout   162
10 A Mature Community and Its Meaning   186

Appendix A: The City Directories
and the Control Neighborhood   201

Appendix B: Census and Tax Information   205

Appendix C: The Occupational Scale   207

Appendix D: The Interviews   210

List of Abbreviations   213

Notes   215

Index   249

Illustrations follow p. 66.

PREFACE AND ACKNOWLEDGMENTS

This book began as an attempt to understand how Hamilton Park, an African-American community in Dallas, Texas, came to be planned. Then it shifted to the problems of comprehending how a community is developed and maintained. The first residents moved into Hamilton Park in 1954 and from necessity began to create a community. At buildout some six years later Hamilton Park contained more than seven hundred houses, three churches, a primary and a high school, a public park, and a shopping center. In 1990 it retained its identity despite the cataclysm of physical change around it and the social transformations that had enveloped it.

Hamilton Park began life as a black community, and has remained—to use again the phrase so often employed—predominately African American. The fact of the community's ethnicity adds an important dimension to its development and existence, as comparisons with a nearby white subdivision of approximately the same socioeconomic standing will demonstrate.

Hamilton Park's residents were middle class in outlook and aspirations, which explains their devotion to one physical and intellectual expression of the community—its school. Community values surfaced in a different dimension during a mid-1980s proposal to purchase Hamilton Park for commercial redevelopment. Almost from the beginning, Hamilton Park's inhabitants formed community-based organizations dedicated to the subdivision's preservation and improvement, social life, enhanced educational opportunity, youth development, and spiritual enrichment.

The organization of the text reflects all the phases of the community's formation and growth. Chapter 1 places Hamilton Park in the context of Dallas history, urban history, African-American history, and the history of community; chapter 2 recreates the Dallas context of the search for a viable, sizeable black subdivision. Chapter 3 recounts the creation of Hamilton Park and chapter 4 moves from the dedication of the community through the founding organization's withdrawal from active involvement in its affairs. Chapter 5 recalls some of the life experiences of pioneer Hamilton Park dwellers, as well as the flavor of the subdivision's first years. Chapter 6 deals with community organizations, their concerns, and their effectiveness. Chapter 7 recounts the relationship between the community and its school and chapter 8 explores the legal, educational, and emotional issues surrounding the transformation of the Hamilton Park School. Chapter 9 concerns the changes in and around the community leading to its proposed purchase. The final chapter, chapter 10, considers the mature Hamilton Park at the end of the 1980s.

Because this study is a work of historical narrative and analysis, it is not overtly concerned with theories of urban politics and society, nor with those of community growth, structure, and activism. It is not a work of theory. It does, however, mirror theory in the unfolding of events, critically examined. It rests upon a variety of sources, such as documents, collections of letters and other papers, quantitative material extracted from city directories and censuses, the daily and weekly press, and extensive interviews. Its first fundamental conclusion is that Hamilton Park was a worthwhile if inadequate response to the serious problem of housing middle-income Dallas blacks. Its second is that establishing Hamilton Park allowed a remarkable community to flourish in a way that commands the attention of reflective students of urban communities.

Many people helped with the preparation of this study, although they share no responsibility for its result. Each interviewee contributed greatly to my understanding of Hamilton Park. All but two either left their interviews open to scholarly use or allowed me to use them with restrictions. Among Hamilton Park interviewees I am especially grateful to Doris Robertson, who endured two interviews, and Sadye Gee, Freddie M. Nance, Charles E. Smith, and Curtis J. Smith, all of whom submitted to at least one interview and provided me with indispensable personal papers for photocopying. Charles Smith and Le Verne Fields arranged for me to photocopy important minutes of the Hamilton Park Civic League. Arzell Ball, the superintendent of the Richardson Independent School District, gave me unrestricted access to the district's files, from which I learned much about the community and its school. Paul V. Harris, the executive vice-president of the Hoblitzelle Foundation, opened the foundation's papers related to Hamilton Park and provided for the photocopying, without charge, of any material that I selected. Attorney Reuben M. Ginsberg granted me access to his papers related to the Hamilton Park Buyout. Ronald D. Henderson, the senior pastor of the Hamilton Park United Methodist Church, allowed me to use archival material concerning the church and its community relations. Vincent L. Rohloff, a member of the Dallas Citizens' Interracial Association (DCIA), gave the surviving papers of the association to me for photocopying; he later donated the papers to the archives of the University of North Texas. All of the titles and descriptions of persons mentioned above are those that applied at the time these individuals assisted me. In addition, one person who wished to remain anonymous allowed me to use extensive papers concerning issues related to Hamilton Park on condition that the papers be cited as a confidential source.

The staff of the J. Eric Jonsson Library, the main building of the Dallas Public Library, and especially of its Texas and Dallas History and Archives Division, greatly assisted my work. The staffs of the Willis Library, University of North Texas, the National Archives in Washington, D.C., the Texas Department of Transportation, District 18, the Dallas city archivist, located in the Office of the City Secretary, the Office of the Clerk, United States District Court for the Northern Division of Texas, the Fort Worth branch of the National Archives and Records Administration, and the Dallas County Tax Assessor's Office also deserve my thanks. The staffs of NationsBank, a successor to the Republic National Bank, the Dallas Citizens' Council, the Dallas Black Chamber of Commerce, and the Fidelity Union Life Insurance Company searched for records related to Hamilton Park, without success.

Several colleagues helped in various ways. Three chairs of the Department of History, University of North Texas, William Kamman, Robert S. La Forte, and Richard M. Golden, were enthusiastic about the study and gave it assistance from time to time. La Forte arranged for two research assistants, Rebecca Durrer and Pamela S. Blanco, to whom I am grateful. Randolph B. Campbell and Richard G. Lowe shared their expertise about quantitative data with me. Campbell generously spent hours helping me with data-entry problems, then he organized the data using an SPSS software package. Ronald E. Marcello, the head of the Oral History Project at the University of North Texas, permitted me to interview under the auspices of his project, which transcribed most of the interview tapes. All but one of my interviews were conducted for the project. They are housed in the Oral History Collection of the university archives. Constance B. Hilliard read the manuscript and offered valuable suggestions for its improvement, as did Robert B. Fairbanks of the University of Texas at Arlington. Andrew Wiese of Barnard College of Columbia University encouraged me to view Hamilton Park in the context of African-American subdivision development.

The Faculty Research Committee of the University of North Texas awarded me three grants. Two of these were for partial summer salary, while another paid a transcriber at the Oral History Project. The university's Faculty Development Leave Committee awarded me a leave during the spring semester 1995, a leave that allowed me to advance the work on this book significantly.

Grateful acknowledgment is due Michael V. Hazel, the editor of *Legacies: A History Journal for Dallas and North Central Texas,* for allowing me to use, with revisions, "'This Negro Housing Matter': The Search for a Viable African-American Residential Subdivision in Dallas, 1945–1950," appearing in his journal's vol. 4, fall 1994 issue, as the basis for chapter 2; and Ron Tyler, the editor of the *Southwestern Historical Quarterly,* for permission to use, as the basis for chapter 8, a revised version of "Desegregation of the Hamilton Park School, 1955–1975," in vol. 90, July 1991, of his journal. Permission to use a few sentences and phrases from "Growing Up Black in East Texas: Some Twentieth Century Experiences," vol. 32, fall 1994, was granted by Archie P. McDonald, the editor of the *East Texas Historical Journal,* and I am grateful for his generosity. The G. B. Dealy Library, Dallas Historical Society, allowed the use of three photographs from the library's collection. That source, and other illustration sources, are included in the photo and map captions.

At the Johns Hopkins University Press I received indispensable help from Albert S. Broussard of Texas A&M University, the reader for the Press; George H. Thompson, president of the Center for American Places and my editor; Dennis Marshall, my copy editor; and Carol Zimmerman, my production editor.

Katharine L. Wilson, my wife, deserves a paragraph to herself. She has always supported my work. Her commitment to Hamilton Park, both as a community and an object of study, is as great as my own.

HAMILTON PARK

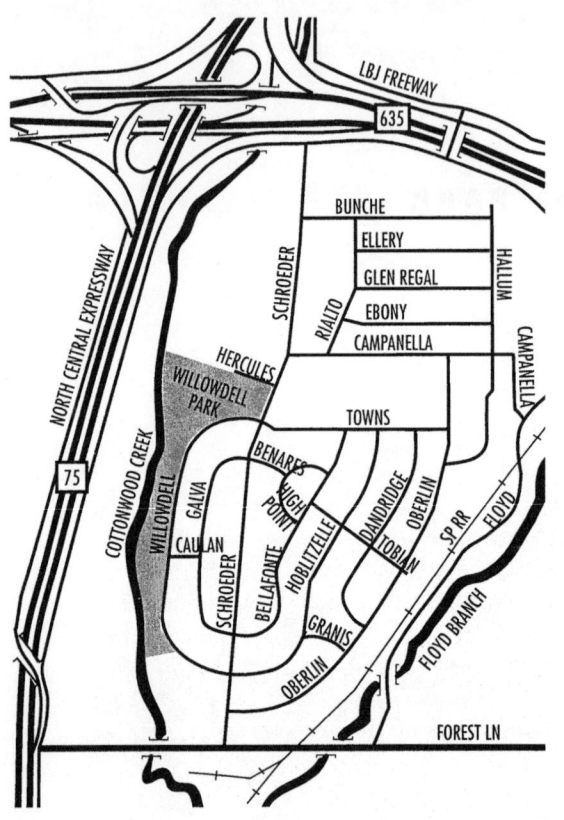

Map of Hamilton Park showing streets and immediate surroundings. Center for Instructional Services, University of North Texas.

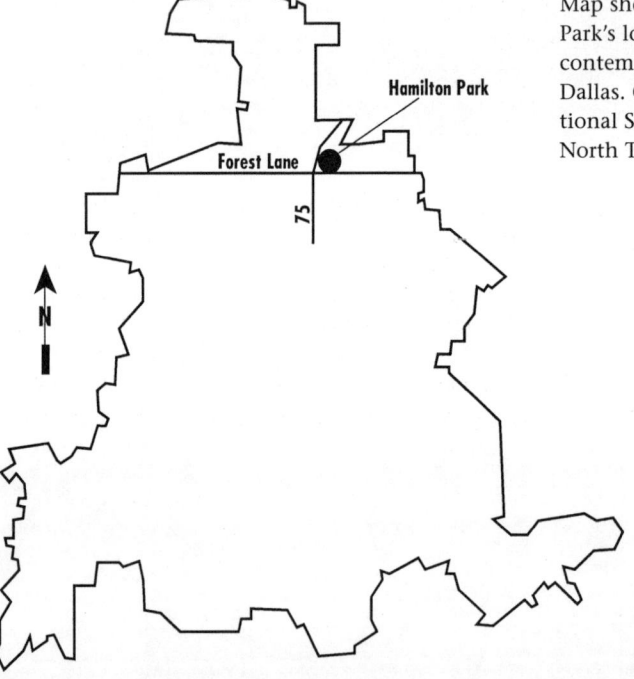

Map showing Hamilton Park's location within the contemporary boundaries of Dallas. Center for Instructional Services, University of North Texas.

1

COMMUNITY AND THE HISTORY OF HAMILTON PARK

Hamilton Park stands at the intersection of four paths of American history: the history of Dallas, urban history, African-American history, and the history of community. Each influenced it, each illuminated it, and each is refracted in Hamilton Park.

Two intertwined strands organize Dallas history: the rapid growth of a banking, commercial, and transportation center, combined with the remarkable degree of control over major city developments exercised from the mid-1930s through the 1950s by an elite group that included bankers, insurance company presidents, department store executives, and newspaper publishers. The word *elite* should not imply that its members withdrew from the rest of humankind to a rarified environment of paneled suites and perfumed drawing rooms. A hardworking, hard-driving, highly intelligent lot, their number included the banker Fred Florence, polished in manner and appearance, and banker Robert L. Thornton, a gruff, cigar-chomping man who sprinkled his speech with brash colloquialisms. Keenly concerned with advancing their own interests, they also nourished a vision of a prosperous, expanding Dallas offering urban amenities and contentment to a diverse population. These were the men who founded Hamilton Park.[1]

Urban historians place Hamilton Park in the formation of the "second ghetto"; that is, the new black settlements created during the movement away from the original African-American neighborhoods developed or expanded under the impact of the rural-to-urban migrations of the nineteenth and twentieth centuries. Following the lead of Arnold R. Hirsch's superb study of Chicago, the "second migration" is dated from the interwar period to about 1960. It involves three distinct but related issues: the development of public housing for blacks, the movement of blacks into formerly all-white neighborhoods, and new housing, often suburban or built within the city limits in the middle-class suburban style.[2]

The same historians, again following Hirsch, write little about the new African-American subdivisions, preferring to concentrate on the local conflicts over slum clearance, urban renewal, and the rehousing of the people displaced by clearance and renewal. There are reasons why this is so. The issues of public housing and residential racial succession are well known and well documented and therefore the avenues to their exploration are well marked. Beyond the abundance of records, urban historians study these issues because they involve conflict, violence, and drama, and lay bare all the public emotions of which humans are capable. They also involve relatively large numbers of people. But the focus on public housing and residential succession obscures an uncoordinated movement across the South to rehouse African Americans in new and superior, if segregated, subdivisions (see chapters 2, 3, and 4).[3]

These subdivisions were as different from the modest all-black or partly black towns springing up around major cities during the first half of the twentieth century as they were from the urban ghettos. The earlier African-American suburbs often struggled to achieve utilities or did without some of them. If located within a white suburb, they were treated as municipal stepchildren and relegated to the least topographically or aesthetically appealing areas. Some housed the domestic servants of nearby whites, but others were home to commuters, just as were the white suburbs. Still others, perhaps the majority, comprised a variety of jobholders employed in the suburb, in another suburb, or in the central city. However highly prized by their inhabitants, the earlier suburbs were vastly different from their white counterparts, with the latter's broad lawns, stately trees, and paved drives. The African-American bungalow subdivisions of the 1920s were the nearer ancestors of the postwar developments, but Hamilton Park itself drew no inspiration from them.[4]

The post World War II subdivisions were well organized, usually by large-scale builders who took responsibility for the entire development. They were planned for profit, just as was any other residential area. Other efforts, while they might allow a profit in one or another aspect of subdivision development, were, in some feature of their activity, nonprofit. In at least two instances, Hamilton Park being one, they were designed in part to slow the expansion of blacks into white neighborhoods, if not to thwart it altogether. By the time Hamilton Park was dedicated, however, the white elite had accepted residential succession in Dallas as a fact of life for working-class and lower-middle-class whites. The emphasis on Hamilton Park then shifted to its capacity to provide some African Americans with an opportunity to realize the American dream of homeownership in an ideal, suburbanlike setting.[5]

Historians of African America have recognized the existence of a black middle class, although they scarcely agree on its composition, its size, the chronology of its development, or its importance to American society. The starting point for contemporary comments on the black middle class is William J. Wilson's controversial *The Declining Significance of Race,* first published in 1978. Wilson's book is less important for its skillful use of historical materials than it is for generating an extended debate over some of its propositions; for example, Wilson's conviction that class is more important than race in "determining" the "life-chances" of blacks. Respecting the significant development of the black middle class, Wilson dates it from the 1950s and 1960s, arguing that before World War II, the black middle class was too minuscule to matter. The flaw in Wilson's definition of middle class is that he relies entirely on an economic, rather than a cultural, definition. As Alan L. Keys has demonstrated, there were many impoverished blacks who nevertheless believed in, and upheld in their daily lives, "American" middle-class values, including a dedication to family and work, to religion and the church, and to formal education. They believed in individualism and self-reliance as well, but an individualism and self-reliance that did not exclude cooperation. These blacks maintained a house and yard, however humble, not just for the sake of the family residing there, but as a contribution to their neighborhood. They actively involved themselves in voluntary organizations that looked in a general way to human improvement. They wished to be valued for their contributions to society, and not simply for their incomes.[6]

Members of the cultural middle class sometimes suffered from less than desirable housing, and almost always from the slurs and slights of the white majority. Their removal from whites into their own enclaves and institutions, although a removal usually required and enforced by the majority, saved them from racial cruelties on a daily basis. Yet the structural inequities of American life, especially a system of discrimination that forced most blacks into low-wage jobs, did not spare them. They or their descendants were not liberated financially until they experienced the expanding economy of the second half of the twentieth century, as well as its civil rights movement. They were not, however, liberated from the racism pervading American society. Hamilton Park was one container for this growing if still restricted middle class, a middle class whose imperfect integration into American society continues to be a subject for analysis and debate.

The contemporary contributors to the debate, besides Wilson and Keyes, include Ellis Cose, bell hooks, Glenn C. Loury, Robert C. Smith, and Shelby Steele. All address the problems of the African-American middle class with vigor and candor, however much they disagree among themselves—and disagree they do. All think historically and all arrive at their disparate conclusions along carefully reasoned paths. This is so whether they find the solution to the problem in a greater acceptance of personal responsibility among blacks, in the empowerment of black women, in awakening white America from its comfortable assumption that bigotry is dead, or in terminating unhelpful federal government programs—or, indeed, if the conclusion is that there is no solution. Cruel as racism was and is, some of its consequences could be escaped in a place such as Hamilton Park, because, as Walt Harrington so simply but elegantly phrased it, "black people live complete lives beyond the matters of race and racism."[7]

The thorniest nettle to grasp along the road to comprehending Hamilton Park is, surprisingly enough, the history of community. The meaning of Hamilton Park, in the context of community history, runs counter to much contemporary analysis of community, because Hamilton Park is above all a *place*. One historical problem involves the word *community*. Once place-based, *community* has been stretched in recent years to cover virtually all human association, even among people scattered over the globe whose connection with one another is solely electronic. Historians of community share in the stretching. They have a relaxed or, as some social scientists in other disciplines might phrase it, irresponsibly loose, conceptual structure allowing them to define community in multiple ways. *Community* may mean whatever they wish it to mean. Indeed, one historian of community has urged his fellows to accept the idea that people are now members of deeply layered associations, each of which is a valid community from their point of view. Historians of community, the argument goes, must accept and apply these popular definitions if they are to regain a lost credibility with the public. In other words, any effort at rigorous categorization and scholarly discrimination ought to be abandoned if a mass audience might not be persuaded of its validity.[8]

Another, related problem involves the "loss" or "decline" of communities of place amid the distractions, demands, and diversions of an increasingly complex, mobile world characterized by a rapid communication approaching the instantaneous. Historians of community have followed the lead of the urban sociologists who pioneered, first, in the study of communities, and next in tracing out the symptoms of their "eclipse." Sociologists and historians agree that people have always lived in more than one relational dimension. They also concur, some dissenters aside, in the belief that the contemporary layering of relationships has drawn the human focus away from place-based community.[9]

Both these assertions, that community may be legitimately applied to any group activity, and that place-based community has been lost, relate in similar ways to the stubborn, anomalous existence of Hamilton Park. Taking the first assertion first, those who argue that the word *community* could and should be defined however one wishes, have in fact expropriated a word having positive overtones of neighborliness, closeness, mutual commitment and concern, and familial intimacy and applied it to groups that are essentially nonterritorial. Such groups are better defined as organizations, subcultures, interest groups, friendships, kinship networks, or other interpersonal relationships, or collections of disparate individuals drawn together for a specific purpose, which dissolve as soon as the purpose is realized. The expropriation of the word *community* to describe such aggregations is understandable, because the more accurate descriptions seldom convey the warmth and comforting associations of community. Ripping community from its original context creates problems for the expropriator, however, as three examples demonstrate.

In 1972 Seymour J. Mandelbaum argued that a person's community "is quite simply, the set of people, roles, and places with whom he communicates." Mandelbaum hypothecated a worker in Oshkosh, Wisconsin, whose job requires him to be away from his place of residence for much of the time and may even force him to shift his residence. He may take little interest in his neighbors, preferring to spend time on the telephone with family or friends. "His entertainment may come from New York and Hollywood, his children go to college in Madison, his political attention be riveted on Washington." The difficulty with Mandelbaum's characterization is not that such people exist in every community of place; they do. The problem arises from assuming that great numbers of people are so intellectually and emotionally disjoined by the centrifugal forces of contemporary life that they cannot or will not focus on a community of place. The worker in Oshkosh, for example, would soon find his life in his residence unbearable if all or most of his neighbors were similarly fixed on work, distant family and friends, New York, Hollywood, Madison, and Washington. Who would report the burned-out streetlight, the pothole near the intersection, the unsatisfactory refuse collection? Who would warn of the zoning change impending nearby? Who would take the initiative to control roaming dogs? Who would ask our working man, if necessary, to get his head out of work or out of the distant abodes of family and friends, New York, Hollywood, Madison, and Washington long enough to take care of his peeling housepaint, brushy yard, and junker at the curb? That is exactly what happened in Hamilton Park—to the indignation, perhaps, of those so advised, but for the physical betterment of the community.[10]

Fifteen years later, M. Scott Peck, the group-therapy guru, published *The Different Drum: Community Making and Peace.* The burden of Peck's argument is that unconditional love and the resulting openness of communication create viable communities. To Peck, communities are individuals called together to deal with an issue or problem who must first come to terms with one another. That done, the problem solving proceeds in an almost mystical atmosphere of "love and commitment" transcending the problem to be addressed. A skeptic could well ask how enduring such groups are. Peck's community, for example, must be guided to its achievement by "leaders" who appear to be highly manipulative. Peck insisted that such communities must be inclusive and be maintained indefinitely. His few examples suggest, however, that community success is based—at least sometimes—on place. They also suggest that his communities cannot be inclusive but must be limited to some reasonably small number of people, to allow the operation of the therapeutic process by which they are formed. Peck has covered these difficulties by appropriating *community*— because other words or phrases do not "imply the love and commitment, the sacrifice, and the transcendence required to build community." But calling a therapy group or a working group or a focus group a community does not make it into one. The group remains fragile and, once its purpose is achieved, liable to dissolution. None of this calls into question Peck's skill or the sincerity of his desire for global peace and understanding. It does suggest that a word that has come to mean a definite place with certain characteristics—a place such as Hamilton Park—should not be ripped from its context because thinkers find its application to some other situation to be useful or convenient.[11]

Howard Rheingold, the cyberspace maven, published *The Virtual Community,* subtitled *Homesteading on the Electronic Frontier,* in 1993. Rheingold's theme is that Peck's ideal community is alive and well on the Internet. Peck admits that creating and maintaining his groups are difficult tasks, but Rheingold discovers them easily, after merely pressing a few keys. Rheingold is nothing if not perceptive; thus, he warns about "the fragility of communities" on the Net, the shallow nature of Net Bulletin Boards, the reality of addiction to the Net, and the deceitfulness of some of its users. The veritable flood of information on the Net and the positive bonding that develops there sweep aside these defects, Rheingold insists. The value of the trade-off may be less than he thinks. In place-based communities, withdrawal, superficiality, compulsive absorption in neighborhood business, and mendacity are possible, of course, but antisocial behavior is not likely to go undetected for long when the interaction is face to face. The best refutation of Rheingold is the cover illustration of his book: the neat houses and lawns depicted there testify to another kind of community—a foundation for nighttime flights into cyberspace.[12]

Another use, or misuse, of *community* has special reference to Hamilton Park, and that is the term *black community.* In many books and articles, the two words define all African Americans living in large urban areas. These books include those by Albert S. Broussard, Christopher Silver and John V. Moeser, and Quintard Taylor. This is no criticism of the content and analysis in these excellent studies. They are examples, nevertheless, of the historian's habit of following popular use in applying the word *community* to situations it does not fit. While it is true that blacks were forced into a common mold in the sense that most members of the white majority denied them their full humanity, they did not all live in the same place in any of the cities under examination. It is also true that African-American voters overwhelmingly favor "liberal" measures and black candidates who are legitimized by major party or other significant endorsements. Otherwise, though, African Americans are divided by income, class, status, religion, and a kaleidoscope of individual preferences and experiences, as are other Americans. The blacks of Dallas, therefore, do not form a community in any meaningful sense of the word. Hamilton Park is a black community, but it is not, nor are its residents, part of a larger group bound only by the city limits of Dallas and defined solely by race.[13]

The argument that people live in multiple "communities," defined however they may be, is related to the second proposition: that place-based community is in decline, has been eclipsed, or is lost in the welter of impulses characterizing contemporary life. The work of two historians will illustrate the situation. Thomas Bender's thoughtful essay on community argues for a gradual but persistent erosion of place-based community in the United States. He finds hope, however, in applying the word *community* to the emotional and experiential web of human relationships. For Bender, the contemporary existence of a place-based community is somehow suspect. He finds "instances in which localities are also communities . . . rare today. Where it does occur, it is often the result of the economic and political defeat of groups who have been excluded from full participation in the larger society." That Hamilton Park represented defeat or exclusion would amaze those who founded it or who lived there. Rowland Berthoff, though hoping for a "new birth of freedom" in America, was more pessimistic than Bender, because he found even the first English settlers unable to transfer a fully developed, place-based community to the inhospitable American shore; then, after individualism and economic change did their work, few Americans experienced any genuine community for any length of time.[14]

One historian who studied a place-based community, Zane L. Miller, found it surviving as a locale but subject to the influence of shifting modes of social thought during the 1950s, 1960s, and 1970s. Forest Park, Ohio, an incorporated suburb of Cincinnati, is much larger and more complex than Hamilton Park. Here Miller found at the outset a "community of limited liability" formed when people were assumed to be able to "make partial commitments to the welfare of a variety of communities, including territorial ones," but able, as well, to withdraw commitment in favor of other types of "communities" such as "churches, fraternal and social organizations, ethnic and labor groups, businesses, and professions." Indeed, the "loyalties and ties to non-territorial communities," not to mention job opportunities and alterations in the family cycle, loosened the commitment to community. Miller pronounced the "death of the community of limited liability" after 1970, when Forest Park became either fragmented into small, sometimes competing, groups, or became a "community of advocacy" in which citizens used community institutions "to protect individual interests." This brief outline cannot do justice to Miller's highly structured and subtle exposition, but his conclusion is clear enough: enchantment with selfish goals has replaced commitment to the whole community, prompted by shifts in social values as well as by the attractions of other kinds of community; *community*, in other words, is not a continuum, but abruptly shifts its meaning within short spans of time.[15]

It is difficult to know what to make of all this scholarly conviction in the face of the prideful propensity of urbanites to identify with their residing in named, and at least vaguely bounded, communities within their cities: Back-of-the-Yards, Lawndale, Whittier Heights, or Hamilton Park. One suggestion would be to call such aggregations as kinship networks and therapy groups by their right names and return *community* to the restricted definition given to it by the sociologists of the Chicago School, whose heyday was the 1920s and 1930s. The Chicago sociologists defined a community as an urban location of comprehensible size, projecting a dominant culture, and having a self-identity grounded in its institutions and activities. Community identity also included a clearly defined role for the community. The community, finally, could be the locus of a profound change that it could not control, and which could in fact undermine it. In other words, a community did not have to be eternal in order to have a value for its residents and for students of community. A Chicago School descendant later gave the name *defended neighborhood* to those communities. "Sharp boundaries," such as those defining Hamilton Park, were one of the ways that a defended neighborhood could delimit itself.[16]

Hamilton Park is not eternal. It opened in 1954 and may eventually give way to commercial redevelopment. Nor is it static. It is not the desirable residential enclave it once was, but this reality has less to do with its built environment than it does with the dynamics of urban change and the improving material circumstances of many African Americans during the 1960s and after. But community, as the Chicago sociologists wrote, in part concerns change over time. The history of Hamilton Park is, then, about the history of a particular place.

2

SEARCHING

FOR A BLACK SUBDIVISION

Understanding the creation of Hamilton Park involves clarifying two issues central to African-American housing in Dallas. First, black housing in Dallas was as dilapidated and overcrowded as it was anywhere else. Second, the financial and commercial elite organized into the Dallas Citizens' Council and the chamber of commerce could do relatively little about the situation, even when it wanted to, which was only when the black housing problem reached crisis proportions. The business elite of the 1930s through the 1950s has been credited with operating an "empire of consensus." The statement reinforces the conviction that Dallas then was "run—or strongly led—by a group of at most ten, at fewest three men." It strengthens the belief that elite leaders established Hamilton Park in part to appease blacks, who were suffering under virulent racism, and to assuage their own guilt in the matter, for it was they who were "exercising control."[1]

The elite did not in fact control outcomes so closely. It is generally correct, however, that most of its members cared little about minority housing on a day-in-day-out basis. The reality of black housing could be ignored just as long as it did not tarnish the city's bright image of progressive commercial prosperity. Because publicized housing deficiencies occurred rarely, the plight of blacks usually could be dismissed—and it was. From the city's incorporation in 1856, blacks lived in those locations marked out by white insistence or indifference.[2]

By 1940, Dallas had grown in the shape of an irregular pinwheel, spreading out from its founding site on the east bank of the Trinity River. The city embraced 294,734 people. Burgeoning Dallas registered a population increase of 13.2 percent over 1930, despite the Great Depression and its crushing effect on the rural-to-urban migration. Most of the 50,407 blacks were squeezed into some three and one-half square miles divided into six neighborhoods scattered around the city. Several thousand more African Americans lived in alley dwellings or unincorporated areas nearby.[3]

In 1940, two black homeowners led an attempted breakout into adjacent white areas. The bitter white response of violent demonstrations prompted the city to intervene. Overt racial conflict spelled trouble because it threatened the business elite's carefully cultivated view of Dallas as a city of harmony, contentment, and industriousness. Yankee firms were unlikely to relocate to, or expand their branches in, a place rent by racial antagonism. The city's intervention established new boundaries between white and black residential areas and calmed the situation for a decade. It did little to relieve the near-explosive pressure for better black housing. Nor did an active public-housing program, begun by the Public Works Administration in 1935 and continued, after 1939, under the auspices of the Dallas Housing Authority. By the time the authority's Roseland Homes for blacks opened in 1942, the prewar defense expansion had become the World War II boom. Building materials were virtually unobtainable and people, drawn by high wages at North American Aviation and other factories, were pouring into Dallas.[4]

The black housing problem was submerged but not forgotten. Intransigent whites held the line against black residential expansion, which was in any case limited by the lack of materials and the natural or land-use barriers surrounding most black neighborhoods. One postwar solution lay in black suburbanization or in its simulacrum, suburban-style dwellings within the city limits to insure proper utilities extension and services. The later Washington Shores in Orlando, Florida, was one such example. A solution of that sort appealed to the distinguished planner Harland Bartholomew, whose prestigious firm began issuing its stream of reports on postwar Dallas, *Your Dallas of Tomorrow,* in 1943. Bartholomew posited black expansion into white neighborhoods as unthinkable. On the other hand, he expected the black population to increase. Blacks had to live somewhere. Excepting a "limited amount" of space in the Elm Thicket or North Park area south of Love Field, however, "land surrounding the six major concentrations of negro population is now occupied by white residential and other uses or conditions that make impossible any logical and unhampered expansion of the city's negro areas."[5]

Bartholomew's suggestion, one that the city's business elite would adopt eight years later, involved nonprofit or philanthropic corporations assisting with the construction of mostly single-family "low cost housing . . . in and adjoining outlying non-white areas." Given Bartholomew's planning orientation, he probably had in mind as a model the private, philanthropic efforts that traditionally accepted a lower rate of return on their investment in superior housing. These efforts reached back into the nineteenth century and enjoyed a suburban culmination in the development of Radburn, New Jersey, during the late 1920s. The Washington Shores inspiration, although organizationally quite different from these traditional philanthropic real-estate ventures, sought the same end for its target population of underhoused African Americans. Meanwhile, Bartholomew proposed four expansion zones: two would be in then unincorporated West Dallas; a third would be due north of West Dallas near the city's airport, Love Field; and a fourth would be in an extension of the easternmost section of South Dallas, near the junction of the Trinity River and White Rock Creek. All the areas were peripheral; none would intrude on whites. The noted planner was confident that in the four zones "fine negro residential neighborhoods adequate in area and conveniently located" would raise the square miles devoted to African-American homes from 3.5 to 11.6.[6]

But would they? Three of Bartholomew's proposed sites were in the Trinity River levee district. The two in West Dallas were behind the west levee and the one near Love Field was protected by the east levee. The fourth, the eastward extension of South Dallas, Bartholomew admitted, "requires the building of a levee in the White Rock Creek Valley to protect the area against overflow." Bartholomew pointed out that some blacks already lived in the levee district but that fact scarcely qualified his projected residence tracts as "fine negro residential neighborhoods." They were, at best, undistinguished. Like most bottomlands, they were low-lying, flat, and viewless, with few tall trees to shade their hot, baked ground. That anything "fine" could be made of them was doubtful. The tenor of Bartholomew's report was neither inhumane nor insincere, but the noted planner was trapped by segregation's rigidities into suggesting only those black expansion areas that whites would not contest.[7]

Meanwhile, African Americans were flooding into Dallas in a swelling stream that would raise their population in the metropolitan area from 50,407 in 1940 to 83,352 in 1950. The pressure against the barriers to black expansion mounted steadily.[8]

By 1945, when the Bartholomew firm was issuing the last of its reports, black leaders and housing contractors had formed an alliance to suburbanize black housing. They intended to pursue by planned devel-

Searching for a Black Subdivision

opment what blacks had been doing for years on an ad hoc basis. But three circumstances limited their effectiveness. First, none of the allies, not even the most successful housing contractors, were members of the elite. They had relatively little political influence—a serious limitation in the face of white opposition to their plans. They could not tap the local capital necessary to buy land, subdivide their property, and build houses. Despite their pledges to build to Federal Housing Administration (FHA) standards, the regional director of the FHA was remarkably cool to most of their proposals—an attitude that doomed any effort to secure FHA-guaranteed mortgage money. Thus the allies were caught in a vicious circle: they lacked the financial clout to secure advance pledges of funds and they lacked the political power necessary to down white opposition and, in some cases, to overcome the FHA's doubts about the soundness of their proposals. The sad reality was that no commitments of FHA-backed, low-interest mortgage money would be made.

The allies' second problem was the lack of black institutions or individuals able to bear the weight of financial obligation to new, improved African-American housing. The initiative that strong minority insurance companies in Atlanta and Memphis made possible in those cities would not be repeated in Dallas, an urban area relatively young, with a relatively modest African-American population on the western fringe of heavy black settlement. The third difficulty they faced was to find suitable, inexpensive property in a large tract, far enough removed from whites to escape their opposition yet sufficiently close to established black employment to allow easy transportation.

Attempts to find building sites, commit interested contractors, and awaken the public to the problem began in 1945 and continued into 1950. These efforts involved, among others, A. Maceo Smith, the local racial-relations advisor of the FHA, and John W. Rice, the secretary-manager of the Dallas Negro Chamber of Commerce (DNCC) and chairman of its housing committee. Early in 1948, Smith encouraged a sympathetic reporter and columnist for the *Dallas Morning News,* Lynn Landrum, to write an article about the problem. Landrum blended a discussion of the white man's "debt" to blacks with a denial that integration was a solution to minority housing. Blacks, he wrote, inhabited grisly, segregated slums and grim segregated public housing in officially desegregated northern cities. "A good, all-Negro addition, run as the Negroes themselves want it run, is better than any other solution," Landrum asserted. Rice then wrote Landrum a letter combining an analysis of the minority housing crisis with praise for "the directness of your reasoning and the sincerity with which you raised the question of Negro housing"—a letter that the columnist reprinted with approving comments. The symbiosis between black leaders and the white journalist would continue.[9]

The black leaders and various other groups and individuals, both black and white, also established a pattern of meetings, formal and informal, publicized and unpublicized, in organized efforts to alleviate the minority housing crisis. In March 1948, Rice appeared before an evening meeting of the Dallas Home Builders Association (DHBA)—a meeting large enough to be held in the Dallas Power and Light Company auditorium. Rice was an astute man who knew how to present a problem to a white audience. In his letter to Landrum he had invoked a favorite phrase of the business elite: "Dallas as a whole." In the letter, Rice had declared his "unshaken belief in the sincere desire of Dallas as a whole to make of itself a model American city in which the basic needs of all its citizens are adequately cared for"; now, standing before the DHBA, he continued his appeals to mortgage lenders and home builders to accept certain, if reduced, profits in the production of black housing. "Only 10 per cent of the 4,000 Negro families who need homes in Dallas can pay $4,500 to $5,000," he warned. The next 30 percent with family incomes ranging from $1,500 to $2,000 "would like decent homes" but would have to accept housing at a price below $4,500. "The remaining 60 per cent, by no stretch of the imagination, would ever be able to own homes."[10]

Rice tactfully did not mention that some portion of the 60 percent required public housing—a subject on which the DHBA was more than a little phobic. He was, nevertheless, calling for some mix of single-family and multiple-family housing scaled to the needs of blacks. Rice left the discussion of public housing to Edward T. Dicker, a DHBA board member and one of "several builders" looking at sites for African-American housing. Dicker bluntly told his fellows that if they did not build more modest housing, then "government-financed building is the alternative." The DHBA committee pledged to meet further with Rice and his committee during the week following the meeting.[11]

A concern for overcrowded blacks, for profit, for the racial stability of existing neighborhoods, and fears of expanded public housing all motivated the contractors to plan sizeable, well-arranged black neighborhoods. Unfortunately, the announcement or discovery of almost every proposed subdivision engendered opposition from surrounding, nearby, and even not-so-close whites. Whites based their resistance on the threat to land values and future white development, the doubtful suitability of the land for residences, and racial disharmony. The results were frustration for the contractors, black expansion into white neighborhoods and its attendant violence, an elaborate housing scheme rejected by blacks, and the intervention of elite whites. The latter factor ultimately quieted the violence and produced the north Dallas subdivision of Hamilton Park.

Indeed, it was Dicker of the DHBA who first offered to put his money where his mouth was. His 1948 plan, when fully developed, would have blunted the immediate black housing problem to the extent that this was possible under private construction, and without a rent subsidy. Within three weeks of the DHBA meeting, he and some associated builders proposed a black subdivision of six thousand units in unincorporated territory ten and one-half miles southeast of downtown Dallas and less than a mile from the western boundary of the all-white suburb of Mesquite. The tract, an old ranch on rolling terrain now within the Mesquite boundary, faced Scyene and Peachtree roads. It contained 1,400 acres. Dicker proposed to establish a park and a shopping center and to erect five thousand frame houses and one thousand brick apartment units. Dicker's company submitted its plans for a two-bedroom house of 607 square feet, priced about $3,900 to $3,950, to the Dallas Negro Chamber of Commerce housing committee for its endorsement. If FHA financing guarantees could be secured, total monthly payments on the houses would be between $24 and $30 and the one-to-three bedroom apartments would rent for $35 to $45 per month. Full city services and utilities were to be provided.[12]

Dicker's proposal drew immediate and mounting protests from surrounding whites. Bailey Johnson, himself a real-estate developer, condemned Dicker's plans. "A project with 6,000 units included would mean a Negro population of about 30,000 would suddenly be placed right in the middle of a fast-growing area containing many first-class homes" costing from $7,000 to $10,000. Hal F. Buckner, president of the Baptist-funded Buckner Orphans Home was another principal objector, despite there being nearly four road miles between his buildings and Dicker's site. In April a group composed of "officials" from the Mesquite Chamber of Commerce, the Mesquite Lions Club, the Mesquite Woman's Club, and the city of Mesquite, protested to Dicker in writing.[13]

What began as a protest group soon became the East Dallas Chamber of Commerce, a collection of fifty people representing nine incorporated or unincorporated communities in the area, "prepared to raise funds and to employ an attorney." Johnson's claim that forty thousand people lived within a six-mile radius of Dicker's site implied a devastating impact of the black development on surrounding areas. The assumed detrimental influences of the subdivision included the decline of existing property values, inadequate services to the site, the proposed inexpensive homes generating taxes insufficient to support the necessary new schools, and the depressing effect on future white residential development. Johnson asserted that his group was well aware of the need for black homes and suggested that public housing provided a solution. The protesters' flawed reasoning was nowhere better illustrated than in their letter to Dicker. The Mesquite Negro School, built to serve a small population west of the city, "is now operating beyond its physical facilities, and additional enrollments would seriously impair its efficiency." In other words, the problem was not an already inadequate, underfunded school, but the desire of relatively prosperous blacks and their allies to improve a deteriorating situation.[14]

Dicker's success hinged on FHA approval for low-cost mortgage loans so that he, in turn, could obtain long-term construction financing. He would not succeed. At first the FHA's district director, R. E. Shepherd, assumed a superficially noncommittal, neutral stance following a mid-April interview with Dicker. Shepherd stated that the FHA was "tremendously interested" in black housing. "FHA does not want to become interested in any way when there is a controversy over location," he declared. But in the next breath he asserted that a black housing development "should be located as near as possible to downtown and industrial areas and should have good transportation to residential sections that would employ domestic help." Because the center of Dicker's site was more than ten miles from downtown and because the white protesters had criticized the plan for its lack of adequate transportation, the district director's reservations foreshadowed his rejection.[15]

In late May, following a visit to the site, Shepherd "turned thumbs down" on the tract. The FHA director offered three reasons for his refusal: the area was too far from Dallas, lacked transportation and utilities, and failed to meet FHA standards for subdivisions. Shepherd echoed Bailey and his protest group when he argued for duplex or multifamily housing in two existing black neighborhoods. Shepherd's solution did nothing for aspiring blacks who wished to own homes. The neighborhoods that he suggested could not be developed on the unified scale that Dicker envisioned, nor would their complete infilling have solved the black housing crisis.[16]

Dicker was stunned. He had delivered strident comments on behalf of his project before—its opponents were "selfish" and "there is too much talk and no action" about African-American housing. Now he was more outspoken. He was "extremely disappointed" with Shepherd's decision, which came as a "shocking surprise." "By no means is this going to stop me. I will start looking right away for another location." Dicker chafed, too, over the FHA's prior insurance of "loans on homes all around that location"—actions casting doubt on Shepherd's stated reasons for rejecting the black development. To be fair to Shepherd, he opposed any threat to FHA construction standards, and Dicker's under-$4,000 houses may have cut too many corners to qualify for FHA loan guarantees. Shepherd's emphasis on duplex and multifamily housing reflected a belief that builders were misjudging the market. Early in 1950 he applauded efforts to secure black housing while urging builders to concentrate on rental units because "most Dallas Negroes can't afford to buy homes."[17]

With all that conceded, there was a racial reason for Shepherd's action—one that became clear in July 1948 when two other builders, Tom Lively and Ira L. Rupley, proposed a $1 million project of 247 houses on a sixty-one-acre site in the Cedar Crest section. At the time the land was an airport, across the Trinity and four and one-half miles south-southeast of downtown. Bus transportation and utilities were available, while a substantial black community, a black shopping area, several black churches, and a park and a school for blacks were within a mile and a half. With the exception of potential drainage problems on a portion of the site, it seemed to meet FHA requirements. But Shepherd interposed a fresh objection. It was not FHA policy, he said, to approve black housing projects in the face of significant opposition.[18]

Cedar Crest whites probably were already circulating a petition against the Lively-Rupley project, and Shepherd's statement did nothing to discourage them. Meeting in a church basement two days after his declaration, they organized the Cedar Crest-Skyline Improvement League. The organization's formal objective, to oppose "by all legal and reasonable means any attempt to impose conditions and situations detrimental to personal and property rights," did not mention the Lively-Rupley development, but one member of the organization made the reason for the protest abundantly clear. "We are not going to lie down and let them put a Negro settlement five blocks from our doorstep," she said. "No nice section of Dallas would stand for it and we won't either." The improvement league appointed an executive committee to present a petition of 614 signatures to the city council, Shepherd, and a congressman.[19]

At first, Rupley appeared determined to see his project through, as had Dicker before him. "There is no question we will go right ahead with our plans with no hesitation at all," he said. "We are not disturbed about this clatter. We anticipated it." Whites would be no closer to blacks than two hundred feet, he said, and a "planting screen" would separate the races. "But if you set up a Negro community on an island in the Pacific Ocean," he concluded, "I guess the fish would rise in protest." Within a few days the terrestrial protesters presented their petition to the council and suggested as an alternate site an area about a mile north of Cedar Creek on the south bluffs of the Trinity. By then Rupley was feeling the pressure and promised to give the bluff site "every consideration." Neither he nor his partner Lively built the black apartments eventually located there; nor did they develop the Cedar Crest area. Despite the dubious validity of the protesters' contentions, they were able to generate enough heat to force the partners into abandoning their plans.[20]

In August, another developer, John J. Stuart, charged that the FHA had "arbitrarily blocked" his proposed development for African Americans. Stuart's site, on two hundred acres, was an east-west rectangle in the Trinity levee area, south of the settlement proposed by city planner Bartholomew. The Stuart location was scarcely elegant, bounded as it was by the levee on the west, busy Irving Boulevard on the south, and the Rock Island railroad tracks on the north. Yet the old farmstead would accommodate five hundred to eight hundred units, mostly two-bedroom frame houses priced from $5,000 to $6,000, but including some rental duplexes. As an officer of the firm likely to be the mortgage company pointed out, the U.S. Army Corps of Engineers certified that the levee would protect the area from a flood "of considerably greater magnitude than the greatest known flood." Utilities crossed the property or were nearby and bus service was available. The housing committee of the Dallas Negro Chamber of Commerce approved the project. It was west of Arlington Park, a developing if small black subdivision that had encountered no white opposition. The location five miles from downtown was convenient to public transit transfer points and to most sections of the city where blacks worked.[21]

Nevertheless, Shepherd maintained that "from our investigation of the site, we would not be able to approve it because of the possibility

Searching for a Black Subdivision

of floodwaters should the levee ever break." Other places behind levees were eligible for FHA-insured mortgages. "New Orleans is the first city that comes to mind, when discussing properties protected by levees," the mortgage officer wrote. When the FHA commissioner upheld Shepherd, Stuart promised an appeal above the FHA, repeating language often spoken during the frustrating search for black homes: "The need for adequate Negro housing is acute." Despite Stuart's determination he received no help from the FHA.[22]

The most poignant of all the 1940s searches for black homesteads was Joseph B. Martin's. Martin, a white, small-scale home builder, observed that in post–World War II Dallas, "hordes of builders, large and small, were building homes for the white veteran, but none were interested in the negro veteran." Beginning early in 1948 he searched for a location away from any substantial white development certain to oppose a black settlement. He and his associates found and purchased a black-owned, eighty-seven-acre farm "just outside the city limits," on the northeast edge of White Rock Lake, about seven miles northeast of downtown. He named it Bel Aire Estates. The adjoining farms were, by his count, "occupied by some four or five white families and some 50 to 60 negro families." Martin "could not foresee that anyone could object to negroes living on land that had been negro owned and occupied for so many years." But Martin quickly discovered that blacks engaged in farming and blacks living in a subdivision near substantial white homes were different matters. A prominent white landowner from nearby obtained a state district court injunction closing a county road giving access to Bel Aire Estates through his property. The landowner strung a barbed-wire fence across the road. From the summer of 1949 blacks had to find other ways to and from their lots, or prospective lots. Martin sued. In February 1950 he persuaded another district judge that the road was public property. The white landowner's attorney filed an appeal and the fence stayed up.[23]

Meanwhile Martin turned to the City of Dallas and the FHA for help with utilities and financing. The city informed him that water lines and sewers could not be extended within two to three years' time. He proposed to the FHA office a community water system and septic tanks but found the FHA's requirements too stringent. Determined to proceed, he laid out 350 lots on the elevated, picturesque ground. His flamboyant newspaper advertising was nothing if not attention getting. In January 1949 his company offered a Lincoln Continental convertible to the buyer who wrote the best completion of the phrase "I bought a lot in Bel Aire

Estates because . . ." The same advertisement announced a sale of lots regularly priced at $2,000 for $900. Martin's plans included a country club, a swimming pool, and a shopping center. By April 1950 he had sold 225 lots, an index of the desperate housing situation.[24]

For all that, the prospects at Bel Aire Estates were grim. The lack of available, affordable financing limited actual construction to fourteen houses. The absence of improvements inhibited lot sales. Curtis J. Smith, later a Hamilton Park pioneer, visited Bel Aire Estates but was unimpressed. He recalled an "undeveloped area with no streets. It had a dirt road." Bel Aire "was a wooded area, and the day that I went out, it had rained, and I really had a little problem even getting to it. It was muddy." Henry L. Davis III, another Hamilton Park pioneer, was one of those who bought a lot despite the problems. He "dreamed of going to the screened back porch where I could look [and] see White Rock Lake at night, shining, beautiful." Making Davis's dream a reality required more capital than Martin could command. As early as March, he railed against Shepherd and the FHA for "sitting back and bringing down objections and criticism that have little weight in the eyes of the colored folks who are forced to live in the squalor and crowded conditions while your government bureau spins around in swivel chairs seeking utopia for them."[25]

By April 1950 Martin and his codevelopers were badly overextended. Bel Aire Estates had taken them, Martin admitted, "to the brink of bankruptcy." A loan from the federal Reconstruction Finance Corporation might save the subdivision, but "time is running out and I would not be able to obtain it soon enough." In May a syndicate of twenty "unnamed Dallas developers, builders, and landowners" intervened to end Martin's misery and to uproot the black settlement. The syndicate bought Martin out and arranged to refund the investments of lot purchasers and houseowners. At the same time the syndicate announced its conviction that Bel Aire "should be changed to a white neighborhood to conform with the general neighborhood north of White Rock Lake."[26]

The failure of one subdivision plan after another presented a bleak picture. In the midst of the struggles for decent African-American housing in Dallas and elsewhere, the black Texas public institution Prairie View Agricultural and Mechanical College held a conference on "Better Housing for Negroes in Texas." For two days it mounted "a frontal attack upon the housing problems of minorities." Despite professions of stern realism, the conference, as with most academically sponsored events, was more successful in exhortation and in the identification and analysis of problems than it was in developing practical solutions. Nevertheless, it brought together an interracial group of "200 builders, realtors, financiers, and representatives from governmental housing agencies and consumer groups." Despite some notable progress in developing black subdivisions elsewhere, there was little hope for Dallas. A frustrated A. Maceo Smith spoke from his perspective as racial-relations advisor for the FHA. "It is harder to find homes for Negroes in Dallas than in any other city in the South," he declared. "Dallas is the answer to the question often asked: Does anyone care?"[27]

Smith's question was directed at a worsening situation. On 10 February 1949 he appeared before yet another meeting of some two hundred home-building-industry representatives, this one organized by Shepherd. Smith estimated the African-American population to be 75,000, grouped into 22,000 families. Because only 12,451 dwelling units were available to blacks, 9,459 families lived "doubled up." More than half (9,460) of the units were substandard, while "a ready market" existed in the upper-income category for a minimum of 1,428 houses at prices ranging from $5,000 to $7,500. Finding sites and financing was a major problem, Smith admitted, but he pledged his help to the builders and challenged them to rise to the occasion.[28]

It was not Smith's impassioned statements nor his statistics but city council involvement that signaled the beginning of the end of elite indifference to the crisis. The plan precipitating councilmanic intervention did so because it produced the most fractious donnybrook of all. The whites involved in opposing a black housing proposal were not residents of the city, but they persuaded the council to table a developer's request for extending water to the proposed subdivision.

The furor began in 1949 after J. Hub Hill, an experienced builder, led a group investigating a potential site southwest of the city. Hill quietly secured an option on the 576-acre tract. His planned additional purchases would bring the total size to more than 600 acres. The proposed Diamond Hill addition lay seven miles southwest of downtown, south and west of the small, incorporated town of Cockrell Hill and south of Arcadia Park. Cockrell Hill is now surrounded by Dallas and Arcadia Park is now a Dallas subdivision; Mountain View Community College of the Dallas County community college system later occupied a portion of Hill's site.

Preliminary discussions with the FHA brought a favorable response. On 1 August, Smith wrote to Shepherd that the Hill location was practically ideal except for its distance from black employment, but the difficulties of finding a closer site and "the prospects for improved and fast transportation" made the objection nugatory. "More than two-thirds" of the "generally high" area "consists of moderately rolling land with patches of woods that may be transformed into a picturesque development at moderate improvement costs." Gas and electricity were on the site, other utilities were nearby, and Hill's intention to request annexation would bring full city services. Provided Hill's application for FHA mortgage insurance conformed to his plans, Smith gave his "unqualified approval" to the location.[29]

The white residents near Hill's site caught wind of his proposal about a month after Smith's letter and began a spirited version of a 1940s NIMBY. They organized a mass meeting at the Cockrell Hill city hall and elected an executive committee of eleven. The meeting endorsed an opposition resolution directed to various individuals and groups, including Shepherd, the mayor of Dallas, and the Dallas Negro Chamber of Commerce. Hill's first reaction followed the familiar script: the determined builder-developer would not buckle under self-interested pressure from narrow-minded bigots. In early January 1950, Hill announced his $14 million development, including three shopping centers, five parks, sites for a school and churches, and two thousand houses costing $5,000 and up. He quoted figures on the black population, existing black dwellings, and black housing needs—figures disseminated by the DNCC. He pointed out how recent improvements, notably the construction of the central expressway and the expansion of Griggs Park in near North Dallas, had destroyed some black housing.[30]

Hill tried to generate sympathy for underhoused African Americans and simultaneously to reassure the white residents of Cockrell Hill, Arcadia Park, and other residential areas. Declaring that 9,500 black families lived doubled up, the contractor asserted: "Acknowledgement of this situation is not enough—it should be cleared up. It is generally agreed that our attitudes are anxious but our actions are lax. We cannot help these people or ourselves by forcing Negroes into backyards and alleyways." Helping blacks would not hurt whites, he insisted. Whites near Diamond Hill and property owners in future white expansion areas nearby would be unaffected because of the development's "secludedness." Two major roads, a railroad, and "rugged and unusable terrain" would permanently bound "the most modern Negro development in the South."[31]

Moreover, Hill was not just any developer but a proven contractor with wide experience in building military housing on and off post. He and his associates might have been able to finance the subdivision without heavy outside assistance. The FHA's Shepherd retreated from his past obstructive comments and tactics to endorse Hill's project. Although Hill was yet to make a formal application for loan guarantees, Shepherd said, the FHA "had no say in whether the area was to be developed for Negro or white residents." Shepherd's bland comment of January 1950 stood in sharp contrast to his July 1948 statement that "it was the policy of the FHA not to approve projects of this kind where there were a large number of protests." The FHA district director's about-face sprang from a February 1949 policy change from Washington—one promulgated under pressure from "civic groups." The directive declared that no FHA insurance could be denied "on the ground that the introduction of a different occupancy type may affect the values of other properties in the area." Furthermore, the Dallas City Plan Commission had approved the plat, which was to conform to the city's subdivision regulations as well as to those of the FHA and the Veterans Administration (VA). His project, Hill said, had the "full approval and hearty support" of the Dallas Negro Chamber of Commerce and of leading black citizens.[32]

Despite Hill's credentials, his statements carried no more weight with area whites than had those of previous developers. The anti–Diamond Hill group was livid. Its leader, George Owens, a minister and mayor of Cockrell Hill, predicted "trouble out here" if Hill followed through with his plans. "We've been trying to fight this thing on a high plane but there's tremendous bitterness." There was "plenty of room" for a black development elsewhere, he maintained. "Transportation out here would be very bad. There'd be trouble if too many Negroes tried to climb aboard our buses. They'd have no schools, no churches out here."[33]

A packed chamber of some 120 people listened to Owens's formal protest to the city council on 10 January. Owens spoke for 29,500 people, he said, most of whom lived in Oak Cliff, a Dallas area south of the Trinity, northwest of Diamond Hill. Owens declared that he and his constituents, not builder Hill, were concerned for blacks. Hill and his associates were making "an effort to exploit the Negroes for money gain." Diamond Hill was too far from black employment, lacked transportation, and "would produce friction to the flaming point of race riot." Other protesters claimed that Hill's proposal had been stealthily advanced, would ruin property values, and stymie development. Owens urged the council to work with the DNCC and the "realty board" to find a suitable location, "a place where Negroes won't have to spend one-third of their salaries getting to and from their jobs."[34]

For his part, Hill promised to meet the city code requirements and to bring water "into the addition at our own expense," provided that the council would supply it at "regular rates" to his company. Rice, of the Dallas Negro Chamber of Commerce, supported Hill. He urged the council to ignore the inflammatory and emotional statements of whites. The difficulties of black housing, he informed the council, "must be solved only deliberately. Leaders must be as unsentimental in their approach to the problem as possible. In doing this you will make possible the orderly development of one sixth of the Dallas population, who have the same interest as you in homes, health, sanitation, fire prevention and the progress of Dallas." Despite the pleas from Hill and Rice, the council deferred action on selling water to the subdivision.[35]

By mid-January it was evident that there were not enough votes in the council to supply Diamond Hill with water. Under the circumstances, Shepherd's statement about loan guarantees was little more than academic. The protesters organized a permanent association and in mid-February were planning to buy Diamond Hill for industrial development. Hill's defeat once more frustrated the hopes for better black housing. Marion Mitchell, a Hamilton Park pioneer who had worked for Hill and knew him well, recalled how the contractor had promised to help. "If they ever start a black neighborhood," he told Mitchell, "I'll build you a house for costs." Mitchell was delighted: "I was going to get a house out there for costs." After Diamond Hill collapsed Mitchell and his family continued to live in a small house in the Trinity Valley addition, behind a river levee, until Hamilton Park developed.[36]

The failed Hill project at last forced the council to face the issue of African-American housing. It charged one of its members, Roland Pelt, to find an acceptable residential site. The councilman, himself a housing contractor in Oak Cliff, probably opposed the nearby Diamond Hill project, although he did not take the lead in tabling it. Pelt specialized in "GI homes," inexpensive frame houses for veterans, houses of the type likely to be built for most black homeowners. He was first elected to the council in 1947 and so enjoyed a useful experience in politics as well as in the real-estate and construction business. He was thirty-three when he resigned from the council for business reasons, shortly after unveiling his plan to provide black housing. A segregationist, Pelt was not a militant racist, as he demonstrated by his election to a directorship of the Dallas Citizens' Interracial Association, Inc., in 1954.[37]

Pelt's appointment heralded a new level of council commitment to a solution of the problem. In a departure from its standard policy of charging a portion of water, sewer, and storm-drain extension costs to developers, the council was "willing and able" to spend public money to bring these utilities into a new black housing area. The publicly paid costs would not be passed through to the black homeowners, enabling builders to sell their houses for less than usual. Later the council decided against the subsidy, but the fact that a subvention was considered at all was an affirmation of the council's concern. The council, Pelt said, would "do everything to encourage this entire program," and "I can't emphasize strongly enough how the council feels about the need for Negro housing. We're really going after it." The council wanted fast action, too. Pelt expected his search for the property or properties to last but two or three weeks and for "a big part of the problem [to be] met satisfactorily by the end of the year."[38]

Pelt's quest for a black housing area occupied, not two or three weeks, but from mid-January to late February 1950. Then violent events in South Dallas forced his hand. South Dallas, a fan-shaped area spreading southeast from downtown, was home to both whites and blacks, with the blacks segregated into some nine separate areas. Pressured beyond endurance, blacks began buying modest houses in previously white blocks at premium prices. By January 1950, some whites were demonstrating against, and threatening, real-estate agents who were showing houses to blacks. Other whites were beginning to leave South Dallas. The resulting racial tensions could be scarifying when directly experienced. Henry L. Davis III recalled pulling into traffic on a South Dallas street one day during the turbulent period, only to find himself in the midst of an automobile protest parade of white families. The whites did nothing hostile, but the frightened Davis turned into a side street at his first opportunity.[39]

The threats escalated into violence in February when a bomb splintered a newly purchased black home in an area of residential succession. It was the first of at least twelve residential bombings over the next year and a half. Those bombings were potentially deadly. One May evening Robert Shelton was relaxing, reading the newspaper in bed after moving into his South Dallas house. A bomb tore through the bedroom roof, shredding the newspaper Shelton was reading and cutting him on the face, shoulder, and legs. His wife, though lying next to him, was uninjured. Her escape seems miraculous when the bomb's enormous power is considered: its blast was heard five miles away, drew two thousand onlookers, and nearly blew patrolman B. C. Garrison, four blocks distant, "out of the police car." When Garrison and his partner reached the scene they found a bloodied Shelton stumbling through his house, pistol in hand.[40]

The bombings had the intended effect of frightening some blacks away from South Dallas. In 1951, when a Dallas Housing Authority project displaced black homeowners, the owners objected to their removal because the only place to go was South Dallas, "a Negroes' no-man's-land." One property owner, already distressed over what he considered a low offer for his house and lot, followed a suggestion from the housing authority's relocation office to investigate a house in South Dallas. When he arrived he found an intimidating sign, "Keep this place white." He told a County Court at Law that he did not want to live in an area where he had to go to bed "with a steel helmet—like in a foxhole." The more than one hundred black spectators so "boisterously agreed" that the judge threatened to clear the courtroom.[41]

Threats and bombings were frightening to individuals but they failed to stop the turnover from white to black, as they usually did when tried in other times and places. They were not the only response. A week after the first bomb shattered a black residence, Lovell Turner, a white real-estate man, proposed a careful change from white to black in one part of South Dallas, mediated by a nonprofit corporation that would buy homes from whites on a block-by-block basis, then resell them to blacks when the whites involved had found other housing. The plan, Turner said, "would merely help speed a consolidation of the Negro areas that is already taking place. My plan," he said, "is to give Negroes the go-ahead signal to live in areas in which they already live and to consolidate such areas."[42]

Turner's idea raised a storm of protest, with the thunderclaps loudest among South Dallas whites. In a series of tumultuous mass meetings, the Reverend John G. Moore, pastor of the Colonial Baptist Church, emerged as the leader of a South Dallas Property Owners Association pledged to seek loans to rehabilitate or refinance white houses, find white purchasers for houses sold by whites, and to raise money to repurchase homes recently sold to blacks. The group also discussed creating new and expanded, but inviolate, black housing areas, worked out in cooperation with African-American leaders. Moore's organization engaged the sympathy of some city officials and of such leaders as James Aston, a banker and former city manager. Realistically, however, little could be done to stop black expansion. *Shelley v. Kraemer* (1948) and other federal court decisions as well as federal administrative action had destroyed any basis for prohibiting anyone of any race from buying a house whose owner wished to sell or for forcing anyone out of a house that he had purchased and occupied. Nor was there any legal way to enforce Moore's proposed new housing restrictions.[43]

In September 1950, Moore spoke to a meeting of the Dallas Interracial Committee (see chapter 3). He estimated the cost of achieving his plan to be at least $100,000 and possibly as much as $150,000—large sums at the time. It would involve the removal of 150 to 160 black households. Given the modest incomes of most white South Dallas residents, the reluctance of some blacks to move, and the doubtful outcome of a citywide fund-raising drive based on something as problematic as unenforceable boundaries between white and black, the chance of slowing the African-American surge through South Dallas was remote.[44]

The actions of those officials and leaders who were open to Moore's solution spoke volumes. The city council seemed in sympathy with his plan to sell vacant, city-owned lots in South Dallas to his group, Moore thought. He planned to purchase the "sixty or seventy vacant lots," build new houses on them, and sell them to blacks who would move from their recently purchased, previously white-owned homes. Instead, the city sold the lots to a private developer who had no such understanding with public officials. Aston, an early leader in the elite's efforts to solve the black housing problem (see chapter 3), supported the idea of realistic new boundaries between blacks and whites in South Dallas, Moore declared. Once Moore's suggested lines were accepted, Aston promised to have the police talk with any white determined to sell to a black; that failing, the police would ask representatives of a new interracial group to reason with the white. If those tactics failed to influence the white, they would be tried with the black. Moore also insisted that Aston pledged cooperation with his efforts to move blacks out of some previously white-owned houses, sending them back into the area designated for blacks. "We are going to get both newspapers to . . . carry a picture of the first negro signing the deed," Moore remembered Aston as saying, "and carry the story that others are going to move out." Whether or not Aston made those commitments, they were not fulfilled, dooming Moore to bitter disappointment.[45]

Moore was accused of being a militant racist, but his alleged connection to the violence was never proven. When the black weekly *Dallas Express* asked Moore for an interview, he invited a reporter to his home. During the interview Moore denied responsibility for the bombings and declared that his group had an option to purchase a new, controversial, all-black apartment building in South Dallas. The black expansion was unfair to African Americans because some post–World War II houses "only cost three thousand five hundred dollars to build but your people are paying six thousand five hundred and seven thousand dollars for them." There is little doubt that Moore expected the bombing to continue. There is also little doubt that he felt most deeply for elderly, low-income whites in South Dallas who would not receive enough for their small, substandard houses to allow them to move elsewhere; they would live out their days in an integrated setting.[46]

Despite his rhetoric and bravado, Moore saw the handwriting on the wall for white South Dallas. The city administration would not support him, he could not raise the funds necessary for his scheme, and the white communities that had solidified around the churches and schools of South Dallas were melting away. Already, by the time of his 1950 appearance before the committee, a black congregation had bought a white church and another white church could not "survive many more months." Moore deplored the "bitterness and hatred in the hearts of hundreds of people in South Dallas," but blamed those feelings on the city's public and private leadership, whose concern for South Dallas ended with sympathetic rhetoric and unfulfilled promises. "Now, frankly," he said, "I think I am going to leave the area. I think that so far as the growth of our church is concerned, it is about gone. I have something in my heart that has been killed over this. I think I have given eighteen years of my life for nothing, as far as the future growth of the church is concerned."[47]

It was in this atmosphere of threats, violence, and racial tension that Pelt rushed to unveil his plan on Saturday, 25 February 1950. He was neither able to secure the formal approval of all African-American leaders and organizations in advance nor to consult with all the landowners in the project area. These considerations should have tempered Pelt's optimism, but he was under severe pressure to pose a solution to the grave, dual problem: African-American overcrowding and the conflicts in South Dallas.

The Sunday newspapers carried the details of Pelt's plan—a vast, comprehensive scheme for housing 35,000 to 40,000 blacks on three thousand acres, three to five and one-half miles from downtown. The land lay in a rough triangle with its apex pointing west: its two sides, shaped by the east levee of the Trinity as it ran west, then bent to the northeast; the meander of the old Trinity bed, by then a branch of the Trinity's Elm Fork, formed the triangle's base. Within the area Pelt envisioned what was called "an entire Negro city," including a black university, three grade schools, a high school, a major business district, five smaller shopping centers, parks, apartments, duplexes, single-family residences, and paved streets, all controlled by a master plan. Pelt was exultant. "I believe this program would be the answer to the Negro housing question for 15 to 20 years," he said. In addition to his preliminary consultations with black leaders and some property owners, Pelt had met with his fellow council members, builders, developers, the planning commission, real estate dealers, and consulting engineers. The black leaders, though uncommitted to the plan, were understood to be preparing a meeting to discuss it.[48]

Pelt's plan had much to recommend it. As the councilman insisted, the levees had held against all high water since 1932 and, with the construction of lakes in the Trinity watershed—Garza-Little Elm (now Lewisville), Grapevine, and others—the area would be safe from river flooding. Four hundred acres of the three thousand experienced no high water whatever; construction could begin on them at once. Proper drainage systems, to be installed prior to construction, would eliminate local flooding on the remaining land. Other black communities were close. Arlington Park, a postwar development of two hundred acres, lay immediately east of the site, across the Elm Fork branch. Trinity Valley, another African-American area, occupied part of the south border of Pelt's triangular tract. Builders Lively and Rupley of the failed Cedar Crest project had recently completed 114 apartments on a thoroughfare nearby. The prewar black settlement, once too remote for whites to worry about, that whites called Elm Thicket and blacks called North Park began about a mile east.[49]

Pelt wished to forestall any more rag-tag settlements such as West Dallas, an unincorporated area stretching west from the west levee, where low-income whites, blacks, and Hispanics, each in their own sections, bought or rented cheap land and built modest dwellings. The pending incorporation of West Dallas required the city to correct the local flooding and poor sanitary conditions there. The east levee area, Pelt warned, was "ready for development of some type right now. We must prevent another West Dallas from growing up." Heavily traveled streets ran through the Pelt site, accenting its accessibility. Pelt had various development schemes in mind for the tract.[50]

But black leaders rejected the Pelt plan. Rice, of the Dallas Negro Chamber of Commerce, led a delegation of about fifty blacks to the city council at the end of February. He took up the task of scuttling Pelt's plan while maintaining his ties with sympathetic whites. "We are more grateful for Mr. Pelt's and the council's interest than we can say," Rice began. The DNCC and the Council of Negro Organizations, representing thirty-seven groups, rejected the plan "because of its location, and the location alone." Despite the statements of developers and an engineer, blacks believed "that this site . . . enclosed as it is on three sides by the levee and traversed by a railroad, will never be freed of flood hazards and other similar situations not conducive to . . . comfort or pride in ownership of homes." Rice also complained of the "smoke, fumes and other nuisances" from nearby industrial areas. Pelt, stung by the statements of Rice and others, challenged them to come forward with locations as good or better and disputed Rice's conclusions. But the black leaders were unmoved. Most of them walked out of the council chamber when a black real-estate man rose to defend Pelt's selection. Another councilman presented a motion to commend Pelt's labors, which, the councilman asserted, were "received somewhat lightly here today"; the council passed the resolution. Rice rose to his feet to tell the council that the black representatives "hardly concur with that action."[51]

The African-American leadership had two compelling reasons for rejecting Pelt's plan. Pelt had, as A. Maceo Smith explained, promised black leaders "that no announcement would be made of the Levee District #5 proposal" until his site had been exhaustively studied, all reasonable alternative locations explored, and a consensus reached on the best area for development. Pelt justified his "breach of faith" by the need to "relieve the pressure" of racial tensions in South Dallas, but his "precipitous public announcement" presented "a grave dilemma" to black leaders. They had "no recourse" but to reject Pelt's scheme, because "the terrain is low and the proposed flood control is subject to nebulous congressional action."[52]

Rice suggested the real reason for the rejection when he mentioned "location." The site was a river bottom—and a river bottom, however nicely improved, remained a river bottom. Rice was circumspect, but blacks who could speak anonymously denounced Pelt's plan. "All their lives my people have dreamed of a time when they could live somewhere besides in the river bottoms," a black leader remarked. "I don't know whether times are any better or not," was a black clubwoman's bitter comment. "It seems that these people still think that anything is good enough for a Negro. We came out of river bottoms. Some of us are still either in them or are so crowded into slum areas that decent home life is not possible."[53]

Related to the river-bottom antagonism was a concern that Pelt's location would be the only black expansion area allowed. "You know," the clubwoman continued, "we women are going to fight with our leaders to stay out of this place where they are trying to put us and where we'll have to live the rest of our lives among mosquitoes, frogs, dampness and smoke." Given the contemporaneous efforts to hold the line against black residential succession in South Dallas, a reasonable person could believe that the Pelt plan was an effort to reconcentrate African Americans, however impossible the task would appear in retrospect. The plan, in any event, attempted to buttress the falling racial barriers of the post–World War II era. The *Dallas Express* editorialized against "the future housing of 35,000 to 40,000 Dallas Negroes in a single segregated unit. . . . It would emphasize the segregated pattern in a way that is wholly out of line with the trends of this great nation." At least one white man shared the clubwoman's suspicions. He wrote to Rice of his pleasure over the blacks' rejection of " 'Pelt's Folly' " and declared that even "if such a ghetto were placed on the highest hill around Dallas, I do not believe you should ever submit to this large scale segregation idea." Rice's correspondent noted that blacks "work all over Dallas and have many sections where you are living happily, although in need of better houses, and if these builders can ever get it through their heads to do something besides create a builders [sic] paradise out of the Negro housing problem, maybe something can be accomplished."[54]

Other whites questioned the levee solution in an atmosphere of growing anxiety over the underlying problem of inadequate black housing and its notorious symptom, the South Dallas bombings. The failure of the city council to solve the housing problem brought matters to a critical point. It was evident that no successful, large-scale housing could be built in the levee area despite some developers' continuing interest in the location. The previous failure of Hill's Diamond Hill project demonstrated that no builder could crack the wall of white opposition to a black subdivision without elite intervention. Evidently, more important whites than Pelt or Hill would have to become involved, and quickly.

The elite's spokesmen began by accommodating to the black rejection of the Pelt proposals. They did so in order to reach a humane conclusion, to preserve the city's good name, and to maintain Dallas's superior record of postwar expansion. The *Dallas Morning News* commended Pelt's effort but sympathized with black objections to "the lay of the land." Because blacks would be spending most of the money on any selected area, "their views on a site are more than weighty." The chamber of commerce in Irving, a suburb to the west, protested the site because, first, "this area is low, flat, hot, mosquito infested and unhealthy," and second, because it was "the most ideal location for industrial development in the vicinity of Dallas." John W. Carpenter, utilities magnate and president of the Dallas Chamber of Commerce, delivered the most telling statement against the Pelt plan. "If I were a colored man, I don't believe I'd like it either." Industrial development, he said, would be "much better" for that location. Although he emphasized that he was speaking as an individual, Carpenter insisted that the chamber of commerce "should deal with the problem because Negroes are valuable citizens of our community. They are valuable to commerce and industry and should be treated in a fair and equitable way."[55]

The comments of Carpenter and the others signaled the elite's involvement in the black housing issue. For A. Maceo Smith, Carpenter's statement was proof of the chamber's "assuming leadership in this Negro housing matter." Many problems lay ahead, however. It is doubtful whether Smith, Carpenter, or anyone else interested in black housing knew that more than four years would pass before the first resident would move into Hamilton Park. But a beginning had been made.[56]

3

ORGANIZING FOR HAMILTON PARK

Carpenter's conviction that the chamber of commerce "owes a debt of responsibility to every citizen of Dallas regardless of race or color" began the lengthy organizational, social, and financial arrangements leading to Hamilton Park. The day of his statement, 7 March 1950, he appointed a five-man committee on black housing to coordinate its efforts with the Dallas Negro Chamber of Commerce and other groups, a committee including the prominent bankers James W. Aston and Robert L. Thornton. The committee broke with past complacency. In 1949 the chamber contented itself with a four-man committee to cover the spectrum of race relations, not just minority housing. The 1949 race-relations group was the same size as the committee on the chamber's pension plans, or the committee on providing farm youngsters with lunches during Rural Youth Day at the Texas State Fair—a token of the minor importance of race issues in the chamber's scheme of things.[1]

The chamber's commitment reinforced the efforts of the homebuilders' association to build housing for blacks. Under a city council "ultimatum" to construct black housing units or face the prospect of new public housing, the home builders bragged on their 1,808 units built or under construction. At the same time, they insisted on their enthusiasm for public housing for blacks. African Americans who ached for single-family houses took little comfort from these developments, for practically all the new buildings were apartment houses. Any hopes pinned on a revival of Councilman Pelt's scheme were dashed in mid-March with the failure of a new plan to build houses on a portion of the levee area. The fresh effort by a coalition of five builders to construct 2,200 homes collapsed when part of the property was sold for industrial development.[2]

Meanwhile the organizational evolution continued. Late in March the Dallas Citizens' Council (DCC), "the city's top organization of civic leaders," fulfilled an earlier promise by announcing its own five-man committee, headed by banker John E. Mitchell Jr. This heavyweight group, DCC directors all, was appointed to work with the chamber committee. The joint committee began a series of meetings with African-American leaders, the home builders, "residents, business men and ministers of South Dallas, and with the entire City Council."[3]

In April the committee conducted a five-hour bus tour of actual and prospective black housing sites, accompanied by city officials, black leaders, white representatives from the South Dallas area of black residential succession, builders, and others. The group viewed both recently built black dwellings and others under construction. The new buildings were, mostly, well-constructed, inexpensive apartments, but the party also saw wretched slums. In the Mill Creek area, one mile northwest of downtown, the delegation inspected five hulks of retired city buses, without partitions or window curtains, that were renting to blacks. The buses rested on a small lot that also contained a few shacks. Only one of the buses was vacant. The nine families on the lot shared the same pit toilet and the same outside water faucet. In West Dallas, then outside the city limits, the group found twenty-two families living in two-room shacks "not two feet apart," using one outdoor toilet and one outdoor water faucet, the whole permeated by "a stench from the open drainage ditches."[4]

After more study and consultation, in late May the joint committee issued what was known as the Aston-Mitchell report. The report posited two conditions for successful housing: first, that it be built within the city limits or wherever regulations "insure that future construction will not develop into slum areas"; and second, that "the only satisfactory and permanent solution to this problem can be realized where there is racial segregation." The "basic factor" of segregation was "recognized by the Negro leadership of our community, so long as segregation in the sense that it is applied here does not mean discrimination." A bow to strict residential segregation was necessary in the Dallas of 1950, but, segregation aside, the report was an exhaustive and enlightened document. Using A. Maceo Smith's analysis of the Dallas black housing market as supplied by Rice of the Dallas Negro Chamber of Commerce, the report rang the latest changes on the "acute and critical" black housing shortage. The African-American population of metropolitan Dallas had increased from some fifty thousand in 1940 to about eighty thousand. The thirty thousand gain comprised about eight thousand families, but the net increase in black dwellings was approximately one thousand, leaving seven thousand families doubled up or tripled up, "living conditions not conducive to good health or good citizenship."[5]

There was no easy way out of the problem, because only 20 percent "of the Negro families can afford to rent or buy standard dwellings, on the present market." The problem for the other 80 percent pointed toward the committee's recommendation for expanded public housing. The committee's call to expand the existing 900 black public housing units by 1,500 new units in eighteen months was a slap at the "free enterprise" proclivities of the home builders (the DHBA). The committee tried to mollify the builders, "men of the highest integrity and ability," who were willing to build for the private market "at a close margin of profit so as to give the Negro purchasers and renters the best possible value for their investment." But the only practical alternative to wretched slum rentals for many blacks was constructing the shacks that the committee deplored. "Much of this is being done, to the great discredit of our city." The committee asserted that "Dallas is not only acquiring slums by the slow process of economic obsolescence; Dallas is actually building brand new slums. This is folly and a disgrace." Shack building was unlikely to end, however, because there was no alternative immediately available. The Dallas Housing Authority had "about 7,000" applications for its 900 black units, while one rental builder "advises that he has on file 2,000 applications in excess of available apartments." A committee recommendation for "lower standards" of construction from the FHA "so as to attract private capital" for cheaper black housing stood little chance of approval. Shepherd, the local FHA administrator, was already on record against any lowering of standards. The committee itself admitted that the required "amendments" to FHA regulations would "perhaps be slow to obtain." The only decent, relatively short-term way out for the 80 percent of lower-income African Americans lay in public housing.

Whether the housing was public or private, the "lack of building sites" meant "displacement" of whites, resulting in "forced sales and losses, disturbed and distressed communities, unrest, tension and trouble." Despite its recognition of the severely " 'hemmed in' " African-American circumstances, the report's only recommended suburban tracts were Arlington Heights and the ill-fated Bel Aire subdivision for future black dwellings. It rejected the aborted Diamond Hill plan because of a lack of public transportation and "the absence of Negro development in that area at the present time." The last phrase suggested how firmly the committee intended to confine most black housing expansion to areas adjacent to existing black homes. It reinforced its designation of underdeveloped sections in the miscellaneous and topographically dull South Dallas with a plea "that all interested groups and parties respect the present boundaries between white and Negro sections in South Dallas." The committee asserted that if its recommendations were heeded, "there will be no further encroachment of Negroes into areas of South Dallas that are now occupied by white people."

But would the continuing encroachment cease simply because the current demands for African-American housing were satisfied? That outcome contradicted the elite's commitment to growth, which would attract more blacks to the city, precipitating a continuous crisis of residential succession. The only solution was a massive, systematic African-American suburbanization to areas outside the city—one reason for the committee's recommendation "that the Dallas County government take immediate steps to initiate in the Texas State Legislature at Austin such legislation as will permit the County government to impose zoning and building restrictions in the County."

Although the committee tied its recommendations directly to its fear of shack-type slums springing up outside the city, the encouragement and control of quality housing was an important consideration. It was a progressive, not to say radical, proposal, that would be doomed by the county's inaction. Worse, zoning would have made no difference to the white opponents of black suburbanization. Nor would zoning have eased the elite's leadership burdens. The committee refused to confront enraged white homeowners around the proposed Diamond Hill subdivision, instead capitulating to the whites' arguments about the lack of transportation and the dearth of nearby black-oriented development. It is doubtful whether county zoning by itself would have emboldened the elite. Nor, even taken together, would the relatively modest public-housing program, a strict prohibition against shack building, and all the other proposed measures answer the needs of poor blacks drawn to a prosperous Dallas. The scope of the problem was beyond the will or ability of the elite to solve, though the elite could meliorate it.

The committee in some measure understood its limitations even though it did not articulate them. Despite its calls for county zoning, public housing, and participation "in the urban redevelopment program," it focused on a cooperative effort between local governments and private builders to produce middle-income African-American housing, "carefully zoned and properly restricted by the City or county," that would "attract Negro families of good character, people who, under proper environment, make citizens of whom our community can be proud." Citizens, in other words, who could pay their own way in the housing market. By providing housing for those blacks who could afford to buy into white neighborhoods, the committee hoped to prevent the residential succession that was a hallmark of social change in cities after World War II.

Indeed, the committee lumped succession with other undesirable outcomes: "We remind the people of Dallas that if we do not provide home sites for Negroes who want to, and can afford to, buy or rent suitable and decent homes, the alternative is terrible overcrowding, dissatisfaction, disease, tension resulting from Negroes buying into white neighborhoods, and many other serious consequences." In the next sentence, however, the committee hedged. "The white citizens must choose between some inconvenience that may be involved by providing suitable new residential districts for the Negroes in various areas or, what would be a thousand times worse, the bad results that inevitably will follow if we continue our present course of action, or lack of action." The possible "inconvenience" would be unlikely to affect the members of the committee, who were warning their less-advantaged white fellows that some unpalatable concessions would have to be made. When it became evident that no committee, however distinguished, could hold back the wave of residential succession, it was clear to embittered whites such as the Reverend Moore that their immediate interests would be sacrificed on the altar of racial peace.

Most important for the creation of Hamilton Park was the committee's recommendation for systematic elite involvement in racial issues. That involvement would occur through "the creation of an interracial committee consisting of not less than 15 outstanding citizens representative of our community, the primary function of which would be to promote better understanding among the various peoples of our city," to "become a clearing house" for interracial issues, and to "prevent the disgraceful bombings which have occurred in our city in recent weeks."

About two months later, on 19 July, the Dallas Interracial Committee organized at the chamber of commerce building. M. J. Norrell, a retired oil-company personnel executive and chairman of the chamber's interracial-relations committee, was elected as chairman and executive director. Samuel W. Hudson Jr., the president of the Dallas Negro Chamber of Commerce, was named secretary. The committee was broadly based, its twenty-six members including five prominent blacks. It made several studies of the black situation in Dallas, with far-reaching suggestions for improvement in such areas as public health, schooling, and recreation. Norrell and the others recognized, however, that "Negro housing was the most important problem for the committee to grapple with"—by which they meant the middle-income housing problem. Not so coincidentally, it was the issue that the committee was best equipped to address. After all, as Norrell himself reported in August, one thousand public-housing units were authorized for Dallas; construction would begin soon.[6]

Jerome Crossman, whose name would become closely linked with Hamilton Park, reported on the middle-income housing problem. He urged "the establishment of a non-profit corporation" to buy and develop large tracts "to be sold to private builders for development," and to work with the city "for the extension of utilities." Crossman's proposal closely followed its model, an "Orlando, Florida development," and would eventually become the mechanism for the creation of Hamilton Park. The proposal, though scarcely original, would be known in Dallas as the "Crossman Plan"—an erroneous attribution. Nothing, however, should detract from Crossman's unremitting efforts to realize a new black community. An understanding of the realities of the situation involves, first, a look at Crossman himself and, second, an examination of the actual origins of the Crossman Plan, including why it was attributed to a local business leader.[7]

Crossman, a respected independent oilman, was the president of the Ryan Consolidated Petroleum Corporation, a producing company. He was, as well, an attorney adept at maneuvering toward goals he judged to be attainable. "He was not the type of aggressive individual in that he was going to run roughshod over the community with his own ideas. He was a good negotiator," an associate recalled. A Reform Jew, Crossman was "very concerned about the welfare of all mankind, regardless of race, color, or creed." Fifty-four years old in 1950, Crossman "was optimistic generally; otherwise, he wouldn't have been in the oil business." He "was optimistic that racial relations would improve and that blacks would develop professionally; otherwise, he wouldn't have been interested in Bishop College"—an African-American institution soon to move to Dallas.[8]

Crossman was an optimist but no visionary. He did not foresee a desegregated society living under legal mandates of equality; nor was he a racial liberal attempting to move toward that goal. Spectacles and a receding hairline endowed him with a scholarly, almost ascetic appearance that belied his penchant for hard work, his drive, and his realism. He would labor for racial justice within the boundaries set by enlightened whites such as himself. At the same time, he retreated into generalizations when describing the racial future, a stance suggesting his uncertainty about its precise composition and his unwillingness to limit the present possibilities by speculating on their ultimate effects. Instead he relied heavily on "understanding" to insure racial harmony.[9]

Crossman's call for a nonprofit corporation to buy land, extend utilities to it, then sell it to developers for house construction came against the backdrop of failed and faltering efforts to provide housing for middle-income blacks. Planner Bartholomew had no authority to realize his suggestion that nonprofit or philanthropic corporations build "in and adjoining outlying nonwhite areas." Individual builders lacked the financial resources or the power to secure large sites, have the FHA approve them for loan guarantees, and arrange for the extension of utilities to them. A nonprofit corporation pooling the political and economic might of the city's wealthy and its leading financial institutions could overcome the handicaps of past, uncoordinated efforts. Crossman's ultimately successful solution could not, however, be publicly revealed as coming from its true source—the racial-relations section of the FHA. Nor could A. Maceo Smith, the African-American leader and racial-relations advisor for the Dallas FHA zone, be credited with promoting the idea in Dallas.[10]

It was not that the Dallas leadership reacted phobicly to federal initiatives or to information from blacks such as Smith. As a case in point, consider the DCC–chamber of commerce committee's embrace of public housing and its use of statistics on black housing as developed by Smith and transmitted through the Dallas Negro Chamber of Commerce. Nevertheless, the elite preferred to present its ideas and positions as locally generated by the white leadership. The practice made sense. A discussion of the Orlando, Florida, plan would have drawn attention away from the local problem and risked a debate mired in the applicability of an Orlando solution to Dallas. Smith was an immensely capable man, but as an African American in Dallas in 1950 he was barred by racial custom from working in close association with the variety of whites in the public and private sectors necessary to carry the idea of a new black community to a finish.

The Orlando development of Washington Shores enjoyed a wide appeal because its nonprofit corporation liberated black housing from dependence on developers with limited resources. By pooling funds from several sources, the nonprofit also expanded middle-income African-American housing horizons beyond the search for a wealthy corporate or individual "angel." The Orlando story began in 1947 when a tile manufacturer searched for a house and lot for a black employee who was saving to become a homeowner. Like other well-meaning whites, the tile manufacturer had no conception of the limited housing opportunities for blacks. Dismayed by his findings, he enlisted the aid of service clubs, the chamber of commerce, and the city government to find a solution. The answer was a private, nonprofit corporation designed to purchase the land and develop it for resale. The tile manufacturer and his civic-minded associates set a fund-raising goal of $50,000, an amount exceeded "by more than $5,000." An investigation conducted with the help of a black advisory group discovered a likely site outside the city. Then a problem surfaced: developers could not construct a desirable community without a guarantee of utilities extension to the site, while the city was reluctant to extend utilities to an area that might not develop fully enough to justify the expense.[11]

At that juncture the Orlando Housing Authority cooperated with the city and the developers by constructing attractive, single-story public housing at either end of Washington Shores. The neat, free-standing houses bore no resemblance to the later, high-rise projects that served to discredit the concept of public housing. With utilities-consuming public housing bracketing the area, the nonprofit corporation and the developers could proceed. Soon, 160 single-family homes were built, a shopping center was developed, and a county school for grades one through six was planned. The depth and range of public and private cooperation was unprecedented. Not only did the nonprofit corporation, the city, the housing authority, and the county school board work in harness, but the First National Bank made mortgage loans, the Florida legislature expanded Orlando's city limits to include Washington Shores, the FHA helped with "technical site problems," and an African-American real-estate firm "was organized and bonded to handle the sales promotion." All this activism flew in the face of opposition from the white owners of profitable rental property.[12]

Moreover, the racial-relations service of the FHA evangelized the Washington Shores plan to interested community groups, as the FHA's Douglas Rosenblum did in Richmond, Virginia, during spring 1947. "Distinctive developments were stressed," Rosenblum wrote, "such as the corporation formed by Negroes themselves in Macon [Georgia] and the non-profit corporation formed by white citizens in Orlando."[13]

Smith had to have been aware of Washington Shores from its inception and he probably advanced the Orlando development as a model during discussions with various groups seeking an answer to the black housing problem in Dallas. There was no great enthusiasm for the plan until after the joint committee's unequivocal endorsement of black expansion areas and orderly black suburbanization. As soon as the Dallas Interracial Committee formed, however, Smith was ready with a suggestion for a nonprofit corporation and a letter endorsing the scheme from the national administrator of the FHA, Raymond M. Foley. Crossman's housing subcommittee accepted the idea. Crossman put up a $5,000 option to secure a site until the nonprofit could be formed.[14]

Crossman's initial enthusiasm reflected a confidence in the Dallas Interracial Committee and the elite's willingness to dig into its own pockets to fund the nonprofit corporation. At first things seemed to go well. The full committee approved the scheme on Crossman's recommendation, then appointed a new housing subcommittee to "develop the idea." The appointees, in addition to Crossman and Smith, were a banker, a prominent real-estate man, and Lynn Landrum, the *Dallas Morning News* columnist who wrote sympathetically about the problems of overcrowded blacks. The subcommittee pressed two plans. The first was a scheme to convert fifty city-owned lots in South Dallas from a buffer area between blacks and whites to black residence. The city had purchased the lots from African Americans in 1942. The subcommittee's idea involved resale to those original former owners who agreed to build within a year. The idea fit the committee's drive to stabilize or roll back the residential succession in South Dallas. Ultimately, however, the city sold the property neither to its former owners nor to the Reverend Moore's group but to a developer with no overt racial agenda.[15]

The subcommittee's second scheme involved extensive purchases beyond the Dallas city limits near the site of Hamilton Park. Crossman worked with B. "Hick" Majors, a real-estate man operating in the area, to secure his option on a struggling airport—179 acres near "the Coit Road site." The Coit Road tract, on which "eight or more options had already been secured," was large and expensive: by mid-August, Crossman was speaking of the nonprofit corporation being capitalized at $2 million. Smith predicted that forty or fifty of the elite would join the nonprofit, "establish public confidence," and "offset any possible opposition that may be incurred." Smith also believed that the Coit Road site had "great possibilities and will be finally developed as planned." As late as mid-November the full committee was "working toward" the nonprofit in order to "develop a large tract, or tracts, of well situated land, into a Negro community—with provision made for sites for schools, parks, churches, and shopping center." Crossman recognized that "the task is too large for a single committee to carry through," but expected that the necessary "cooperation will be forthcoming."[16]

Despite Crossman's optimism, the interracial committee proved unable to organize the nonprofit before the bombings resumed in June 1951. The elite's bold definition of the problem contrasted with its hesitant commitment to a solution. Later, Crossman and his fellow laborers would understand that the concern was less for the money involved than it was for the embarrassment of a failed subdivision. The renewed bombing had the good effect of temporarily downing such concerns and again catalyzing the elite. Members of the elite pressed for a special grand jury and—spurred by Crossman—for a definitive solution to the middle-income black housing dilemma. Once more Crossman shrewdly analyzed the problem and offered a solution within the scope of the elite's powers. The bombings, he asserted, were "but a symptom of deep-lying causes, namely, lack of adequate and decent housing for the Negroes of Dallas." Low-income blacks were "well on the way to being taken care of in West Dallas and other sections by the Dallas Housing Authority," he believed. "But the housing gain for other income brackets has been negligible." Action to meet the middle-income demand, he argued, would help all "white citizens," but "particularly" those "in the troubled areas" of racial succession. "All thinkers recognize that the insecurity of one group of people menaces the security of all. Enlightened self-interest alone dictates to the dominant group the necessity of solving the Negro housing problem as quickly as possible."[17]

Crossman garnered fresh pledges of support from businessmen and from Rice of the DNCC, but this time he went to the board of directors of the chamber of commerce. By the end of August the chamber, the interracial committee, and the DCC had agreed to appoint yet another committee of five representatives from each group. The chamber's five included Henry S. Miller, a leading real-estate man; the interracial committee appointed Crossman, Rice, and three others. A month later the DCC appointed its five, including bankers John E. Mitchell Jr. and

Nathan Adams. The committee followed Carpenter's injunction to "get organized and get right down to business." By the end of October it had secured a state charter for the new group, the Dallas Citizens' Interracial Association (DCIA).[18]

Crossman, not surprisingly, became the association's president. The other officers were Mitchell, the powerful Thornton, businessman Louis Tobian, and banker Ben H. Wooten. The association's fifteen directors included the officers plus banker Adams, merchant Stanley Marcus, and two blacks—Rice and Samuel W. Hudson Jr., the manager of the Roseland Homes public-housing units. Committees were appointed within a few months of the founding. Adams was named chairman of the finance and budget committee. H. Leslie Hill, a prominent real-estate man, headed the sites committee, and Karl Hoblitzelle, the founder of the Interstate Theater chain, chaired the ways and means committee. An advisory council of 176 white and black leaders was largely window dressing, but served notice of broad-based support for the DCIA and its objectives. Those objectives were to "consider and act upon any matter of whatsoever character which shall induce harmonious relationships among members of various racial groups residing in [Dallas County]." Adequate minority housing headed the list of specifics. The bylaws set an annual membership donation of $52.[19]

The DCIA moved ahead after the holidays. In February 1952 the directors named Norrell their executive vice-president. On the morning of 26 March the association held a rousing meeting at the First National Bank building, attended by some hundred officers, directors, and members of the advisory council. Crossman told the crowd of the membership donations pouring in. More than $14,000 had been raised, he said, and still more was on the way. But he did not blink at the difficulties ahead. "We're going to have static," he predicted. "It is not a job for one or two or three citizens. It's a job for each of us. I'm not a reformer," he protested, "but it will take spiritual understanding." Crossman added that "platitudes and generalization" would not overcome the sort of attitude reflected in the comment of a white man who said that he did not want black housing within three miles of his residence because he "would have to 'drive through it' to get home."[20]

Following Crossman's remarks, representatives of the DHBA, the DNCC, and the real-estate board pledged their support. Hoblitzelle remarked that "the problem of Negro housing should be considered from an ethical, moral, and commercial viewpoint," reiterating the need for a nonprofit corporation. The meeting concluded with appointing the ways and means committee and the site-selection committee and approving yet another African-American housing survey.[21]

The final moves toward a beginning on Hamilton Park involved not only site selection but also the more difficult issues of airport expansion and the financing of both land and utilities. Selecting the site was the simplest of the three, although it was a lengthy, exasperating process. Crossman probably influenced the site committee to continue looking in the area north of Dallas, well known for its scattering of small African-American communities. A joint meeting on 26 June of the sites and ways and means committees, with Crossman and Norrell also present, heard a recommendation from H. Leslie Hill for the site that became Hamilton Park—"located at Forest Lane, approximately 100 yards east of Central Expressway." The group then toured the site. At a joint meeting on 3 July the sites committee presented its report on the 173-acre area—a report forecasting in its essentials the outcome of events. The report noted that some seven hundred families could be accommodated in single-family houses and apartments in a "high" area, permitting "a high type of development, having proper drainage and ideal home sites."[22]

The report took note, indirectly, of the strident opposition to previous homesites from nearby white residents. It gave veiled assurances that little or no resistance could be expected to the development of the property. "There are at the present time many negro families living in the immediate proximity to this proposed location," the sites committee noted. "There also exists a negro school, two negro churches, and a small negro shopping area." The location included some twenty acres used as a park, which the committee hoped could be taken into the Dallas park system. To that end, and for the purposes of utilities extension, zoning protection, and full city services, the committee recommended annexation of the site. The property would have to be purchased and utilities extended at the association's expense. The committee also recommended placing the property "under the necessary deed restrictions, to insure proper development and future protection," and resales to developers under terms "requiring the area to be developed with streets, utilities, and homes according to deed restrictions."[23]

The presence at the session of city manager Charles C. Ford and C. B. Bunkley Jr., the president of the Dallas Negro Chamber of Commerce, together with Crossman and Norrell, lent weight to the sites committee's recommendations. Absent a definite funding plan, however, the group reached no conclusions. When the ways and means committee met with Crossman a week later, a second site of 150 acres about a mile south of the future Hamilton Park had been offered. Tentative costs, including utilities, had not been assessed, which required a further delay. At the next joint meeting on 24 July an exasperated Crossman read a prepared statement deploring the "considerable loss of time" taken up with "the discussion of relatively unimportant matters" that left "less time for a discussion of the real fundamentals involved." Crossman blamed the circumstances on the relatively large size of the group and the lack of a "definite agenda"; he proposed, therefore, that both "the so-called Majors site" (the future Hamilton Park) and "the so-called Hexter site" to the south be considered. Utilities costs to both would be about the same and the combined area of more than three hundred acres would yield "some 1400 net building sites."[24]

Crossman urged definite arrangements with the City of Dallas for utilities extension. The committees acted on his proposal by appointing a subcommittee to discuss the problem with the city. Turning to costs, Crossman argued that the suggested price of home and lot, $8,000 to $8,500, was far too high. He had been "informed" that the FHA would approve a two-bedroom design to sell for $6,500 to $7,000, which would lower the total monthly mortgage costs from $65 or $75 a month to some $40 or $45. Crossman raised a significant issue. Given the median wage for an African-American working man in 1949 of $1,503, and also given the FHA's qualifying rule of thumb of monthly earnings—that they be five times greater than the monthly payment—the reduction "would immediately bring . . . many times as many folks able to buy and qualify. It may not seem that a few dollars per month should make such a tremendous difference," he added, "but it is axiomatic that each time a price be reduced, even if only by a few dollars, percentagewise the number of prospective buyers increases tremendously."[25]

A meeting of the two committees and others on 31 July brought matters closer to a resolution. In the presence of Louis J. Hexter and B. "Hick" Majors, the sites committee decided to proceed only with the Majors site. A late August meeting involved discussions about developing the Majors location. Crossman appointed a subcommittee that included banker and former city manager Aston to plan the eventual annexation of the property. At a mid-October luncheon, the DCIA's steering committee concluded that the "development was imperative," discussed various ways of financing it, and appointed a subcommittee to bring back "a definite recommendation for financing" the purchase. The members of the committee included Crossman, Hill, Mitchell, a banker who had been active in the effort since 1950, and its chairman, Carr P. Collins, the president of the Fidelity Union Life Insurance Company. Collins, a fresh public face in the drive to secure Hamilton Park, would become a key figure in its development. By February 1953 all the arrangements were in place and the DCIA purchased the property from Majors—the same Majors who had worked with the Dallas Interracial Committee in its unsuccessful efforts to locate land during the summer of 1950.[26]

The future Hamilton Park would not be free from controversy, however. This was because of a simultaneous elite effort to expand the municipal airport, Love Field. Black-owned houses and rental property occupied by blacks lay in the southward path of the expansion—an expansion promising to exacerbate the very housing crisis that the DCIA was laboring to resolve. The area, called North Park or Elm Thicket, was built beginning in the 1930s. A neighborhood of small-to-modest houses, it would lose some three hundred homes and find the new boundaries of Love Field abutting many more.[27]

The elite's willingness to obliterate black housing while offering mostly rhetoric about the plight of underhoused blacks was not lost on Dr. John O. Chisum, an African-American optometrist and resident of the threatened district. Chisum and his white allies near Love Field, few or none of whom would lose their homes, opposed the expansion on the grounds of safety, noise, and the inadequacy of even the expanded airport to handle jet aircraft and substantially increased traffic. Chisum's emphasis, however, was on black residential displacement in the context of Dallas's racial past. The preconditions for a stable black neighborhood, he wrote, were: that blacks settled it originally; that it was not wanted by whites; and, more recently, that any proposed African-American area "must by no means displease one white man due to its proximity." When forced by overcrowded conditions to expand into neighborhoods previously white, "we face the terrors of mob outrage when we seek new homes." Chisum termed the Dallas Negro Chamber of Commerce's efforts to combat violence "feeble at best," while "the boss Chamber doesn't have time to get around to it." He was not questioning the integrity of the leaders of the "boss" Dallas Chamber of Commerce, "but with their multi million dollar programs they seldom find it convenient to give the Negro even passing notice regarding his housing problems."[28]

Chisum's criticism was overdrawn but accurate enough to sting. In an editorial response written by Landrum and published a few days before the 27 January 1953 bond-issue vote, the *Morning News* answered. Landrum anticipated the DCIA's purchase by almost a month when he wrote that the association "has under contract an area on a desirable location, where 700 single-family dwellings will be erected for Negro homeowners at a price they can afford to pay." The next day Crossman assured the North Park residents that they would have ample time to relocate and "be able to buy good homes at reasonable prices with paved streets, gutters, adequate draining, water, sewerage, and all utilities." Although Crossman hoped to down black opposition to the expansion, he failed. Before filing away Landrum's editorial, Chisum wrote across its top margin, "The Big Lie." The bond issue carried handily, but the doubts continued. In March 1953, North Park residents were skeptical of Crossman's statements about a "first class development" where houses would be available for payments of $45 to $50 per month. They thought that the area—some nine and one-half road miles northeast of North Park, by streets and the new North Central Expressway—was too "remote" from schools and transportation. And, as one resident asked: "How do they know we will like the place?"[29]

Crossman persisted. "First preference will be given to families in the Love Field area," he announced in June. "Approximately 300 families in the Love Field area will find it necessary to obtain other homes." Chisum was unpersuaded. Interviewed late in 1954, in the midst of a losing legal and propaganda fight against the expansion of Love Field, he continued to denounce Hamilton Park as a humbug of the white elite. The first houses there sold for $7,500 or more, and Elm Thicket residents who received only their equity in $1,500 to $4,000 homes could not afford down payments and the monthly charges. Inadequate bus service kept out those dependent on public transportation. "Our people are poor," he said. "Owning a car is just out of the question for many of them." When asked how many of his neighbors moved to Hamilton Park, he replied, "I've checked our neighborhood thoroughly, and have been unable to find any who did. Perhaps there were some." Chisum was correct in the main, for most families displaced from Elm Thicket moved to nearby black areas. Relatively few ventured across town to Hamilton Park.[30]

The subdivision was, nevertheless, a significant benefit for 737 African-American families. Financing the land purchase and utilities extension, securing engineering services on the site, and finding a contractor-developer were the remaining major steps toward that realization. Washington Shores continued to be the model for the development, with variations to suit the conditions in Dallas.

Karl Hoblitzelle of Interstate Theaters provided the loan for Hamilton Park through the offices of the Hoblitzelle Foundation. Bringing him into the DCIA was an inspiration, because of Hoblitzelle's abiding sympathy for blacks. Tall, spare, and gray-haired, with a dignified mien and courtly manner belying his humble origin, Hoblitzelle attended few meetings of the DCIA or its committees but stayed in touch with the ways and means committee through a surrogate. As Crossman told it, "I came to Karl one morning, not for money, but for advice. The association had an option on the 173 acres of land we needed for the houses, and we had to act. Mr. Hoblitzelle quickly volunteered: 'Go ahead with your project. I'll see you have the money.' "[31]

It is doubtful whether either man was so naive. As early as May 1949, well before the South Dallas bombings, Hoblitzelle went before the board of his Hoblitzelle Foundation and "presented to the trustees the desperate need of the negroes of Dallas for housing. He outlined a general scheme that contemplated a development embracing from one thousand to fifteen hundred acres that, in addition to various types of housing, would accommodate a park area, with swimming pool, tennis courts, a lake, small golf course, and other recreational facilities; a suitable plot to be dedicated for a negro college; and other areas to commercial development, churches, school, etc." Following an "animated and lengthy discussion," the "trustees enthusiastically endorsed the tentative program," as well as Hoblitzelle's suggestion that a small fund be set aside for preliminary expenses. They also resolved that some $250,000 might eventually be spent to develop the plan.[32]

By January 1950, Hoblitzelle and his trustees—such people as Sara T. Hughes, a federal district judge, Fred Florence, of Republic National Bank, and Umphrey Lee, the president of Southern Methodist University—had decided against a thousand-acre tract. No such large parcel of land could be assembled for a quarter of a million dollars in the Trinity River valley where the foundation's secretary had been scouting out properties; besides, the secretary had learned of "two or three" efforts to build black housing in the area. The trustees shelved their original plan, almost identical to the one that Roland Pelt would shortly propose for the same location, in favor of a 150- to 200-acre site for community purposes, should the valley develop as African-American housing in the future. Thus, the idea of assisting middle-income black housing on a smaller scale survived the failure of the grand plan. Hoblitzelle spoke to the prospect of a more modest project when he said that "the time might very well come when the Trustees will want to seize on such an opportunity as this negro housing development, which would call for a large amount of cash." He advised his trustees "to accumulate and maintain generally a fairly large amount of free cash on hand" to assist with black housing.[33]

The date on which Hoblitzelle first became aware of the "Crossman plan" funding of a black subdivision is not known, but he was well aware of it by the March 1952 meeting of officers, directors, and the advisory council. He and Fred Florence discussed the matter, then Hoblitzelle directed his foundation to lend $216,873 to the DCIA to buy the land that became Hamilton Park. The foundation granted the loan on 13 February 1953, for one year at 3 percent interest. As the DCIA sold land to the developer, it repaid the loan to the foundation. From time to time the foundation renewed the note, which was finally retired in July 1960. The DCIA made no interest payments over the years and the foundation forgave the accrued interest when the DCIA completed the payments of principal.[34]

Hoblitzelle's commitment was careful, prudent, and made in the light of the tradition of African-American settlement around the Hamilton Park site—a tradition that practically precluded white opposition. In the context of elite whites' fears of a failure of any black subdivision sponsored by them, however, his action appears bold. The white fears were unfounded; nevertheless, Crossman would encounter them from time to time as he and others struggled with the details of bringing the utilities to Hamilton Park, extending the city limits around it, financing and contracting for the utilities, arranging the site development, securing FHA approval for standardized house designs, and finding a contractor who would build the designs to FHA specifications.

The details easiest to obtain were getting permission for city utilities and the limits extensions. While it was moving toward a land purchase, the DCIA signed contracts with the city for two utilities extensions— one, a water line west for two and one-half miles along Forest Lane and the other a sewer three and one-half miles north from the nearest useable trunk line. The city agreed to reimburse the actual cost of the lines in annual installments, but not any interest charges. The council subsequently, in August 1953, annexed Hamilton Park.[35]

Crossman convinced a consortium of banks whose officers were or had been active in the black housing movement to loan money for the utilities extensions. The banks loaned $423,620, with Florence's Republic Bank acting as agent and assuming 37.5 percent of the amount, the First National Bank accepting 37.5 percent, and Thornton's Mercantile National Bank following with the remaining 25 percent. The note bore interest at 4 percent, "payable annually on the unpaid balance," sums that were repaid by early 1960. It was a large amount of money then, and in elite eyes it was a considerable risk, whatever the outcome. At least one banker, Ben Wooten of First National, shared the elite's uncertainty about the success of Hamilton Park. He confronted Crossman one day during the negotiations. "Jerry," he asked, "these loans that the bank is making to the Interracial Association—are we going to get this money back, or should we just consider it a donation?" The loan went through, despite misgivings, and on 18 July Crossman could sign the contracts for the installation of water and sewer lines. About the same time, he secured an engineering firm "to survey and sub-divide the land purchased into residence lots, and to supervise the installation of utilities and other improvements." The local offices of the FHA and the VA worked with the association to develop affordable house designs.[36]

Meanwhile, Collins, of Fidelity Union Life Insurance, the Dr. Pepper Bottling Company, and other enterprises, became active in securing a building contractor. At the same time, he was organizing a consortium of insurance companies to purchase the FHA-insured mortgages. He involved himself in the search for a contractor after Crossman "had called the main home builders," asked them to build in Hamilton Park, and received negative replies. "The boom was relatively at a nice pace then, and the builders had just about all they wanted to do with white housing. In fact, they just didn't want to get involved with Negro housing at that time." At least one company with prior experience in building African-American housing refused to become involved for another reason: because of doubts about obtaining "the financing without it being more trouble than it was worth."[37]

Collins was "a humdinger of a dealer; he was a real sharp dealer," unlikely to be deterred by such refusals. He telephoned Thomas J. Hayman, of Inge-Hayman Construction Company, the builders of his life-insurance office tower, and asked Hayman's firm to erect the houses. Hayman admired Collins, but was skeptical. The company built commercial buildings, not houses, Hayman replied. He also expressed doubts about financing the construction, the ability of a significant number of blacks to pay for the houses, and the mortgage market. Collins soon removed some of Hayman's doubts. As the contractor remembered it, Collins backed his own three children as silent partners in an expanded Associated Construction Company, an existing development corporation that consisted of Hayman and two partners. Collins also went to work on the problem of financing the mortgages. Collins's commitment to mortgage financing meant that Associated Construction had no trouble with its own finances. "Now this is a civic thing," Hayman said of the Hamilton Park development, "and First National gave us a very good rate of financing. So we'd go to the bank to get the money to buy the land, and we'd go back to the bank to get the money to build our houses, and then we retired that as we sold houses."[38]

Collins's work with other insurance companies forged the final link making Hamilton Park a reality. His variation on the collaborative theme, already so much a part of Hamilton Park, was to form a consortium of companies agreeing to invest in Hamilton Park house mortgages. Knowing that his own company, Fidelity Union Life, should not or could not assume the entire burden, he urged other insurance companies to share the responsibility. His method revealed just what "a humdinger of a dealer" he was, because he proposed that each company buy mortgages in proportion to its assets. Let Thomas Hayman describe Collins's inspiration: "He hit on the idea that he would go to the insurance companies of the area and impose on them or give them an opportunity—let's word it that way—to be part of this great move to furnish homes for these Negroes. He had a formula that they would participate in the lending in direct proportion to their capital structure, you know, their net worth. Well, that gave just a small portion of this to Fidelity Union and a large portion to Southwestern Life. Mr. Collins came out pretty easy." In addition to Fidelity Union, which pledged $1 million, or 20 percent of the FHA and VA paper, and Southwestern, Republic National Life and five others agreed to come in. Collins's plan was far enough advanced that Crossman could announce the tentative arrangements to the DCIA board on 1 June 1953. On 26 October, at a meeting in Collins's office, the companies made their commitments and the subdivision was assured.[39]

Collins could not assuage Hayman's doubts about the number of blacks who would purchase substantially constructed, FHA-approved houses in Hamilton Park. Smith estimated that thousands of people would qualify. When Albert Cole, the head of the Housing and Home Finance Agency, visited Dallas in August 1953, John W. Rice of the Dallas Negro Chamber of Commerce was one of several people who appeared before him. "It is estimated that 59,566 Negroes are employed in the metropolitan Dallas area and that 21% of the minority group families" earned $3,000 or more per year, Rice declared. Those figures represented a market, as yet unmet, of at least 2,500 new houses. Growing "employment opportunities for Negroes and improved educational achievements" had "produced some income increases and savings," qualifying at least that 21 percent "for participation in the private housing market."[40]

Would these estimates translate into down payments from families with incomes and commitments adequate to the long-term development of a stable community? No one knew. Hayman, acting for Associated Construction, agreed to build two model houses facing Forest Lane. If there proved to be "insufficient qualified purchasers available to warrant further construction or if for any other reason we do not go forward," then the DCIA could reimburse the construction company's costs or sell to the company, at cost, the land on which the houses stood. Hayman never doubted that Hamilton Park itself would be realized. Years later he said that "when you have whites like Fred Florence, Karl Hoblitzelle, Dr. Levi Olin, Carr P. Collins, and Ben Wooten, you were talking about powerful people in that day. They determined that it was right." The development work itself "was not a scary thing at all," in part because "we saw the need" for black housing. Could need be transformed into houses? That was Hayman's question.[41]

By June 1953 the plans for Hamilton Park had advanced far enough for Crossman to make a general announcement about the subdivision. A little more than three years had passed since the joint committee of the chamber of commerce had pointed to the urgent need for black housing, and almost another year would pass before the first families moved into their new homes. The halting, cumbersome move toward opening one black subdivision scarcely seems to justify the white elite's later fulsome self-congratulation. Taken in the context of racial change in Dallas, Hamilton Park was no great leap forward. By 1953, whites had conceded South Dallas to blacks, opening a large area to African-American residence. The year before, Cabell's Dairy had "put the first Negro on a retail milk route in the South," and the Schlitz brewery had hired its first black distributor. The Dallas Eagles baseball team signed David Hoskins, a pitcher, the first African American in the Texas League. Edward L. Newhouse Sr., who moved to Hamilton Park in 1955, remembered that his employer, the Huey and Philip firm, integrated the men's room when the company hired its first woman employee and the Jim Crow rest room became the women's room. These changes affected few whites or blacks immediately or directly, no more than did the contemporaneous federal court decisions relentlessly striking down racial barriers. They were portents nevertheless (see chapter 5).[42]

From the perspective of race relations, however, Hamilton Park should be viewed as one more straw in the wind bringing sweeping changes in many areas of life. Neither original nor unprecedented, it represented close black-white cooperation to improve housing for more than seven hundred black families. But race relations and improved housing opportunities are not the only lenses through which to view Hamilton Park. Influence and control were important, too. The power and determination of the white elite created the subdivision, but white influence over the maintenance and development of the community rapidly dwindled. The residents of Hamilton Park did not always control all areas of their community's development, but their outlook was critical for its future. In a time of national and local racial transition, Hamilton Park shifted from a white-led project to a black-controlled community.

4

A TRANSITION IN WHITE AND BLACK

Hamilton Park resulted from interracial effort but there was no doubt where the locus of the power to effect it lay. The white elite had put it over, but the white elite would not and could not maintain its control over the development. As Hamilton Park grew, whites retreated and blacks assumed increasing responsibility for the community. After 1959, when Hamilton Park was virtually completed, its destiny was in the hands of its residents, as much as a community's fate may be decided locally. The waning of the DCIA, failed efforts to expand black housing adjacent to Hamilton Park, and the Hoblitzelle Foundation's and outsiders' refusal to become involved in two land-use disputes in Hamilton Park, confirmed the shift to community control. First, however, Hamilton Park had to be opened and developed.

Overcast skies and pattering rain greeted the awakening citizens of Dallas on Sunday morning, 4 October 1953. Through the day the rain would diminish to almost a mist, then resume its light but steady fall. Rain or no rain, the dedication of Hamilton Park was scheduled for 4 P.M. An interracial and interdenominational gathering, it was carefully planned and well promoted in the African-American newspapers. By the appointed time some three hundred people had squeezed into the frame shell of a two-bedroom model home facing Forest Lane, a two-lane road marking the extreme north limit of settlement in Dallas.[1]

Crossman presided at the plywood podium. A Roman Catholic auxiliary bishop gave the invocation. C. B. Bunkley, the attorney who was also the vigorous president of the Dallas Negro Chamber of Commerce, delivered the keynote speech. Dr. Marshall T. Steel, the progressive pastor of the Highland Park Methodist Church, gave the major address; bankers Fred F. Florence and Ben Wooten spoke briefly; and a rabbi and the Reverend Ernest C. Estell each pronounced a benediction.

The representatives of each race emphasized their own perspectives on the dedication. Bunkley spoke to an era of the poll tax, the dual labor market and its low job ceiling for blacks, and the problem of decent housing for African Americans. Yet it was also an era of rising expectations. "This," Bunkley remarked, referring to Hamilton Park, "came about through the efforts of those who want to make democracy a reality." After deploring the "economic status and credit restrictions" limiting "the pride of ownership of property," he suggested that more improvement should follow, "for no city can be any better than its lowest scale citizen." In a statement suggesting how far society yet had to travel to achieve equality of opportunity, he declared that Hamilton Park "places on all of us a consciousness of the benefits as well as the responsibilities involved in making democracy work in our city."[2]

Estell, the pastor of the black St. John Baptist Church, was, as builder Thomas J. Hayman remembered him, "one of the greatest fellows on the interracial committee"—a "great character and a sound man." Estell's church choir provided music that emphasized the opportunity for homeownership: its selections included "Swing Low Sweet Chariot (comin' for to carry me home)," "Bless This House," and "Plenty of Room."[3]

Whites also emphasized the value of homeownership. "Men die," Wooten declared, "not to preserve apartments, slums and just ordinary possessions. They fight and die to preserve their homes, the most sacred places on earth." White speeches, however, focused on the idealism, hard work, recognition of duty, and interracial cooperation involved in creating Hamilton Park. They also perpetuated the newly minted myth of the uniqueness of their effort. Despite Washington Shores in Orlando and existing postwar, suburban-style communities for blacks in Atlanta, Miami, Memphis, and Oklahoma City, Wooten insisted that "no other city has had the courage to do what we have done in the creation of this subdivision." Councilman W. L. Miller, standing in for the ailing Mayor Thornton, spoke of "a model of civic interest which will challenge cities all over the nation."[4]

Speakers of both races discoursed on the environmental value of a quality home life. Wooten praised "the men and women who will live here and raise stalwart citizens." Bunkley referred to a site "high, beautiful and well situated," a place "from which future citizens will come to help and to make possible a type of progress that Dallas, our city, has never known before."[5]

Bunkley's hopeful reference to the site was well taken. North from

Forest Lane the land rose, from about five hundred feet above sea level—
well above the elevation of a river bottom—some eighty feet in the
length of half a mile to the future intersection of Schroeder Road and
Towns Street. A gradual ascent led to the ultimate north boundary at
Bunche Drive—about a ninety-foot rise in all. To the west, the surface fell
away, sometimes steeply, toward Cottonwood Creek. From the western
line of the future Willowdell Drive, it sloped over the twenty-acre swath
of park that would serve the community. To the east, the land declined
more gently toward the Houston & Texas Central (now Southern Pacific)
railroad tracks. Save for a cluster of tall trees at the southeastern segment of the Oberlin Drive curve, only shrubby hackberries and mesquite
clumped here and there on the thin, farmed-out soil. Limestone lay just
beneath the surface of the crescent-shaped ledge marking a steep rise in
Schroeder Road—a rise beginning two blocks north of Forest Lane. Limestone outcroppings broke the surface in scattered spots. Ocie Turner, one
of the first residents in Hamilton Park, remembered the shell of a large,
abandoned house near the limestone ledge. A bramble of branches rose
above the bed of Cottonwood Creek. A line of trees ran near the future
location of Bunche Drive.[6]

The site was well known to many Dallas blacks. The Andersons, Bonners, Subers, and other black families lived nearby in what was then
known as the "upper White Rock" area. Some residents of Hamilton Park
had earlier associations with upper White Rock and, in some instances,
with the Hamilton Park site itself. Frank Dixon hunted rabbits there.
Sadye Gee recalled family outings to the area when she was a child.
"Out here was a real treat." On Sundays and holidays the family would
take the interurban from near north Dallas to a station in the Vickery
vicinity, south of the Hamilton Park site, where cousins who owned a
Model T Ford would meet them. "It was a thrill to ride in an automobile."
Schroeder Road "was just a little trail," leading to relatives' homes and to
play places. "We would play and go up and down the cotton fields and
just explore the rural area. . . . We lived in the city, and everything was
so fascinating to us." Freddie Allen drove a long-distance truck north, detouring from Greenville Avenue to the tree line near the north edge of
the future Hamilton Park, where he sat under a tree and cooled off.[7]

Members of the Fields family and their relatives lived in a group of
seven houses along the west side of Schroeder Road, north of the future
junction with Willowdell Street. Some men in the family cut hay on
the nearby northern portion of the community-to-be, across the road

from the Fields houses. Later, when Hamilton Park developed, a few Fields family members moved into the young community. Richard Bonner, although never a resident of Hamilton Park, knew it well. He lived near the site—across North Central Expressway—attended the Hamilton Park School, and started on the Bobcat football team that won the state championship in 1961. He spent "a lot of time" in the community with Hamilton Park school chums.[8]

African Americans further identified with Hamilton Park because they named the community and its streets. The Dallas Negro Chamber of Commerce, or black members of the DCIA, or both groups possibly conducted the contest for which citizens submitted names. The subdivision itself honored Richard T. Hamilton, a prominent black physician and community leader. Hamilton had worked with whites and blacks to restore racial peace after a series of bombings rocked South Dallas in 1940 and 1941. The bombings stemmed from the same cause as those of ten years later: blacks buying in previously all-white residential blocks.[9]

The sources for some street names are now lost; others may have had no significance beyond that of being attractive names not already in use in Dallas. Two streets recognized white members of the DCIA: Hoblitzelle, whose foundation loaned the money for Hamilton Park, and Louis Tobian, the DCIA secretary. The names of local blacks were selected for two other streets: Hallum Street honored Mary E. Hallum, a second-grade teacher at the B. F. Darrell Elementary School, and Towns Street recognized Jerry W. Towns, a teacher at Booker T. Washington High School. Sadye Gee remembered Towns as a strict disciplinarian whose preferred form of punishment was requiring recalcitrant students to remain after school and copy the U.S. Constitution, the number of copies depending on the gravity of the offense.[10]

Other streets commemorated nationally famous African Americans of the era: Bellafonte Drive was for the singer and entertainer Harry Belafonte, Bunche Drive for the distinguished statesman Ralph Bunche, Campanella Drive for the baseball star Roy Campanella, and Dandridge Drive for the film actress Dorothy Dandridge. Oberlin Drive, the first street to be opened, was named for Oberlin College, founded in 1833; soon after opening, the college admitted both women and blacks; Ella Lois Hudson, the wife of a black member of the DCIA, attended the college's music conservatory. Another street name, Ebony Drive, recognized the successful African-American monthly *Ebony*.[11]

It was little wonder, then, that interest in Hamilton Park ran high among African Americans. Cars lined both sides of Schroeder Road for at least half a mile and covered more than half an acre near the dedication site. "Even after the 45-minute dedication service was completed," the black *Dallas Star Post* reported, "a steady stream of cars filled with prospective homeowners continued to approach the site from Central Expressway." Thomas J. Hayman remarked that "we were just absolutely covered with interest from the Negro community." Indeed, some prospective white homebuyers were attracted to the new development. They were told it was segregated and strictly for blacks.[12]

Interest in a house in Hamilton Park was one thing; qualifying for an FHA or VA loan was another. Whites absolutely controlled the gateway to homeownership in Hamilton Park. Associated Construction, Inc.—five related companies acting as one—was determined that its project would succeed and set high standards for applicants. The company opened its sales office the day after the dedication. It hired an experienced white salesman, Matthew Critchlow, to work during the high traffic days, especially Sundays. Critchlow, Hayman recalled, "was financially independent to do this work even if he makes something or if he didn't make something." Prospective purchasers "came out in droves on Sunday. That's when we had our big day." Hayman remembered that "most any Sunday out there you could sign up fifty or sixty applications. The biggest problem we had was knowing who to even attempt to qualify." After eliminating "forty or fifty" by asking questions, the salesman would initiate the paperwork on others. Even after the first cut, "you'd go through about ten to qualify one."[13]

Soon Critchlow and other salesmen developed a quick visual appraisal of prospects. Hayman explained that "if they drove up in a new Pontiac, forget it! If they drove up in any new car, forget it! Chances are nine to one they owed every nickel on the car that they could possibly stand, and they had not one nickel in the bank." The real "prospective purchaser" would "get out of the car with two or three little children following him—he and his wife. It's going to be an old, worn out car like practically all of us were driving in those days." The parents would "be neatly dressed, but there'd be nothing floozy. You could say, 'There's a family that you can check into.'" Hayman's remembered percentage of qualified buyers may have been too low but the spirit of his recollection was correct. Residents of Hamilton Park affirmed that qualifying for a loan could be rigorous and anxiety-producing, with disappointments along the way.[14]

A Transition in White and Black 59

Meanwhile, on the ground, Associated Construction, in overall charge of the project, began realizing its street and house designs. By the third week in April, fifty houses were completed along curving Oberlin and Hoblitzelle Drives. Thirty-six were sold. The utilities were ready and people were moving in. "We'd dreamed about having our own home. Well, here it is," Helen Thomas said to a reporter for the *Morning News* as she and her husband carried their possessions into their new house on Oberlin. Her smile faded when she saw her spouse maneuvering a large box. "Elgin, be careful with that box," she told him. "My good crystal glasses are packed in there." [15]

The community was ready, the DCIA decided, for its formal opening on 2 May 1954. About two hundred blacks and whites crowded the parkings and driveways near the symbolic ribbon spanning Oberlin. It was a sunny spring afternoon, the tall, old trees in the area contrasting with the freshness of the pastels of the modest but trim houses. Crossman presided, as he had at the dedication. The speakers repeated the themes of the first ceremony: congratulations to the members of the DCIA, praise for Hamilton Park as a symbol of progressive Dallas, and hopes for those who would live in the community. A former mayor, James B. Adoue Jr., extolled "men like" Crossman "and Karl Hoblitzelle who had this wonderful thought." Mayor Thornton heralded "the dawn of a new day in Dallas"—the city, he said, had demonstrated its concern for "all its people." Dr. L. G. Pinkston, a prominent black physician, hoped that the new residents would be "a blessing to themselves, the community of Dallas, and the citizenship of the world." Florence, the president of the Republic National Bank, was enthusiastic about the environmental influence of Hamilton Park. "Homeowners are better citizens," he said. "And homeowners, as taxpayers, take more interest in their government—and more interest means better government." [16]

But interest did not produce qualified buyers in the new subdivision. By August, Crossman, A. Maceo Smith, Rice, and perhaps others were concerned enough to meet in Crossman's office and discuss the "lag in the sales and rate of development of Hamilton Park." There was reason for worry. From the opening of the sales office in the previous October, through the time of their meeting, to late October 1954, Associated Construction sold only ninety houses. It was a paltry record for six months of active promotion when contrasted with the confident assertions of pent-up demand of a few years before. The sense of the meeting in Crossman's office was that sales were disappointing because of VA and

FHA processing delays, the VA's "too stringent credit requirements," FHA down-payment regulations, and a "lack of attractive public relations" to increase interest in the community. The group concluded that Crossman should work with the VA and the FHA to accelerate their loan processing. Vincent Rohloff remembered that Crossman "made a number of phone calls to the FHA and VA"; his personal stake in Hamilton Park warranted such involvement. Crossman probably was able to move VA and FHA officialdom, because the developers closed on an additional 170 houses from late October through the end of the year.[17]

In response to further suggestions to increase the visibility of Hamilton Park, Rice helped to establish a "community league which stresses . . . the benefits" to the residents. If, however, a suggestion threatened white control of the community's development, Associated Construction ignored it. The sense of the meeting in Crossman's office was that the builders should improve their public-relations campaign by encouraging news stories and buying advertisements in the "weekly press"—by which was meant the African-American newspapers—and by "an increase in the sales force including representation of Negro sales and public relations personnel." The developers could, with reason, dismiss a renewed publicity effort, because there was no lack of information and no dearth of applicants for houses in Hamilton Park.[18]

Suggestions to hire black sales and public-relations people received equally short shrift. "That would have been a very bad move at that time," Hayman insisted. "If it were done all over today, it would be a totally different thing," but Hamilton Park "was built long before" civil rights breakthroughs. "You wouldn't have any way in the world to qualify that black to be your salesman unless you went to Washington to get him. Then he wouldn't go in with these people here." Selecting an African-American salesman "wouldn't have worked any more than trying to obtain a Negro developer to put it over." Caught up as he was in the prevailing Dallas exceptionalism, Hayman probably did not know of either the black real-estate agents in Orlando or the black developers who built a large subdivision in Oklahoma City. Such African-American business successes refuted his claim that blacks could not then have handled the responsibility. It is more likely that Hayman and his associates desired to retain complete control of the slowly developing community.[19]

But white control was passing away even as the pace of construction quickened. The Hamilton Park School opened in the fall of 1955 and at once became a source of community pride and concern, as well as a community center. Social organizations and volunteer groups flourished. The Baptists began meeting in homes in 1954 and soon acquired a church building near the community. In August 1957 the Methodists held their first worship service at the school, a year and a half before their new building opened. So many organizations sprang up that community leaders formed the Interorganizational Committee in 1957 to represent all the groups in city, county, state, and national politics. In 1961, the Civic League fought the first of many land-use battles, a successful bid to deny permanent zoning to a troublesome concrete-batching plant located south across Forest Lane.[20]

Meanwhile, the DCIA influence declined. The organization continued to be active during the early development of Hamilton Park but its involvement slackened, then ended in 1960 with its final payment to the Hoblitzelle Foundation. About 1955, the DCIA cosponsored a discussion of the school desegregation problem in Dallas; apparently it did little more than briefly touch the surface of that controversial issue. Under its charter the DCIA could engage in a wide range of interracial activity but its principal purpose was to establish middle-income black housing. Having achieved that goal, it atrophied.[21]

Crossman himself was partly responsible for the DCIA's ebb. Vincent Rohloff recalled that after Hamilton Park got under way Crossman became president of the chamber of commerce. "I would guess," said Rohloff, "that at that time he was spending three-quarters of his time on Chamber of Commerce activities, maybe more, plus other civic activities that he was involved in." Rohloff affirmed that Crossman "was devoting almost all of his time to this fight" over the expansion of Love Field. Because Crossman was "the driving force" of the DCIA and he focused his attention elsewhere, the organization lost its fervor. Besides, "he was the type of person that liked to get things over with so he could get on to something else."[22]

The last recorded activity of the DCIA was symbolic of its drift away from Hamilton Park. In 1964 Crossman wrote his board about disposing of the DCIA's remaining money, a balance of $20,000. He had approached Collins, who suggested a new outdoor swimming pool for Bishop College and offered to make up, anonymously, the cost difference of $30,000. The college administration instead desired either a much more expensive indoor pool or a browsing area for its new library building, and the money went to the latter project. The funds could have gone to the sorely needed rest room and shelter for Willowdell Park on the west side of Hamilton Park—a building that instead was financed through the Hoblitzelle Foundation. In 1965, the DCIA forfeited its charter following several years of failure to file annual reports with the state.[23]

But Crossman's flagging interest was not the only reason for the fading away of the DCIA. As the 1950s advanced, black housing spread across Dallas. In the ten years between the 1950 and 1960 censuses, the eight census tracts in South Dallas shifted dramatically from white to black. In 1950, only one was 90 percent or more black, although another had reached 72 percent and a third, 51 percent. Ten years later, six tracts were more than 90 percent, one of the remaining tracts was 88 percent, and the other was 75 percent. To mark the cataclysm in another way, the 1950 census found 22,281 whites in South Dallas. By 1960, only 1,781 lived there. In about 1957, McShann Road opened in a developing area of comfortable homes and spreading lawns. Some three miles west of Hamilton Park, the "street of the doctors" was a much more expensive location than the subdivision, but it lured well-to-do professionals who possibly would have located in Hamilton Park. In about 1958, the first residents moved into the Highland Hills subdivision, near the future campus of Bishop College. Hoblitzelle donated the 103-acre campus, a partial inducement for Bishop's move from East Texas. The area developed rapidly after Bishop opened on its new campus in 1961. Highland Hills, seventeen miles south of Hamilton Park, was closer to some traditional black neighborhoods. Its frame houses, small, two-or-three bedroom models, were similar to the first homes in Hamilton Park. In all, the stiflingly confined African-American housing of the 1940s and early 1950s had given way to much improved if scarcely equal circumstances by the early 1960s.[24]

The third reason for white withdrawal involved the failure either to expand Hamilton Park substantially or to locate planned black housing nearby. The white elite at first regarded the community as an initial move toward a realization of spreading black subdivisions. "I want to see thousands of homes like this," Hoblitzelle exclaimed to a newspaper reporter before the May 1954 opening ceremonies. Landrum, the sympathetic newspaper columnist and active member of the DCIA, applauded Hamilton Park in 1954 because it was neither a "governmental project" nor "the feckless fumbling of a group of do-gooders." He envisioned an African-American complex reminiscent of the 1950 Pelt plan for the Trinity River bottoms. "Suppose now that we could add to the Hamilton Park acreage another tract large enough" to house a group of black colleges, together with a training school and a hospital, he mused. Two or three administratively distinct colleges could maintain their historic integrity while sharing facilities and avoiding "overlapping" curricula. "There are said to be several institutions which want to come to Dallas and locate in such a community." Landrum's program was unrealized except for the later arrival of Bishop College.[25]

Before turning to other matters, Crossman was actively involved in expanding Hamilton Park. In late October 1955 he reported to the DCIA board about his "several conferences with various parties relative to the purchase of additional land in the vicinity of Hamilton Park to provide homesites for Negroes." The directors authorized him to purchase additional land, but nothing came of his negotiations. Some time after Crossman attempted to buy additional property, developers unconnected with the DCIA purchased the sixty acres bounded by Hallum Street on the east, Schroeder Road and Rialto Drive on the west, and the north side of Bunche Drive south to the north line of Campanella Drive. They continued the DCIA's relationship with Associated Contractors.[26]

The final effort to secure land adjacent to Hamilton Park gave way to industrial development. In 1964, a real-estate developer arranged for commercial and multiple-family redevelopment of an African-American enclave east of Love Field. The homeowners in the enclave requested the developer and an associate to locate an undeveloped tract for their new "quality housing" in the northern area of Dallas. The new location would have to meet several criteria, including "a school situation without problems," good access, and "a location which is already identified with a negro community." What the real-estate agents described as the "only" qualified property lay east across the then Houston & Texas Central tracks from the eastern margin of Hamilton Park. The agents had negotiated with the owners for sixty-three acres of their property and appealed to the Hoblitzelle Foundation for help in purchasing the land. The foundation, however, considered matters only "very deliberately," and before it could respond, Charles Inge, a developer active in the area, had secured the tract as part of a 146-acre package. Inge was negotiating for Texas Instruments, which wanted the land for expansion. Inge held the trump hand because he could buy more property than only the land suitable for quality single-family residences and he could pay about 12 percent more per acre.[27]

The Hoblitzelle Foundation and the DCIA refused to become involved in land-use disputes in Hamilton Park—actions that affirmed the white elite's disengagement from the community. In 1961, a land-development corporation sued four Hamilton Park couples, a mortgager, the Hoblitzelle Foundation, and the DCIA to clarify the corporation's privilege to build apartments on a tract on the south side of the community. The land lay at the southwestern curve of Willowdell Drive, south of Willowdell Park and west of the new Hamilton Park Methodist Church. The corporation contended that its some three and one-fourth acres were exempt from single-family restrictions by reason of language in the deed permitting single-family residences but also allowing "shopping centers, schools, churches, parks, community centers, and recreational areas." The developers also insisted that the catch-all phrasing did not exclude apartment houses. Crossman and Hoblitzelle quickly took themselves and their organizations out of active participation in the suit. Both men agreed that they had "no intention to restrict" the tract "from apartment usage" and "any restriction of said property from apartment usage was a mistake of fact and done through inadvertence."[28]

Crossman and Hoblitzelle could have argued that they were merely fulfilling the original purpose of the DCIA, which was to provide both single- and multiple-family housing. Nevertheless, they offered no support to Hamilton Park residents who believed that their subdivision was, except for its shopping center and churches, a single-family area. The corporation continued its suit against the homeowners, eventually winning a judgment. Surprisingly, the developers did not follow through with apartment construction. Eventually the adjacent Methodist congregation purchased the site.[29]

The last effort to summon the aid of the white elite came in 1971, eighteen years after the dedication of Hamilton Park. The issue concerned the elaborate covenants forbidding various uses, activities, or types of construction on single-family lots—part of the effort to create in Hamilton Park a showcase of black homeownership. By 1971, the violations had reached the point at which the president of the Civic League could no longer ignore them (see chapter 6). In November he complained to the Hoblitzelle Foundation and to the DCIA, in care of the author of the deed restrictions, about uncorrected violations. The Civic League, he wrote, had informed violators of their transgressions, but to no effect. It had "exhausted" its remedies. Therefore, he concluded, he was turning to "your organization" to "help us keep Hamilton Park a place to be proud of and a good place to live."[30]

The letter set off a round of correspondence among the addressees and others. The author of the restrictive covenant disclaimed any connection with the DCIA, correctly assuming "that the corporation has long since ceased to exist." He concluded his musings about what could be done to help the Civic League with "what any of us can do, more particularly what I can do, adds up to a grand total of '0.' " A flurry of letters and telephone calls demonstrated sympathy for Hamilton Park but no inclination to become involved. The reply to the Civic League from an officer of the Hoblitzelle Foundation conveyed a polite refusal but none of the sympathy. The foundation's involvement in Hamilton Park, he wrote, was limited to the financing of the land purchase. When the DCIA repaid the loan, the foundation's obligations ceased. Therefore, "those owners of lots complaining of the violations of the restrictions should sue the violators." The foundation does not "intend to go to court for the benefit of the present owners of lots who are complaining." The whites to whom the Civic League president appealed surely were within their rights, and certainly were prudent in remaining aloof from an internal matter in Hamilton Park. Their doing so, however, affirmed that the era of white intervention had passed.[31]

The spirit of racial cooperation and pride of achievement focused on Hamilton Park was transitory, lasting ten years at most. From 1950 to 1960 it was overshadowed on the national scene by remarkable if inadequate black economic and educational advances, notably the landmark *Brown* school-desegregation decisions of 1954 and 1955 (see chapter 7) and the Montgomery, Alabama, bus boycott of 1956, the first of many private, organized efforts for equal access to public facilities. The Kennedy administration's arrival in 1961 would usher in an unprecedented activity on behalf of minorities. Hamilton Park's planning and development was, then, no herald of the future. Segregated in fact if not in law, it was the creation of a dying era. Nevertheless, it provided an opportunity for the realization of the shared American values of homeownership, industry, and thrift, bolstered by family and community life, neighborhood schooling, and the intense organizational activity of hundreds of people.

Crossman could be forgiven his hyperbole when, in 1955, he urged the members of the DCIA to visit Hamilton Park "and see what your labors have brought forth—a project that is unique in America.... Again, Dallas has led the way!" He saved laudatory clippings about Hamilton Park, clippings taken from the African-American press that he evidently interpreted as reinforcing the myth of Dallas's exceptionalism. In 1960 he wrote of Hamilton Park's two churches, of its "most modern grade school and high school," the growing shopping center, and residents who "take a great deal of pride in their homes." The careful screening of applicants, he wrote, had produced the result desired. "I might also mention that to date there has not been a default." Hamilton Park, launched in a spirit of hopeful cooperation, was in the future to make its own way as a community.[32]

Robert L. Thornton, an influential banker and civic leader, assisted with the development of Hamilton Park. He became the mayor of Dallas soon after the dedication of the subdivision. From the collections of the Dallas Historical Society.

A. Maceo Smith, the racial relations advisor to the regional office of the FHA at the time of the development of Hamilton Park, provided important information on African-American housing to individuals and groups concerned with improving minority housing. He is shown here some years after the subdivision opened. From the collection of the African American Museum Archives, Dallas, Texas.

Theater owner Karl Hoblitzelle *(left)* and banker Fred Florence played key roles in opening Hamilton Park. From the collection of the Texas/Dallas History and Archives Division, Dallas Public Library.

Carr P. Collins, an insurance company executive, arranged for the construction of most of the houses in Hamilton Park and for the acceptance of most of the home mortgages guaranteed by the FHA. From the collections of the Dallas Historical Society.

Jerome K. Crossman, president of the Dallas Citizens' Interracial Association, the organization that founded Hamilton Park. Crossman's involvement was so extensive and intensive that the subdivision could not have been developed without him. Crossman, Thornton, Hoblitzelle, Florence, and Collins are photographed as they appeared at about the time of the opening of Hamilton Park. From the collections of the Dallas Historical Society.

Members of the joint committee of the Dallas Chamber of Commerce and the powerful Dallas Citizens' Council touring a slum area one mile from downtown in April 1950, during the aftermath of house bombings in an area of racial residential succession. The tour was a first step toward the creation of Hamilton Park. From the collection of the Texas/Dallas History and Archives Division, Dallas Public Library.

The resumption of house bombings in 1951, after they were assumed to have ended, rekindled efforts to solve the minority housing problem. Here two policemen, Night Chief O. P. (Pokey) Wright and Detective Charles Sansone, examine debris from a bomb blast on 11 July at 4622 Meadow Street in South Dallas. From the collection of the Texas/Dallas History and Archives Division, Dallas Public Library.

Members of the Fields family, African Americans who lived across Schroeder Road from land that later became part of Hamilton Park, are shown haying on what became the north portion of the subdivision. They were among several black families residing in the upper White Rock area— a circumstance that made locating an African-American subdivision in upper White Rock more appealing than placing it among whites, who were likely to contest any nearby black housing. Photo courtesy of Le Verne Fields.

The senior choir of the St. John Baptist Church, photographed in 1953, the year the choir sang at the dedication of Hamilton Park. From the collection of the Texas/Dallas History and Archives Division, Dallas Public Library.

Hamilton Park about 1962. North Central Expressway (U.S. Highway 75) is at the *far left* (west). The trees along Cottonwood Creek east of the expressway form the western boundary of the community. Schroeder Road is the broad, north-south street in the *middle* of the photo. The Hamilton Park School, its campus, and its athletic field are visible at the *upper middle, to the right* (east) of Schroeder Road. This photo originally appeared in Dorothy Neville, *Carr P. Collins: Man on the Move* (Dallas: Park Press, 1963). From the collection of the Texas/Dallas History and Archives Division, Dallas Public Library.

The Hamilton Park School during renovation, 1991. The original window panes, shown here, were replaced by thermal windows. Inside, the renovation removed vestiges of the long-closed high school, such as drinking fountains that were too far off the floor for some Pacesetter youngsters. Photo by Katharine L. Wilson.

Groundbreaking ceremonies were important to the Methodist (later United Methodist) congregation of Hamilton Park. This group is gathered around a sign announcing the church's future home at about the time work began on the first sanctuary. The scene is at the junction of Schroeder Road and Willowdell Drive. Photo courtesy of the United Methodist Church of Hamilton Park.

By 1990 the United Methodist Church of Hamilton Park was planning a major expansion and this groundbreaking ceremony was held soon thereafter. Photo courtesy of the United Methodist Church of Hamilton Park.

Bellafonte Drive, looking north from the south junction with High Point Circle, showing some of the more expensive brick houses. Photo by Katharine L. Wilson.

Glen Regal Drive, looking west toward Rialto Drive. Photo by Katharine L. Wilson.

Many residents remodeled their houses to increase comfort and spaciousness. Hamilton Park pioneers Mr. and Mrs. Alfred W. Dupree Jr. extended and enclosed their garage to provide an additional living area *(left)*, added an entranceway *(center)*, and built a large addition at the rear of their residence. Dupree, an accomplished musician and woodworker, designed and crafted new shutters. The shutter *at the right* depicts a violin *(top)*, a treble clef, and a piano. Photo by Katharine L. Wilson.

Willowdell Park, looking south, with Willowdell Drive *on the left*. Trees shade portions of the park, but open ground is characteristic of this community recreation area. Photo by Katharine L. Wilson.

Cottonwood Creek undermined the foundation of the rest room and storage locker in Willowdell Park *(lower right-hand corner)* until City of Dallas crews built revetments to stabilize the creek bank. The structure was built with funds from the Hoblitzelle Foundation and dedicated to Jerome Crossman. Photo by Katharine L. Wilson.

Cottonwood Creek, looking upstream. Normally quiescent, the creek at flood is capable of submerging much of Willowdell Park. Concrete used to channel the creek is visible *at the right*. Photo by Katharine L. Wilson.

Utilities work along Willowdell Drive undertaken in 1983 in connection with the construction of the Willie B. Johnson Recreation Center. The hill on the near horizon was lowered to accommodate the center and its parking lot. Photo courtesy of Sadye Gee.

The groundbreaking committee for the Willie B. Johnson Recreation Center in 1983. *Left to right:* Rev. J. L. Foster, Freddie B. Nance, Charles E. Smith, Sadye Gee. Photo courtesy of Sadye Gee.

Willie B. Johnson in 1985.
Photo courtesy of Sadye Gee.

Willie B. Johnson, *at center right* (wearing a print dress), attended the 1991 groundbreaking ceremony for the expansion of the recreation center named for her. Photo courtesy of Sadye Gee.

The Willie B. Johnson
Recreation Center at
the north end of Willowdell
Park. Photo by Katharine
L. Wilson.

The Juneteenth parade up Willowdell Drive in 1987, moving toward the recreation center. Juneteenth commemorates the enforcement of emancipation in Texas, 19 June 1865. The parking lane added to Willowdell Drive (see chapter 9) is visible alongside the sidewalk at the edge of the park. Photo courtesy of Sadye Gee.

Willowdell Park. Photo courtesy of Sadye Gee.

The Hamilton Park Civic League notice board on Schroeder Road. The Hamilton Park United Methodist Church is *in the left background*. Photo courtesy of Sadye Gee.

A winning lawn in the civic league's lawn-of-the-week contest. Photo courtesy of Sadye Gee.

Cottonwood Creek, looking downstream. Revetments designed to stabilize the creek and prevent the flooding and washing away of Willowdell Park were built into the left bank. Photo by Katharine L. Wilson.

Bellafonte Drive, looking north toward the Hamilton Park School. Photo by Katharine L. Wilson.

The Hamilton Park School after renovation. Photo by Katharine L. Wilson.

The Hamilton Park School auditorium. Photo by Katharine L. Wilson.

5

THE EARLY COMMUNITY AND BEYOND

Many were called to Hamilton Park but houses were expensive for families with a gross monthly income around $450. They sold for prices ranging from about $8,500 for a two-bedroom, one-bathroom house bought in 1954 on the southern portion of Oberlin Drive to about $11,000 for a four-bedroom, one-bathroom house at the north end of the development bought five or six years later. The price difference reflected inflation, larger quarters, and improved design, but both dwindle away in the face of 1990 assessed valuations of from $52,000 to $58,000 for similar properties. Those prices were no small amounts in the 1950s, considering the median single-earner income of black Dallas families—in 1949, $1,503; in 1959, $3,255.[1]

The developers' demanding screening excluded very-low-wage earners and the casually employed; conversely, few members of the African-American elite bought there. The modest design of the early houses in Hamilton Park plus the ability of affluent physicians, attorneys, and businessmen to buy elsewhere and the opening of McShann Road helped to homogenize Hamilton Park. Common interests and problems, centered on race and neighborhood, coalesced around the school and its community support organizations, civic groups, churches, and social clubs.[2]

Before they could build a community, however, the prospective residents had to select Hamilton Park over other possible places. Arlington Park was then a relatively new westside subdivision near the Elm Fork of the Trinity River. Laurice Stevenson found it to be "kind of in a hole" and "in the wrong side of town, and I just didn't like that." Albertus Edley "had a brother living in Arlington Park, and there were no sidewalks and driveways [there]." Marion and Irene Mitchell owned a house in Trinity Valley, west of Arlington Park, but did not consider it to be more than a way station on the road to something better. The search for housing also led to South Dallas, which by the early 1950s was rapidly turning from striated white and black housing to black. Willie B. Johnson looked at "an old two-story house" there, but a white friend urged against buying it. Freddie Ervine considered a "huge house" in what had been an elite Jewish neighborhood. "I loved those houses. They were beautiful." But the thought of financing and maintaining such a place was daunting, and besides, "I knew they were old, and I wanted something new, really." In the Wheatley subdivision of pleasant housing built for blacks, few houses came on the market. Charles E. Smith and Le Verne Fields found nothing for sale in North Park (Elm Thicket), the African-American neighborhood decimated by the encroaching Love Field. And so it went—poor housing or no available housing in West Dallas, Roosevelt Heights, or anywhere else. "Black housing was a very tough situation at that time," was Ruby Watson's succinct summation.[3]

Having chosen Hamilton Park, would-be residents had to survive the screening, consisting of credit, character, and income checks. For Joseph R. Williams, Myra L. Christian, and others, who owned property or enjoyed comfortable family incomes in legitimate activities, the process was routine. For some, however, the screening evoked powerful memories. "They asked you about your friends, your habits, your everything," Doris Robertson recalled. Sadye and Cleophus Gee's neighbors in near North Dallas were asked, "What kind of people are these?" One neighbor, surfeited with questions about the Gees, replied, "If you want to know anything else, you go and ask them yourself!" Then he told the Gees, "Some people have been around here asking about you—do you fight, do you pay your bills, and this kind of junk." Laurice Stevenson remembered his employer received a form requesting information "about your character and how did you act or how did you produce, were you dependable." His employer showed him the form and exclaimed, "Good God, Steve! What kind of place is that for them to ask all these questions?" The check of Stevenson's credit record turned up "a little electric fan, about a nine-inch electric fan" his former spouse had purchased but not paid for some ten years before. He was told to clear his record or he could not buy a house in Hamilton Park.[4]

Some residents knew from their postquestionnaire experiences just how high were the hurdles to homeownership in Hamilton Park. Willie B. Johnson's white friend, a contractor, who had gone with her to look at the old house in South Dallas, asked, "Willie B., is this what you really wanted?" She replied, "No, sir. What I wanted, I can't get"—because the salesman, Matthew Critchlow, had refused to allow her and her husband Clifford to fill out a Hamilton Park application form. Critchlow gave as the reason the fact that her husband "was too old at that time, and he wouldn't have been able to finish paying for" a house. On hearing this, her contractor friend promised to "carry" her to Hamilton Park. The next week, her friend walked into the Associated Construction office, "me and him and my husband. He said 'Critchlow, where is the blank?' Mr. Critchlow reached over and grabbed one. We filled it out"—and three weeks later they were told that the loan was approved.[5]

White intervention of a different sort saved the situation for Doris and Lincoln Robertson. Robertson applied for a VA loan. Unfortunately his job as a cloth cutter and shipping clerk in the garment industry and his wife's secretarial work together grossed only about $495 a month— not enough for a loan approval when allowances were made for loss of income because of illness or pregnancy. Robertson reported his failure to qualify to the brothers who owned the garment company; they had been anxiously awaiting the outcome of his application and asking if they could help. They became "furious" on hearing the bad news. By happy chance, the VA office was located across the street and the company president walked over there to inquire about the Robertsons' loan. Two hours later, Critchlow and builder Thomas Hayman called Doris Robertson to say that "a mistake had been made and that we certainly did qualify."[6]

Norman and Velma Jackson knew the problems of clearing the financial hurdles both vicariously and directly. When they chose Hamilton Park, only Oberlin and Hoblitzelle Drives were opened. Childless at the time, they selected a two-bedroom model. The house was completed down to the interior colors selected by a hopeful purchaser, but "this girl's loan wouldn't go thorough," so the salesman turned to the Jacksons. Velma Jackson remembered "that we needed—I think—$350 for a down payment. We got the $350, and we had to wait to see if the loan was going to go through. It took forever, but finally our loan went through." Scraping up the down payment meant cashing some of Norman Jackson's World War II savings bonds and Mrs. Jackson's asking her father for help. Her father supplied the needed funds, saying, "That will be your house present."[7]

What drove these residents and hundreds of others like them to submit to and survive the screening process in Hamilton Park? The answer lies in what Andrew Wiese has termed "the proud dream of ownership and personal autonomy" that moved African Americans to suburban locations; Hamilton Park was suburban in its physical arrangements and distance from the central business district. Yet homeownership and the sense of autonomy it conferred had been achieved by—or were within the grasp of—Hamilton Park residents without the added burdens of a move to Hamilton Park. Indeed, they moved from houses they already owned, or they rejected affordable but less desirable housing in other locations. Wiese's language, then, contains more within itself than is at first apparent, and more than merely the characteristically American striving to express in one's physical surroundings one's status and income.[8]

None of this is intended to argue against the importance of homeownership, a concomitant sense of autonomy, or material reflections of achievement, either as social realities or personal goals. Much more than these ambitions, however, was at stake for the residents of Hamilton Park. Understanding what was at issue means moving away from the themes of much of the contemporary scholarly writing on the African-American experience in the United States. Some of this literature emphasizes black social pathology or black disadvantages, especially the income and other disparities between blacks and other segments of the population. Some of it celebrates or analyzes African-American achievement, such as the maintenance of a distinct yet influential culture in the face of majority indifference or hostility, the struggle to found and maintain educational and religious institutions despite great obstacles, and the contributions of individuals to the arts, letters, medical and other sciences, and invention. Other studies focus on the development of desegregation and the civil rights movement, while still others analyze the contributions of the black workforce within the context of the dual labor market.[9]

All of this literature has value but little of it is immediately helpful in comprehending the impetus to suburbanization. Of more relevance are the studies of shared American values contributing to the similarities within the urban centrifuge since World War II. What the residents of Hamilton Park sought, along with millions of their fellow citizens, was a new house, certainly, but more—a fresh environment free from existing mixed land use and safe from the problems of settled neighborhoods, such as an unattractive location, the potential maintenance expenses of older houses, and the threat of undesirable encroachments resulting from dynamic urban change. The judgments of Laurice Stevenson and Albertus Edley against buying in Arlington Park and the disinclination of Willie B. Johnson and Freddie Ervine to purchase in South Dallas are cases in point. So is Vivian T. Starks's memory of her house and its surroundings on Munger Avenue in old North Dallas. "It was a very pleasant house," but "I just didn't like the atmosphere." The three houses close by created a situation "that was too crowded for me."[10]

While it was important for people to leave, or to avoid, undesirable areas, those concerns were essentially negative. The positive "pull" of Hamilton Park was much stronger, involving a skein of values and concerns making the potential humiliations of the screening and the relative remoteness of the site worth bearing. Many residents in Hamilton Park came from families that emphasized sacrifice and perseverance in the disciplined pursuit of a goal, be it education, a comfortable family life, homeownership, or a steady job responsibly performed. Among pioneer interviewees, fourteen of thirty-eight knew of property ownership by grandparents or parents. The new house in a secure environment with modern conveniences brought with it a lot large enough for a spreading lawn with trees, grass, flowers, and a place for a vegetable garden in back. The fresh, new environment would be a fine place for the children, for most homeowners had children or planned to have them. Children or not, the family would enjoy a richer, fuller life in superior surroundings. And the houses in Hamilton Park were, financially, a good deal in the post–World War II era of modest house prices, rising incomes, and long-term, amortized mortgages with little or, in the case of the VA, no down payment required.[11]

Two interviewees remembered family pressure—as well as encouragement—to buy. Curtis and Kelsey Smith lived in the new, comfortable Southern Terrace Apartments in South Dallas when his father came for a visit. "Son," he said, "are you going to buy you a home? Every time you pay rent on this place, you don't own any more of it than you did before you paid the rent. If you made a payment on a home, that means you're closer to owning it." Smith "was always afraid of buying a home. I was afraid I couldn't afford it, and I never wanted to go spend money on a home and lose it." So he replied, "Dad, I'm not making enough money." His father was unimpressed. "Well, you're making enough money to pay your rent and live here, and you could live in your own place." The elder Smith's talk with his son and his daughter-in-law eventually had its desired effect. Sadye and Cleophus Gee faced the same parental pressure. Asked why she and her husband could not have rented, Mrs. Gee replied: "No way! Daddy wouldn't have that. As a matter of fact, that was one of the things that he wanted most for his children—to purchase their own places." But not just any place. The Gees purchased in Hamilton Park partly because it was north of the Trinity River and her father was prejudiced against locating south of the Trinity. They bought their corner lot because her father "had always said that whenever we buy a piece of property . . . we were to buy a corner lot."[12]

Traditions of family-centered life, disciplined hard work, and living within the family's means powerfully influenced some Hamilton Park residents. Marion Mitchell grew up near Wheelock, Texas, where his parents owned and operated a farm and his father made regular wagon trips to Hearne and Bryan, hauling goods for residents and businesses in the community. Mitchell and his three brothers were required to wait up for their father's return from his business trips, sometimes as late as 11 P.M. Then they unhitched and stabled the horses. Sometimes they ran the wagon into a "water tank"—a small pond on the farm—to prevent the dry, wooden wheels from shrinking away from their iron tires. The sons chopped wood and kept the wood box filled while their mother concentrated on cooking, kitchen tasks, cleaning, and tidying with the help of her three daughters. J. B. Simpson attended the Italy Colored School, in Italy, Texas, a two-room frame building with a wood-and-coal stove but no plumbing or electric lighting, through the seventh grade. Because he was "the last child, my daddy was determined that I got a better education." The family sent him to Dallas to live with his sisters while he finished grade and high school. Each summer he returned to work on the farm, just as he had before. While attending Booker T. Washington High School he "had odd jobs, like, setting pins at the bowling alley, caddying on the golf course." Le Verne Fields worked on her grandfather's farm outside of Tyler. She dug, sorted, and loaded potatoes into her father's wagon or truck for the haul to town, where her father sold potatoes and other produce to passersby.[13]

The discipline of work extended to other areas of life. Children were expected to behave and were punished when they did not. Le Verne Fields remembered that the failure to complete a school assignment meant "a whipping from the teacher, and from your parents, too." George Brewer's Corsicana, Texas, high school experiences were similar. He recalled that "at that time you could be whipped. . . . It wasn't so much that it hurt; it was embarrassing because you could get whipped in the classroom." Recounting those days, he said, "I don't think . . . it made us any more violent and probably did an awful lot to remind us how we should act." Velma Jackson was raised near Hawkins, Texas, where kindly neighbors would feed children but discipline them, too. "This was the environment that I grew up in, and I really liked that. I feel sorry that the kids now do not have that environment. I felt we were disciplined by the neighbors, the aunts, the uncles, whoever, and there was no problem." City kids had to meet the same expectations. A. W. Dupree first revealed his musical talent after his mother spanked him in the backyard of their Dallas home. "I was three years old, and I left where she was, and I walked straight to the piano and started playing on it. She looked at me, and she discovered I wasn't just beating; I was playing a tune. Then she started to give me lessons when I was five—she made it possible—on the piano."[14]

Thus, the Hamilton Park environment represented values absorbed from childhood, clustering around material comfort, family, discipline, work, and ownership of the best possible home, to reflect and to perpetuate the other virtues. Albertus Edley had a long-standing ambition to move to Hamilton Park because the addition was to the north and "the black folks in North Dallas were more informed, and they dressed well, and they had nicer cars than the people on the south side." To Doris and Lincoln Robertson, Hamilton Park represented "something a bit different—a step up in life, a little progress." Few residents had to be convinced that homeownership was superior to renting. "Well, if I had been in an apartment for forty years, I still wouldn't own anything. If I'd have stayed in an apartment, I would have been paying rent, rent, rent. If I bought a home, eventually it would be mine," was Edley's conclusion. "I was *excited* to have something to call my own, working on ownership," Pauline Dixon said. "Oh gosh! There's no collateral in renting," Freddie Nance exclaimed.[15]

Hamilton Park was desirable because it was new. "The advantage we had was that all these houses was brand-new," as J. B. Simpson put it. Once Curtis Smith decided to buy, "I wanted my own new home. I really didn't particularly want to buy a used house." Pauline and Frank Dixon "wanted a new home. This was new." Beyond newness, the addition offered a desirable, child-centered family environment. Apartment living dissatisfied Cicero Bruton because, when he "worked on the night shift, I didn't feel that my family was safe. So, my burning ambition was to get them out of there, I wanted something they could be proud of." Robert C. and Barbara Darden lived in the Roseland Homes public-housing project—a situation that was "fine" for Mrs. Darden. "But with children, you felt like you need your own yard, your own place." Hamilton Park was within the Richardson school boundary, and "I really wanted my children in that type of school district." A. W. Dupree lived on Redman Circle in the Fair Park section of South Dallas, but "the family was growing, and I didn't particularly like the way that the neighborhood was going." Le Verne and Willis Fields wanted "to buy a home that we felt was really safe for the youngsters." Would South Dallas have filled the bill? "No," Le Verne Fields replied, "not for my kids—no. At that particular time, it was not a good place to raise your kids. . . . I just wanted something better and different for my kids."[16]

The symbolism of home was so compelling for some future residents that they went out to Hamilton Park after work and on weekends to watch their houses being built or to note the daily or weekly progress of the crews. "We would come every weekend," Freddie Ervine recalled. "We'd come out and look and watch and everything. That was a good feeling." Lincoln and Doris Robertson enjoyed a similar experience. Joseph Williams took a series of photographs of his house—one of the larger brick homes on High Point Circle, where residents bought lots then hired their own contractors. "I'd come out twice a day at least," said Williams, who recorded progress from site preparation to the finished house. Cicero and Naomi Bruton would "meet out here and see what they did, see where they were now." Visiting the site was such a compulsion that, on occasion, even though they might have agreed *not* to go to the site after work, "by the time we got off, we would slip out here, and sometimes we'd meet up out here. This was after we'd already said we weren't coming. Yes, we'd meet up out here. Oh, we got a big kick out of that."[17]

Moving day arrived at last. With the screening done, the down payment made, the house completed, the families arrived in loaded cars and trucks, pulling up to their pastel-colored houses. It was a day many remembered as they would any other important anniversary. They came from all parts of the city where African Americans could find homes. Of those 432 pioneers who could be traced (see appendix A), 170 were from South Dallas, an additional 41 from the area of South Dallas immediately around and east of Fair Park, 28 from West Dallas, 14 from near North Dallas clustered around the State-Thomas commercial district, and 51 from old East Dallas, the area across North Central Expressway from near North Dallas. Many East Dallasites came from the Roseland Homes public-housing project, then a carefully-tended cluster of apartments that carried none of the stigma later attached to public housing. Twenty-six migrated from areas south of the Trinity River. All other parts of the city accounted for 143, including 12 from the elite Highland Park,

University Park, and Preston Hollow areas. People from those sections were butlers, chauffeurs, and maids moving out of servants' quarters into their own homes. Thirty-six moved from North Park–Elm Thicket, in or immediately around the Love Field expansion area. This relatively small number of 36 mocked Crossman's widely publicized setaside of three hundred houses for those African Americans displaced by the runway extensions. The setaside was, in any event, promptly forgotten in the eagerness of Associated Construction to accept any qualified buyer to counter the slow development of Hamilton Park. The moves from North Park also refuted the claims of Dr. Chisum, the black optometrist, that few residents could afford to live in the new development.[18]

Some families could begin settling in with no fear that they could not make the payments. Even with the strictures of the dual labor market, they did well enough. Others faced years of scrimping and hard work. "I was just drawing manual labor wages," said Cicero Bruton, who worked for a subsidiary of the Texas & Pacific Railroad. When the family moved in, he was "just as broke as I could be." To make the $70 per month payments, maintain and improve the property, and feed and clothe a growing family, he "just sacrificed myself and my time. On my job I could work long hours. I could work overtime. Then in the neighborhood there were people who needed yard work done. . . . Where there was an honest dollar to be made, I was there trying to make it." Willie B. Johnson usually took food from home to eat during the break from her night-shift nursing job at Parkland Hospital. One evening she took no food and instead spent twenty-five cents at the lunchroom vending machines. Her extravagance, "that Mrs. Johnson was really putting it on," was a subject for comment among the staff. During his early years in Hamilton Park, Charles E. Smith held down two porter's jobs to make ends meet. His day was "very long. It was night when I left home and night when I came home."[19]

Freddie Ervine worked at three jobs to save for her and her husband's down payment. Then she developed a successful catering business to help pay the family bills. Doris and Lincoln Robertson paid $9,500, with $250 down, for a house on Galva Drive, just at the southwestern bulge of its gentle ellipse. The monthly payment was $50.87, not that much more than the rent of some $45 on a shotgun house in old East Dallas. But that $50.87 was relentless, and it was only the beginning. "I had to budget mightily," Mrs. Robertson remembered. "We did a lot of sacrificing. I made my own clothes so that I wouldn't have to go and buy clothes. We bought only that that absolutely had to be purchased ready-made." She stretched the gross family income of $5,820. "I planned our meals, and I had to plan wisely ... in order that we could meet our monthly payments and not be late, pay our utilities and not be late, pay for our gasoline for our car, and pay that car note and not be late."[20]

The determination to make payments was so strong that Crossman could report to the DCIA in 1960 that there had been no defaults in Hamilton Park. It is possible, of course, that financial stringency forced some of the early move-outs. By 1960, twenty-four of the original householders had moved, but their migration does not alter the truth of Crossman's statement. In any event, the benefits of homeownership in a new subdivision outweighed the anxieties. The raw newness and remoteness of Hamilton Park in the early 1950s could scarcely be imagined a quarter of a century later. North Central Expressway, just west of the community, had thrust far out into the penumbra of Dallas by the time it crossed Forest Lane. Hamilton Park's more than ten miles from downtown was in the sticks, the far edge of scattered settlement. "There wasn't anything but a field," Pauline Dixon remembered. "At that time," Charles E. Smith said, "it was just out in nowhere, because when you left Mockingbird Lane, some six miles from downtown, there was nothing." The site of Hamilton Park was then called "the country," Ruby Watson recalled, as in "why would you want to move to the country?" As Curtis J. Smith put it, "This was just plain land out here when we came out here."[21]

The distant hillside was breezy and, relative to urban temperatures in North Texas, cool. Before the area built up, as Joseph Williams remembered, "there was a precipitous drop in temperature from Loop 12 [Northwest Highway] on out to Hamilton Park." Laurice Stevenson affirmed that the subdivision "was very cool. You didn't need any air conditioner or anything. It was very, very cool at night." Sadye Gee recalled squirrels and "lots of rabbits playing in the yard early in the morning. The breezes were so nice; the air was fresh. . . . You had to put a sweater on to sit out in the yard in August late at night, and that's where we spent most of our time after we'd get through digging and mowing the grass and everything." J. B. Simpson remarked on the squirrels and rabbits. "Oh, it was beautiful," Dorothy Simpson said, "and I could just look out this window and see Pegasus on the Magnolia Building," the "flying red horse" of the Mobil Oil Company atop the downtown skyscraper. Pauline Dixon and George Brewer remembered how "quiet" Hamilton Park was in the early years.[22]

The commitment to the maintenance and improvement of houses

and yards was almost universal. There was a lot of yard work to do because Associated Construction's commitment to a modestly priced house precluded much attention to the lot, once the costs of land, streets, utilities, and building to FHA standards were figured in. Typically, the contractor graded the lot and planted two or three shrubs and a tree, often a mimosa or a fruitless mulberry, in the front yard. Establishing turf, correcting any surface drainage problems, adding to or replacing the original plantings, and maintaining the house and yard were the responsibility of the new homeowners. They turned to the task with enthusiasm. They were youthful, energetic, and determined to create a home environment emblematic of their values.

J. B. and Dorothy Simpson arrived home from work to begin working in their yard. "Of course," Dorothy Simpson remarked, "we were very young then, and we had lots of energy. We could come home from work and work until 11:00 or 12:00 and didn't feel a thing." Easter and Freddie Nance resloped both front and back yards. Freddie Nance recalled going over to her next-door neighbor "and she pulled some shoots out of her yard, out of her flower bed, and put them in a bucket for me. I went over and got them and stuck them there in the yard, and they've grown." Norman and Velma Jackson faced a bare, unsatisfactorily sloped yard when they moved into their house on Hoblitzelle Drive. Fortunately for them, the contractors were excavating house sites on Bellafonte Drive, the next street up the hill. The contractors gave them the excavated dirt, but to transport it they had to push their wheelbarrow up their lot, across the alley, into the lots on Bellafonte, and return. Once their lot was leveled, they planted grass. "We were hard workers," Velma Jackson said. George Brewer remembered the "challenge" of "having something to do with making something yourself."[23]

Once the grass was in it had to be mowed, trimmed, watered, and fertilized. "On Saturday morning, it would be a symphony of lawn mowers," said Donald Payton, who spent part of his childhood in Hamilton Park. "On Saturday morning, starting at about 7:00, everybody would cut their yards at a certain time. . . . After the mowing, you could almost hear the harmony of hedge clippers and edgers." The cooperation involved in yard planting and the concurrent maintenance activity had a purpose beyond individual self-satisfaction or display. "The idea was ownership and the pride to build up a place which had been labeled as not going to last," Pauline Dixon maintained. The mutual fondness for home and community helped to promote a strong familial sense. Some residents had relatives in Hamilton Park and others had friends, though neither friends nor relatives were essential to familialism. Curtis and Kelsey Smith knew none of their new neighbors well, "because we'd come from different areas of the city," but "we became about like a family." Joseph Williams, on the other hand, knew so many people from the beginning that "it was almost like one family." In the early years Hamilton Park residents "had that close-knit community. We were like a family," declared Zan W. Holmes Jr., who left Hamilton Park and the pastorate of its Methodist church to minister to a larger congregation, win a seat in the Texas legislature, and assume a leadership role in Dallas and the state. To Sheila R. Allen, who grew up in Hamilton Park, "it was like a great, big family." Families may have disagreements, or have individual members who may not prosper, but, she said, "other members of the family are the ones who keep it together. That's the way I understand it."[24]

Pauline Dixon could rely on her neighbors for help in a crisis. "We cared," she said. If, late at night, "a light popped on across the street and I was up, I went over to see; if a light popped on over here, they came over to see. If we heard an ambulance, we would call somebody on that street and say, 'What's going on? I heard the ambulance.'" A neighbor's absence from the yard-tending ritual brought a similar reaction, Donald Payton said. "If you didn't cut your yard, people would come by and check on you: 'I noticed Mr. Smith wasn't out this morning cutting his yard. Is there something wrong?'"[25]

The neatly kept yards and trim houses attracted scores of weekend visitors—black and white—who made Hamilton Park a destination for their Sunday drives. So many drove by the Nance property on Oberlin Drive, the first street opened, that "it was just like a parade every Sunday," Freddie Nance recalled. Streetman Watson, whose family occupied a house on Galva Drive in February 1956, said that the sightseeing continued "even after we moved in." He remembered that "on Saturdays and Sundays and some evenings during the summer, it was a tourist attraction." "People did that," Barbara Darden said, "because everybody here kept up their houses in tip-top shape. It was a perfect place. It really was." Donald Payton remembered the "bumper-to-bumper weekend traffic" interfering with boyhood football games. "We didn't know that we were being 'show cased' because that was just home for us. On Saturday evening, and especially on Sundays after church, people would come up our streets and just look at us as if we were something really special. Here you are—you have houses, new houses. Nothing filtered down here."[26]

The Early Community and Beyond

The residents sometimes joined the "parade." Velma Jackson remembered that "we got in our car and would go and see what the other people were doing." Occasionally an African-American sightseer would stop to inquire about a resident's satisfaction with house and neighborhood—questions that could lead to the sightseer's becoming a resident. Willie F. Smith knew Hamilton Park from his visits to a brother who was an early homebuyer. "I was not at first really impressed with it because I did not want a carport, and most of the houses were smaller than what I wanted. Then, as I continued to come out here, they continued to improve the houses," making them larger, with enclosed garages, and discarding the wall heaters in the early homes in favor of central heat. "So I came out in February of 1959 and decided to buy one." On 29 May 1959, Willie and Jessie Smith and their two children moved into a four-bedroom home at 8425 Glen Regal Drive, in the north section of Hamilton Park. The house sold for $10,800, with monthly payments of $72 on a 4 3/4 percent VA loan.[27]

Hamilton Park's appeal was undeniable, and part of its appeal lay in its remoteness. "This was done in the fly-to-suburbia days, and that was the dream world—escape the city to get away," Zan Holmes remarked. Commuting "was just something you did." But distance from the still-centralized industrial, commercial, and retail core did not always lend enchantment. As Willie Smith put it, not all the initial discussion of the new addition was positive, "because Hamilton Park then was in the country. To get in the car and drive from South Dallas to Hamilton Park was like driving forever. There was no traffic on Central Expressway to amount to anything." The distance exacted a price from a husband and wife who had committed themselves to a new house, who held jobs in different parts of town or went to work at different times, and who could afford only one car.[28]

George Brewer, who compared the isolation of Hamilton Park to "being on an island," did not own a car when he moved in. In the mornings he rode with a neighbor who also worked in an industrial area south of downtown. "In many cases, though, if we got off at different times, I had to walk home—if he got off early." The walk took him out of the industrial district, through the elongated downtown, and out to Central Expressway. "Sometimes I'd be three or four or sometimes five miles out before catching a ride. On one occasion, maybe two occasions I walked all the way home or nearly home"—a distance of twelve or thirteen miles. When he did buy a car, Brewer discovered that living in remote Hamilton

Park could be expensive as well as inconvenient. His first car, an "old box-type Chevrolet," improved the commute for a while. One evening, after a family outing at the State Fair of Texas, the Chevrolet's fan flew off its mounting and crashed into the radiator, disabling the car. The hour was late and the family was stranded near Fair Park in South Dallas. The only solution was to call a taxicab. Brewer "had enough, to the penny, to pay the cab fare."[29]

Others carpooled or drove to pick up spouses at the end of the work day. Pauline and Frank Dixon and his mother, who lived with them, all held jobs on different schedules, in different locations, and in the early years there were few neighbors to help out. Their "two raggedy cars" were in steady use as either of the Dixons, depending on the demands of her beautician's job, drove his mother to and from work. Velma Jackson took her husband Norman to work early in the morning then drove the family car to her part-time job. Usually, "someone . . . would bring him home. If not, I'd go back and get him. We just went back and forth in that one ol' car. We made it." There were no acceptable alternatives to making it. Freddie Nance learned to drive the family's "old DeSoto" as a condition of moving to Hamilton Park. Pauline Dixon recounted the situation of two neighbors: "Take the lady next door. She didn't work, but they had one car at a time, which means she was trapped. They had three children. The lady across the street . . . worked over in South Dallas at a school, and she was a single lady; and, if her car went out, she didn't have transportation."[30]

Demands for bus service arose from these problems. The first petition for improvements including bus service circulated in 1954, soon after the addition opened. Not until the late 1950s, after Hamilton Park was built out, did the Dallas Transit Company experiment once or twice with bus service. Buses ran during the morning and evening rush hours at widely spaced times. Leaving Hamilton Park in the morning, they drove a block east to North Central Expressway, turned south on the expressway, and rolled down the four-lane road until they reached the exit ramp for near North Dallas. After a stop for passengers at Hall and Thomas Streets, the decaying commercial heart of the once-thriving African-American neighborhood, they continued on to downtown. The trip to Hamilton Park reversed the morning ride. A Saturday bus ran in the morning and at noon. Not surprisingly, the service garnered an inadequate ridership. It appealed only to those with jobs in or near the retail area, who worked normal hours and who rarely or never put in overtime. J. B. Simpson

The Early Community and Beyond   81

"rode it while it was running." Cicero Bruton rode the bus when he could, but his "odd-ball hours" precluded dependence on a bus. The express-style run from Hamilton Park to near North Dallas, then to downtown, was more rapid than local, off-the-expressway travel would have been, but it bypassed potential riders. The rush-hour trips were no help with shopping, after-school activities, or children's visits to the movies on Saturday afternoons. The end of the experiment left Hamilton Park residents as dependent as ever on the automobile.[31]

Hamilton Park's remote location worked a hardship on women, who often traveled long distances to shop. The Hamilton Park shopping center could not meet the demand for comprehensive family shopping. Its filling station, barbershop, and other small proprietorships enjoyed a steady trade, but they offered a limited range of goods and services. Its grocery store, while useful for convenience items, set its prices higher than those in the big markets. Before, and for years after the center opened, major shopping trips were virtual expeditions. One pioneer resident remembered the nearest large grocery as almost seven miles away. Unless another family member could stop by that or some other store, the trip was an inconvenience for women burdened by other responsibilities. The closest commercial center was in Richardson, about four miles north, but Richardson in the mid-1950s was "a clean little country town that did not welcome blacks." Doris Robertson remembered that her "best girlfriend," who did not, in spring 1956, own a washer or dryer, patronized a washateria (laundromat) in Richardson. A presentable, personable woman, the friend used the washateria twice without trouble. On her third visit she encountered "a huge sign" reading "Maids, wear your uniforms," and was instructed to leave and put on her uniform. When she protested that she was not a maid, she was told, "Niggers are not allowed!"[32]

Sadye Gee's experience confirmed how little the Richardson merchants welcomed African Americans. Soon after moving in during December 1957 she paid for groceries in Richardson with a check, "and you would have thought that I was robbing the store. 'Where did you get this check?' I said, 'It's my check.' " A store employee "rushed to the telephone and dialed the number, said, 'Nobody answers! Where did you get the check?' I said, 'It's my check. Did you expect me to answer while I'm standing here?' " The store finally accepted her check, avoiding "a real nasty scene. I was watched until I got back into my car with my little groceries and went home."[33]

Hamilton Park's isolation, then, was no shield against the sometimes harsh realities of the workaday world beyond the subdivision. Some residents fared better than others, of course. Those women with education, ambition, and family support could look forward to teaching careers. Within the limits of segregation, residents such as Mary Garnett, Sadye Gee, Pauline Dixon, and Vivian Starks encountered only the usual frustrations of teaching—frustrations far less significant than the rewards of their profession. Vivian Starks's experience broadened when she worked for the United Service Organization (USO) near various military posts, North and South, during World War II. At Cheyenne, Wyoming, she was a program director for the desegregated USO club catering to nearby Fort Francis. There she met a young soldier, Sammy Davis Jr., who "helped me out so much when I was in Cheyenne." Davis, a performer since his childhood and later the entertainment star, "helped me plan programs, like, the dancing programs. He knew a lot of good music. . . . He was the smartest person." Davis not only helped to plan the entertainments, he volunteered to participate with his song-and-dance routines. "He was very good," Mrs. Starks remembered, but he was also "a fine young man" who "used to come and clean up my office for me."[34]

Other capable women moved from the hard, long hours of "day work," cleaning white families' houses, to better-paying, more responsible jobs. "Day work" was not the sort of occupation most women interviewees wished to recall in detail. But Willie B. Johnson remembered generally positive experiences with at least two families for whom she had worked. Freddie Ervine's desire for "beautiful things" was fueled partly by the interior decoration and furnishings that she saw while in Highland Park, an elite, separately incorporated community near downtown Dallas.[35]

Freddie Ervine, Easter P. Nance, and J. B. and Dorothy Simpson owned catering businesses in addition to having other employment or home responsibilities. Exploiting such a niche within the dual labor market was one way of easing the economic pressures of homeownership and growing families. For the childless Simpsons, it was a way to earn money to provide "extras," such as indulging their fondness for travel. Some women broke out of the barriers of limited African-American job opportunities in the 1950s and 1960s. Those were the years that the walls against black participation in many desirable jobs began to crumble.[36]

Barbara Darden and Willie B. Johnson took advantage of a program to expand the number of licensed vocational nurses during the Korean War. By the time Mrs. Johnson finished the program it was racially integrated, as was Parkland Hospital, the sprawling public hospital where she began working in late 1954. Pearlene Smith began working for Southwestern Bell Telephone Company as a cleaning woman but retired in 1989 as a long-distance operator. Velma Jackson began in 1964 with a clerking job at a credit-reporting agency, retiring in 1989 as a supervisor.[37]

Myra Christian did day work in the "biggest houses" in the Lakewood district. "I wasn't afraid of the house. The bigger the house, the more money you made." In 1948 she enrolled in a school for beauty operators, earned her license, and went to work for a shop in old North Dallas. Right away she learned the difference between a beauty shop for blacks and one for whites. "It's always two jobs for us," she said. "White women go to [the] beauty shop all day long, but our customers have to go to work." That meant getting up mornings to take care of the few nonworking African-American women, or those working late shifts, then returning in the afternoon to take customers who were leaving their own jobs. The shop remained open through the evening hours. Later Mrs. Christian transferred to a barbershop–beauty shop in the Hamilton Park shopping center, then bought the beauty shop from the barber when he moved to a larger location. In 1991 she worked in the shop she owned for twenty years, employing a barber and eight beauty operators.[38]

Work opportunities did not necessarily free blacks from racial comments, as Willie B. Johnson discovered. She encountered bigoted supervisors and physicians who made Parkland Hospital a "battlefield" for the first group of African-American licensed vocational nurses who worked there. On one occasion a doctor looked up from a conference with his colleagues to notice the white blotches on Mrs. Johnson's face. The patches probably resulted from vitiligo, a fairly common disorder characterized by the loss of pigmentation in irregularly-shaped spots. "Look at Mrs. Johnson," the doctor blurted. "She's got two colors." "I'm going to show you how it can be done," the combative nurse replied, after which the offending physician made no more such remarks. A combination of "being just as ornery as they were," black competence, and some whites' insistence on equal treatment for African Americans had dramatically improved the situation at Parkland by the time she left in 1969.[39]

Doris Robertson's was one of the most insulting racial experiences in the world of work. Before her marriage in 1949 she had taken a maid's job at a downtown retail store. As happened in other small businesses, the manager recognized her talent and gave her additional responsibilities. Soon she was operating the elevator and decorating windows. When the bookkeeper fell ill and resigned, the manager added bookkeeping to her tasks at an increased salary. In the midst of these developments, a representative of the American Friends Service Committee (AFSC) visited the store, was impressed with Mrs. Robertson, and asked her to call after work. The result was that she joined an AFSC program designed to place blacks in jobs for which they were trained and qualified—in her case, secretarial work. Because of President Harry S. Truman's announced commitment to civil rights, the AFSC concentrated its efforts on defense contractors—firms more sensitive to federal pressure for minority hires. Robertson and other participants in the program were told to dress correctly for the interview, to be polite but not fawning, and to answer all legitimate questions. They also recorded their interviews. Mrs. Robertson taped a small microphone to her wrist and carried the bulky recorder in a large shoulder bag.[40]

Mrs. Robertson secured an interview for a secretarial position with a Dallas-area firm. The company personnel director's curt behavior bordered on rudeness; she insisted that Mrs. Robertson take a battery of tests and appeared flustered when she figured the results. She called Mrs. Robertson into her office, seated her beside her desk, and told her that her scores were exceptionally high. Then the personnel director leaned over her desk, spat on Mrs. Robertson's shoes, and exclaimed, "But we don't have any jobs for niggers!" After the AFSC released the results from the recorded interviews, Mrs. Robertson was assured that she could find work with several firms, but she declined, preferring that the companies promote qualified blacks already working for them at menial tasks. In an unrelated development, she was soon fired for no stated reason from her bookkeeping job. Later she found secretarial work in pleasant environments with Sears and with the Dallas Independent School District, but her earlier experiences with job-holding and job-seeking were indelibly impressed in her memory.[41]

Hamilton Park's heads of household, overwhelmingly male, experienced similar uneven progress in the world of work. After taking the jobs open to black adolescents in the late 1930s and early 1940s, many had been inducted into the armed forces during World War II. Some wartime experiences belied any notion that, because African Americans usually served in noncombat roles, they were spared danger. J. B. Simpson was assigned to the Red Ball Express—the truck convoys that raced across France and Germany to keep advancing Allied forces supplied. Simpson drove the big trucks that on trips to the front carried gasoline and ammunition for Allied tanks; on the return journeys they ferried back the dead and wounded. William J. Edmond careened over French, German, and Czech roads at all hours of the day and night and in all weather conditions. At times he couldn't see, yet he and his fellow truck drivers always drove "as fast as we could." Ocie Turner, one of the first few thousand blacks admitted to the U.S. Marine Corps, was assigned to a graves-registration detail. He vividly recalled the "gruesome" task of retrieving corpses from the beach at Iwo Jima under deadly Japanese fire. Curtis Smith, drafted into the navy, stood watch on a troop transport in the Pacific during the bitter campaign to retake Japanese-held islands. He experienced plenty of action, including a torpedo hitting his ship.[42]

A. W. Dupree did not undergo combat-area duty but his military life was not the more bearable for that reason: Dupree—a mechanic and later a crew chief—confronted bigotry. Stationed with the pathbreaking Ninety-ninth Pursuit Squadron, the first African-American fighter unit, he trained at Tuskegee Army Air Field, near the famed Tuskegee Institute and the white-controlled town of Tuskegee, Alabama. Dupree chafed at the virulent racism. "We'd go to town, and they treated the dogs better than they treated us." Those experiences "just drove me to the point one time where the sergeant asked me, 'Well, don't you love your country?' I said, 'Well, just about as much as my country loves me.'" The army's politics and promotion policies alienated him, too. During his service his father told him, "I want you to at least be a lieutenant." Dupree replied, "Daddy, I'm PFC—Praying for Civilian." He stayed at Tuskegee Field after the Ninety-ninth's departure, became a truck driver there and at other posts, and refused to consider a career in the service.[43]

With the war won, the men who would later live in Hamilton Park returned to take the jobs that were available to them. The wartime Double-V campaign of the black leadership (victory over fascism and racism) had little immediate effect in Texas. The scarcity of steady jobs within the dual labor market in rural areas and small towns encouraged the continuing migration to Dallas. The city grew from 294,734 in 1940 to 434,462 in 1950; the black population went from 50,407 to 57,263. The population surged to 679,684 in 1960, with the number of African Americans in the city rising to 130,311 (156,726 in the metropolitan area).[44]

In burgeoning Dallas, the labor market for blacks was expanding, but it was also changing, if slowly and fitfully. Henry L. Davis learned through an unhappy experience that desegregation was one thing, racial harmony another. After active army service in World War II, he joined the U.S. Army Reserve in 1945 and was assigned to the 277th Engineer Camouflage Company. In 1948, President Truman issued Executive Order No. 9981, establishing the Committee on Equality of Treatment and Opportunity in the Armed Services, and in effect ordering the desegregation of the armed forces. In about 1949, however, First Sergeant Davis's outfit remained a traditional black unit—black enlisted men officered by whites. "I was praying that some way or another I could bring about the integration of the company," Davis recalled. A captain who temporarily commanded the company agreed to accept anyone with an MOS—a military occupational specialty—useful to the unit. "By doing that, I integrated the company with his blessing." The men in the integrated company "got along" without incident, but drew the hostility of the all-white companies. Davis and his men discovered just how the white units could show their displeasure in an incident that occurred on their return from summer camp. They found the headquarters company truck fully loaded, and an officer ordered Davis to unload the headquarters truck as well as his own. When Davis protested that the truck was the responsibility of headquarters company, he was told to unload both trucks if he wanted a clearance slip. He called his men together and told them: "Sometimes in this life, we have to swallow a bitter pill. So, let's just swallow this and go in and unload that truck." The men unloaded both trucks in the time usually required to unload one.[45]

Joseph Williams's experience confirmed that desegregation did not necessarily lead to integration or equal treatment. He was admitted to the Dallas County Medical Society and shortly thereafter to practice at St. Paul's Hospital. Williams insisted that "there was no altruism involved" in that decision. At the time, "all black patients were in the basement, where the hot water dropped on them in the summer and the cold water dropped on them in the winter—from the overhead plumbing pipes. Of course, we had no special privileges. All you really were there effectively for was to bring your patients in and refer them to Majority physicians." The only other reason for admitting blacks was that the administrator of St. Paul's "was playing to the NAACP annual meeting in Dallas."[46]

Yet the falling barriers were portentous. By the time of Davis's experience, the armed services were moving, however gradually, toward becoming the most integrated, meritocratic organizations in the country. In 1955, when Williams joined the county medical society, the U.S. Supreme Court had already enunciated its famous *Brown* school-desegregation decision and the country was firmly in the civil rights era.

In the mid-1950s environment, the administrator of St. Paul's Hospital was wise to cater to the NAACP. The rising tide of post–World War II prosperity and the collapsing barriers against African-American economic opportunity affected almost all the other heads of household among the pioneers in Hamilton Park, if very unevenly. Those first residents held jobs reflecting the sort of work open to most blacks in the Dallas of the 1950s. They tilted to the menial, janitorial, and clerical kinds of work most widely available, with 268 in maintenance or other unskilled activities. Another 152 were in semiskilled occupations such as service-station attendant, driver, and red cap; 22 held lower professional or managerial jobs, including bookkeeper, manager of a small business, and department supervisor. A minuscule number—only 3—were in the upper professional category, if pioneers involved with education and church ministry are not included. There were 17 small proprietors, who typically, in those independent businesses, catered to blacks: barbershops, filling stations, restaurants, and independent groceries. Another 23 were skilled laborers and 5 worked in public-safety or service jobs such as nurse or firefighter. Another 14 were domestic servants; many spouses of household heads also were employed in that category. Of 55 in the upper professional and managerial ranks, 47 were schoolteachers or administrators and 5 were church pastors. For 10 of the pioneers, the move to Hamilton Park coincided with a move up to a better job.[47]

The prosperity of the 1950s and 1960s probably touched most Hamilton Park residents, but the expanding opportunities for African Americans never reached some of them. Of 242 pioneer heads of household listed as gainfully employed in 1990, 34 were in janitorial, maintenance, and other unskilled jobs, or in the self-described category of "employee." A substantial number, 204, rose on the occupational scale at least once during their years in Hamilton Park; 98 dropped to jobs that were less prestigious or less demanding. Typically those who rose made modest gains, such as a move from maintenance to clerical employment. Of 99 pioneers who could be traced to new Dallas addresses and who listed occupations, 31 improved their financial situations; it was an improvement they expressed by relocating. Five move-outs coincided with a lowered occupational level.[48]

Granted some economic advancement among Hamilton Park dwellers, a comparison with a random sample of pioneer residents in the nearby Spring Valley Park addition demonstrates how seriously African Americans lagged behind whites. The easternmost section of the Spring

Valley development opened a few years after Hamilton Park, for whites only, with houses comparable to those in the black subdivision. Of 161 in the sample, none were in the maintenance category when they moved to Spring Valley Park, and but 17 were in the undifferentiated "employee" group, which placed them arbitrarily in the unskilled-labor category. Thirty-six, or 22 percent, began life in Spring Valley as lower professional-managerial people, compared with 3 percent in Hamilton Park. Upper-level professionals and managers totaled 38, or 23.6 percent, contrasted with Hamilton Park's 7.4 percent. A larger percentage of whites suffered from downward mobility (4.3 to 1.3), perhaps because of the generally higher level of jobs and their greater instability. Of the Spring Valley pioneers, 8 of those traceable (or 5 percent) moved after obtaining a better job, compared with 31 (4.2 percent) in Hamilton Park.[49]

For all the limitations on black progress, the economic and social system allowed some capable, determined Hamilton Park residents to rise. Freddie Allen, a construction-crane operator, was accepted into the equipment operators' local in 1957. Charles E. Smith eventually was promoted from his janitorial job with the telephone company to a craft position. In the 1960s he moved through the ranks of the crafts before retiring as a communication technician, "the highest craft title at Southwestern Bell."[50]

Marion Mitchell worked at a variety of jobs, then became an airplane cabin cleaner for Braniff Airlines. Promoted to head an all-black cleaning crew, he confronted a white worker who was complaining "about the black people this and the black people that and the niggers and . . . one thing and another." Mitchell told the white, " 'I don't think it's necessary to get all out of sorts about this.' So, he came over to me and said, 'Well, if you ain't a nigger, what are you then?'" Mitchell, "provoked," felled the man with one punch, "jumped on him and choked him. It took three or four guys to get me off of him." Fired for fighting, he went to work as a maintenance man, but with a schedule flexible enough to allow him to drive a contract mail truck, if or when he garnered a contract. About a year later, in October 1965, he landed a contract to haul mail between Dallas and the suburb of Garland. There were four trips every day in one truck, with either Mitchell or his part-time driver at the wheel. Mitchell scrupulously maintained his good relationships with his banker and truck dealer, meanwhile keeping careful track of his costs. His close figuring of bids based on a comprehensive knowledge of costs won him contract after contract. "I built that thing up from one truck to twenty-two tractors, five bobtail vans, thirty-one trailers, and forty-two full-time employees. I went from about a $1,500-a-year operation to somewhere close to [a] $3,000,000-a-year business." He sold out in 1989 and retired.[51]

Other whites who were willing to recognize individual ability without regard to race helped at least two Hamilton Park residents get ahead. Curtis J. Smith began working for Braniff Airlines in 1949 at Love Field as a member of an airplane cleaning crew. The white manager of the department noticed his work. One evening in 1950, when a shift supervisor called in sick, the manager called the eighteen or nineteen workers together and announced, "I'm going to appoint 'Smitty' to be in charge tonight." The manager repeated: "He's in charge," and he advised anyone who did not like the arrangement to leave. No one left and the shift worked with no problems. For a year Smith filled in whenever a supervisor was absent. In 1951 the manager asked him to be the full-time supervisor of the graveyard shift, bossing integrated crews. Smith was doubtful. "You know how things are," he said. "We've got some people out here who don't like black people telling them what to do." The manager's response was, "Maybe they don't want their job." Smith accepted the promotion. Later he became manager of the passenger-service department, in charge of placing on board every aircraft all the in-flight materials for passengers and crew, except for meals. His experience with the forms and procedures for handling in-flight materials on international flights stood him in good stead when the original Braniff went bankrupt and ceased operations in 1982. A catering service that had suffered through customs fines and confiscations in foreign countries hired him to straighten out its methods of moving its equipment on and off the international flights of American Airlines.[52]

Willie F. Smith's rise formed the quintessence of American success. Smith's war was the Korean conflict. A combat infantryman, he endured "four or five" separate human-wave attacks from the Chinese army, when "our guns and machine guns fired as fast as they could" and the Chinese troops would "just die like flies." He was discharged in 1953 and began looking for work. While downtown, he passed the Lawyers Title Insurance Company. Looking through the glass front, he "didn't see any black people in there," but he went in, and met a "very cool" reception when he asked about employment. The company's state manager interviewed him on a Monday, asked him to telephone on Friday, and, when he did, told him to come to work the next Monday. Smith and the manager settled the terms of his employment. Then the manager leveled with him. "All those people out there and all those people out in the courthouse are not going to help you." The manager promised him that he would have to "scratch and dig to make it," and when he felt his "back against the wall" he could appeal directly to the manager. Smith went to work in title research, investigating properties to determine whether his company could insure a new title for the buyer or the buyer's lender.[53]

Smith's responsibilities increased as the years went by. A restructuring in 1974 required a hundred layoffs, but he was one of thirteen survivors. About the same time, he put together a complex title-insurance package for the Southland Corporation, then the owners of the 7-Eleven chain of convenience stores. Southland was expanding rapidly, leaving large amounts of working capital tied up in earnest-money payments. It was also paying attorneys substantial sums to check titles. Smith's plan arranged for the company to issue debits and credits to Southland's account in the place of earnest-money payments, and for the company to move the title work to a point at which Southland's paralegals could complete it. The Southland Corporation accepted the package and "it worked. I put one together like that for Phillips Petroleum when they were expanding; I put one together like that for Pizza Hut when they were expanding; for Steak & Ale when they were expanding; and probably twenty to twenty-five other companies." His clients included the Church of Jesus Christ of Latter-day Saints in the days before the Mormon church accepted African Americans to equal membership. Smith knew the problem, but, as he did when confronted with a difficult situation, "brought the Lord in." Despite a snub from one member of his welcoming delegation at the Salt Lake City airport, he carried through, leaving the conference with church leaders with "all their business—a pledge of all of it."[54]

Whether or not a resident of Hamilton Park enjoyed stunning economic success, he or she occupied the community and the world of work and other activities beyond the subdivision, physically, mentally, and emotionally. The worlds beyond Hamilton Park were not compartmentalized but reciprocal. Steady jobs and good reputations in the worlds outside the community made residence in the community possible. Good or improving jobs, when the dual labor market is considered, allowed residents to realize their values in a house and lot in Hamilton Park and to escape neighborhoods that were a less adequate expression of a satisfactory family life. The improving economic circumstances of many Hamilton Park residents suggest, too, that the 1950s and after were a time of organic progress in the world of work—not a series of advances inspired by dramatic events. It does not diminish the *Brown* school-desegregation decision of 1954 or the successful Montgomery, Alabama, bus boycott of 1956 against white-supremacist seating arrangements to note that Curtis J. Smith's and Willie F. Smith's job breakthroughs occurred earlier. Hamilton Park, for that matter, preceded any of the great civil rights advances of the 1960s. Finally, however compelling or demanding the world outside Hamilton Park, its pioneer residents also focused on their community. Their focus, to be sure, was on family, house, and lot, but it was also collective, and was expressed through a variety of organizations.

6

ORGANIZING IN HAMILTON PARK

It is not too much to claim that its organizations and its easily comprehended size insured the survival of Hamilton Park as a community. The claim does not spring from an institutional or geographical determinism: active, dedicated people did the necessary work. The residents of Hamilton Park founded and built their organizations in the early years of the community, well before the final size or shape of Hamilton Park could be known.

Several groups focused on community development, in a variety of contexts. The Civic League, nonpolitical in a partisan sense, was committed to community betterment by bringing residents together to improve the addition's private property and public places, and involving government in the effort. The Interorganizational Committee (later the Interorganizational Council, hereafter IOC) developed to concert and harmonize the activities of all programs and citizens of Hamilton Park. In practice this objective involved, first, the IOC's serving as a community clearinghouse for organizational activities; second, holding candidate forums, nominating a slate of candidates and taking a position on bond issues before each election; and third, organizing voter-registration drives. The purpose of the last two objectives encouraged a high level of bloc voting.[1] Both organizations were deeply involved in the struggles over the desegregation of the Hamilton Park School (see chapter 8).

Churches played a large role in the community. The Hamilton Park Methodist (later United Methodist) Church, the First Baptist Church of Hamilton Park, and the Hamilton Park Church of Christ attended first to the spiritual needs of their congregations but they also cooperated with other organizations. After 1963, when their education building opened, the Methodists enjoyed the most ample space for community meetings.

There were several clubs, primarily social, including the Hamiltonians, a men's group, its auxiliary the Hamiltonettes, and a smaller group for men, the Hamonites, although each of them also carried on some charitable activity. The Gold Cup Garden Club was an active group with city and national affiliations. The Parent-Teachers Association (PTA), the Dads Club, and the Band Parents revolved around the school (see chapter 7). Adults organized and led the Boy Scouts. Other residents responded to community problems as they perceived them on an ad hoc basis or under the umbrella of one or another organization. Still others maintained or developed ties with institutions and groups outside Hamilton Park—activities not precluding community involvement.[2]

The Civic League was the most important secular organization. It was also one of the earliest—the brainchild of John W. Rice, the secretary-manager of the Dallas Negro Chamber of Commerce. In the summer of 1954 he received a petition from ninety Hamilton Park residents asking the chamber to "help us to solve" a serious school transportation problem. When resident Claudia Gaines spoke with Superintendent Joseph Jones Pearce of the Richardson Independent School District (RISD), he informed her that state law required bus transportation for students living beyond two miles from their school. Hamilton Park children, who lived about a mile by street routes from the Anderson Bonner School, could walk along Forest Lane and Coit Road, neither of which had sidewalks, all the while tempted to take a dangerous shortcut by running across North Central Expressway. Or they could be driven to and from school in private cars. Pearce was willing to supply a thirty-five-passenger bus, but would not operate it if the Hamilton Park school population exceeded thirty-five. Because there were already eighteen schoolage children and thirteen younger children in the subdivision, with more families expected by September, the bus could be no more than a temporary solution.[3]

Nor was moving the children into the Dallas Independent School District (DISD) a feasible solution. Mrs. Gaines spoke with a member of the DISD board, who informed her that parents who sent children outside their home school district paid $20 per child per month. At the existing price and income levels, the payment was prohibitive for most people who had just assumed a new mortgage. The added transportation costs of Hamilton Park's remote location led thirty-three residents to ask, in the same communication to Rice, for city bus service.[4]

Rice could do nothing more than could the residents concerning schooling and transportation problems. As Crossman pointed out, the

RISD would not have its grade and high school building in Hamilton Park ready for another year. Nor could the small population of the addition justify city bus service. Rice could, however, establish a community organization, a civic league, of the type he had helped create in past years. He wrote to Crossman "that since such requests as these must be handled . . . on a long range basis, it would be well to form a civic league through which not only these matters can be discussed, but others looking toward the orderly development of a good community." After laying the groundwork, Rice met on 20 August 1954 with "several of the residents of Hamilton Park and assisted in the organization of [the Civic League]."[5]

The Civic League soon developed a constitution and a full-fledged committee structure. The league dedicated itself to "a better understanding and appreciation among the residents by working together" to improve "our homes, streets, schools, churches, businesses, and living conditions in general within [Hamilton Park]." The league opened membership to any resident "of legal age" and to anyone else "proving" an interest in the community. Voting was limited to members in good standing who paid their dues. The usual offices and an executive committee were established. Standing committees oversaw membership, program and social events, public relations, and parks and recreation. A sunshine committee was charged with relieving the suffering in "all homes in this community that are darkened by accidents, sickness, death, or any other crises." Special committees would be appointed as needed.[6]

The Civic League, as Rice suggested, took steps "looking toward the orderly development of a good community." During the first thirty years of its life the league focused on situations both within and without Hamilton Park, but a substantial shift in emphasis bisected this era. Into the late 1960s, the organization sustained the familial atmosphere in the community and pressured the city government, and sometimes private interests, to enhance its quality of life. Henry L. Davis III, the president from 1961 to 1963, started a newsletter and appointed block captains who went from door to door, soliciting membership dues. Then from the late 1960s, the inner-directed as well as the outer-directed activities transferred their focus. Inwardly, more attention centered on homeowners who failed to meet the original standards of maintenance or decorum and those who violated the deed restrictions.[7] Externally-directed activity during and after the late 1960s paid relatively less attention to the maintenance and improvement of public ground, the shopping center, and undeveloped space around Hamilton Park. Civic League activists devoted relatively more time and energy to fending off commercial encroachments as development northward from the city center reached, passed, and then crowded around Hamilton Park.

The Civic League created programs for children and youth because of the subdivision's isolation from the usual centers of recreation for African-American youngsters, because of the initially undeveloped state of Willowdell Park, and because of the commitment to the rising generation implied in the families' moves to Hamilton Park. In a Hamilton Park household, both parents often worked, and one or the other sometimes worked at more than one job. The resulting lack of supervision for children exacerbated the youth problem. The youth of Hamilton Park, league president Davis wrote, "are our pride and joy. If given something to do, they make us happy. If not given something, they find something to get into and there are times when their finding makes us very unhappy." As the dynamic activist Willie B. Johnson phrased it, "You will either treat the kids right and do what's right when they are coming up, or later on around the corner, you are going to meet them with a gun in their hand."[8]

Pauline Dixon, the first long-term league president, recalled that the organization encouraged many private efforts to create positive diversions for the young. Several women acted as chaperons for backyard parties, organized discussion groups, and persuaded other women to join them on field trips, taking their own and other children in their cars to such places as the zoo, the fine-arts museum, the planetarium, and the main library. During summers, the mothers took the youngsters to picnics and swims at the city parks. The backyard and house gatherings presented a problem of safety and security, because word of them would spread to teenagers in other communities, who would attempt to crash the parties.[9]

Most of the young outsiders were simply in search of novelty or a good time in a subdivision of new houses that was attracting much attention. A few were bent on mischief and undeterred by the chaperonage of older women, and for that reason the women called on men to assist. Pastor Zan Holmes recalled that on one occasion the male presence was an insufficient deterrent: "There were kids who would come from North Park [the neighborhood south of Love Field], and we were looking out for them." Also looking for them were "a couple of boys from Hamilton Park" who "had guns and shot up that place. Fortunately, they didn't kill anybody, but several kids were wounded." Holmes pointed out that the

Hamilton Park youths were "protecting their turf. The boys from Hamilton Park didn't like it because these boys from other places were coming out and being with their girlfriends." On another occasion, Pauline Dixon remembered, "we had a group from [old] North Dallas, and they were really looking rough. We called the police. The Civic League had previously informed the police what we were going to do. We got rid of them. We let them know we were not glad for crashers out here." Richard Bonner remembered the indignation over outsiders "coming to crash our parties and to run off with our girls. We just didn't accept those guys."[10]

The league cooperated with others to expand opportunities for youth. Working with the Hamilton Park School administration, the league secured the services of a YMCA youth worker in 1958. The youth director organized after-school sports and expanded the program of educational and recreational tours. That year he took a group to the East Texas oilfields, the Richardson school district supplying the buses. In 1961, the high-school senior tour went to Monterrey, Mexico. Other destinations through the years included Hot Springs, Arkansas, and the Houston Astrodome. In the years before the public accommodations provisions of the Civil Rights Act of 1964, the tours were planned with exceptional care. Pauline Dixon said that "if you go through [a town], you go through tour guides, the city council, the bus company—all those things. You tell them you don't want any problem, and then you get people who have access and knowledge, that know how to do that."[11]

Some residents worked with youth independently, but along lines parallel to the Civic League's. High schoolers respected Holmes, then in his early twenties, who was regarded much as a wiser and sympathetic, but firm, older brother would be. Young people went to him with their problems; parents spoke with him about their youngsters' difficulties and arranged for him to speak to them. Holmes was not merely reactive. Early on, he worked with "some of the toughest boys in the community" to form the Crusaders, a name the group selected itself. The Crusaders met midweekly at the Hamilton Park Methodist Church, quickly becoming a constructive "social force." Holmes recalled, "They'd come and play games. They'd clean out the little hall and the overflow area under our supervision. We would serve them refreshments, and it was a big thing. They'd jam in there in just huge numbers." Vacation bible school and summer camps also attracted youth.[12]

Scouting provided an important outlet for young people. On Saturday mornings, Donald Payton remembered, "the boys would go to the

Scout meeting. We had Mrs. Wilhelmina Rettig," a light-skinned Cub Scout den mother "who looked just like a white lady, and she had us all in tow" at Scout jamborees and other functions. Whites would look at the group and think, " 'Colored kids! What are these kids doing here?' " Then they would "look at Mrs. Rettig, and she'd have her uniform on with a scarf and everything. They'd look like: 'Well, is this . . . is this a white lady?' You know, you could just see it on their faces. They'd look at us, and then they'd look at Mrs. Rettig, and they'd look back at us; then they'd say, 'Well, maybe she knows what she's doing.' "[13]

George Brewer, a Boy Scout in his youth, organized one of the two troops in Hamilton Park because of the contribution that Scouting would make to "a good, clean community." After meeting with a representative of the Boy Scouts, he "began to inquire as to which boys wanted to have a troop. Then, I decided to organize it." Brewer required parental attendance at the organization meeting "because, in the final analysis, the boys' participation is going to depend a lot on the attitude of the parents." Brewer also organized a "father's group" to help take troop members on outings. "I had pretty good cooperation throughout the community because people knew I was busy, they knew I was involved in community activity; and a lot of people who see that you have an interest, other than your own interest, will stretch a point to work with you." The scoutmaster took his turn at the wheel, too. Brewer "had a 1956 Rambler and tore that thing up driving out into the rural areas and sometimes across plowed fields and things like that—carrying them on trips, overnight trips, camping, that sort of thing."[14]

Concerns for young people were in part responsible for the Civic League's steady pressure to improve Willowdell Park, a twenty-one-acre swath bounded on the west by Cottonwood Creek and on the east by Willowdell Drive. Aside from the brushy hackberries lining the creek, the park was almost entirely bare of foliage. Occasional heavy rains in the Cottonwood Creek watershed forced the usually insignificant stream out of its banks. Sometimes the water rolled over the park and approached Willowdell Drive; when it receded, it left behind a litter of scummy mud, driftwood, and trash. The first need was, however, for play equipment to create an inviting atmosphere for the youngsters. A 1957 Civic League petition and repeated visits to the park board during the next few years from the chairman of the league's park and recreation committee eventually bore fruit. Playground equipment and a wading pool came first. In 1960, the city completed a lighted baseball diamond with bleachers and a fence. The city also installed a lighted tennis court, planted trees, and built sidewalks within the park. The same year, the league sponsored the community's first annual picnic, held in the shopping center because of construction in the park. It was a family-oriented gathering featuring a band, refreshments, and a well-known disk jockey who gave out awards. In 1961 the annual picnic moved to the park, where it became a community fixture for more than a quarter-century. A baseball game between Little League teams and a dance contest were among the youth-oriented activities.[15]

All these functions, plus several more connected with the school, together with the sense of discipline and closeness prevailing in most families, produced a generally good atmosphere for youth in Hamilton Park. The "good atmosphere" did not mean that the young people lacked spirit or exuberance or that they did not become involved in some of the usual shenanigans and scrapes of childhood and adolescence. Ordinarily such activities were no more serious than sneaking a few bottles of beer, or attempting to sneak them, into backyard parties. In "those days," Holmes remembered, "adult authority was respected. We looked out for each other's kids. If I saw a kid doing something, I could challenge that kid, knowing that I would have the support of that kid's parents. It was that extended family concept that comes out of the African culture that was operating out there at Hamilton Park during those days."[16]

A few incidents, "isolated instances," were more serious. Holmes knew about them because of his close, sympathetic relationship with young people. He recalled some home burglaries and automobile thefts and two youths who "robbed a milkman." Those youngsters "were sentenced to the penitentiary. I would go down and visit them at the penitentiary." They were, Holmes believed, "good boys, but they just made a mistake." In general, however, a "strong family orientation," a "high respect for adult authority," and concerned adult involvement limited most juvenile delinquencies to minor offenses.[17]

Besides the problems of children and youth, the Civic League addressed issues involving the physical development of Hamilton Park. The community was thoughtfully, if not perfectly, designed at the time of its virtual completion in 1960. Its compact layout and carefully planned, connecting streets made for easy interaction among residents. Holmes remembered that "one of the things about the Hamilton Park community is that it was a real neighborhood, a real community, primarily because of the way it was built. You could walk through Hamilton Park easily, and I could do pastoral visits by walking. We knew each other; everybody knew each other. So, we had that close-knit community."[18] The 1953 subdivision requirements, paved streets with cement gutters, curbs, and sidewalks, enhanced mobility and mutual activity.

Other physical aspects of the subdivision were less appealing, but the Civic League considered them a challenge to its mandate. Every household in Hamilton Park had an alley. Most of the alleys were graveled, not paved, a savings in the infrastructure costs added to the price of each house and lot. The contractor paved only short stretches of alley—for example, along the north end between Galva and Willowdell, because, as Ruby Watson put it, "there was no way the garbage pickup truck could climb that hill" in rainy weather. Elsewhere, "they graded the alleys, and then they put maybe four inches of gravel on top of that, and for a while it worked," George Brewer said. "Then the [refuse collection] trucks would begin to bog down when the gravel would sink into the mud. They'd have these long rains, and the trucks would just sink into the mud. Then, they wanted us to put our refuse out on the . . . front parkway. We were having all kinds of problems with the garbage and stuff getting knocked over and the dogs distributing it up and down the street, that kind of thing, so we decided in the Civic League that we needed to do something about that."[19]

What the Civic League did under Davis's presidency was to assume a task already begun. Homeowners along a portion of Oberlin Drive had successfully circulated a petition for paving, submitted it to the city, and had the gravel in their alley replaced with concrete. The league sponsored so many petitions that in January 1962 Davis reported fifteen alleys— about two-thirds of the total—paved. Brewer and others worked hard, both at that time and during Brewer's 1963 presidency, to line up petitioners. Brewer's custodial work kept him out until late, but he often arranged to leave petitions in screen doors to be collected later. "On several occasions I called people as late as 10:00 at night." The overwhelming majority gladly paid the paving assessment to rid their backlots of mud and their front yards of rubbish. By early 1966, Willie Smith, then the president, could boast of all but three alleys being paved.[20]

The Civic League aggressively addressed other issues concerning the physical environment. In the beginning, the community was so dark after sundown that one pioneer resident remembered no street lights at all. The league secured a sheaf of street-light petitions and by early 1962 one petition had been filed and a light installed. The league worked to increase the number of stop signs and crosswalk markings. It requested and received additional police patrols to curb speeding. After the Hamilton Park School opened in 1955, league members raised money for trees and shrubs on the grounds and around the building. Some men of the league set out the plants themselves. To stimulate pride in well-kept yards, the league established a "lawn of the week" award during the growing season. A prize for the best house and yard decorations turned the community into a blaze of light at Christmastime.[21]

Other problems were less tractable. Schroeder Road, the main stem running north-south through Hamilton Park, created three such headaches. The contractors did not heavily regrade the venerable road before installing curbs, gutters, sidewalks, and repairing its surface. They saved money when they raised the street over the limestone brow of the south-facing hill a few yards north of the junctions with Galva and Bellafonte Drives, but they reckoned without a sizeable depression in the road north of the stony outcrop. This hollow was large enough to hold a southbound car out of sight of the motorists below on Galva and Bellafonte for a few critical moments. Often enough, when drivers turned south onto Schroeder from Bellafonte, or either direction from Galva, a speeding car suddenly appeared bearing down on them. There were a "number of accidents" at the location. Police speed traps helped the situation but, short of a stop light or stop signs, which the city would not install, there was no permanent solution.[22]

Flooding at the junction of Schroeder Road and Forest Lane was the second and most spectacular problem. The same heavy rains that sent Cottonwood Creek out of its banks and over Willowdell Park also forced floodwaters east along Forest Lane, through the shopping-center parking lot, and over Schroeder Road. The grade of Schroeder fell gently as it approached Forest Lane, then rose abruptly to meet Forest. Water flowed into the pocket, deep enough to trap a driver attempting to negotiate "that little hill" on Schroeder north of Forest, Doris Robertson remembered. "Your car would stall because it would get flooded with the water. You would try to cut through that little shopping center area and the same thing would happen. So what did you do? If your car flooded, you'd have to get out, lock it, walk home, and wait until the water ran off. Then you would have to call in [to an employer] and then try to make it to work." Some of the rising water caused little damage. When severe floods came, they invaded the drugstore at the southeast corner of the shopping center. Then the water would flow into Myra Christian's beauty shop, around the corner on the east side. "That water would be in that shop," Mrs. Christian said, "so that it would be boiling in the commodes [toilets]."[23]

When the vegetable stand was in seasonal operation, the flooding sometimes provided lighthearted diversion. Myra Christian remembered that "the vegetables would be floating out in the water. Watermelons would be floating in the water. It was just so much fun. When you're young, anything is funny: 'Look at that water!' And we'd get the watermelons and eat them." Reality returned when the water ebbed. "Then we'd have to clean the beauty shop up before we could work." City crews tried to correct the problem. "The city came out, and they worked and they worked and they worked," Mrs. Robertson said, but the effort produced little improvement. The reconstruction of Forest Lane and the regrading of Schroeder Road in the later 1970s eliminated any serious flooding problems at the intersection.[24]

In the worst of times the high water never halted travel over Schroeder for more than a few hours, but during those hours there was no easy way in and out of Hamilton Park. A narrow, poorly blacktopped extension of Schroeder led a determined driver north to Valley View Lane. Elsewhere, rutted tracks ran from the north end of the paving on Hallum Street, across undeveloped prairie for a quarter of a mile to Valley View. Wet weather was the most difficult time to negotiate the substandard roads, especially in a passenger car. By 1968, Schroeder was widened and repaired to the freeway access road, and by 1985 the city had completed an extension of Campanella, east across the Southern Pacific tracks to a new, north-south thoroughfare. Until the improvement of Schroeder north, however, Hamilton Park's main stem was the only all-weather way in and out.[25]

The problems with the trough in Schroeder Road, flooding, and access, suggest that external relations with governments and other entities were uneven. One signal success involved three unlikely protagonists: Mable Davis, a teacher at Hamilton Park Elementary School, her husband, Henry Davis, then the president of the Civic League, and Karl Hoblitzelle, whose Hoblitzelle Foundation had loaned the money to purchase the original 173 acres for Hamilton Park. The issue that brought the Davises and Hoblitzelle together was the lack of shelter and rest-room facilities at Willowdell Park. Amenable as the park authorities were to some improvements, they stonewalled the Civic League on the rest-room issue.[26]

Searching for a stopgap, Davis persuaded three families on Willowdell Drive, across from the park, to open their bathrooms to properly supervised children attending picnics or other family outings. Their gesture "was mighty nice," but not the answer for a large gathering such as the league's annual picnic. In 1961 Davis rented portable toilets for the first picnic to be held at the park. Meanwhile the Davises prayed for a solution. Soon Mable Davis dreamed that "God spoke" to her, telling her to have her husband write to Hoblitzelle. In September 1960, Davis wrote the distinguished-looking theater tycoon about the need for a "clubhouse" containing rest rooms and a meeting area for use during "inclement weather." Hoblitzelle responded. By the end of the year the foundation and the city parks and recreation department were discussing a more modest building than Davis envisioned—one containing a small shelter area, rest rooms, and storage for playground equipment. A year after Davis's letter, the contract was let for a cost of $10,190. The foundation arranged for a plaque honoring Crossman to be placed on the building. "The plaque down at the rest room doesn't say 'Mable Davis' on it, but it don't bother me about that," Henry Davis remarked. The improbable trio had achieved its goal.[27]

Other external struggles of the early years produced a mixed bag. The league worked with the Interorganizational Council to secure, in 1961, a new voting precinct, then numbered 180 and located at the school. The new precinct ended the mile-long drive to the nearest polling place. It persuaded the post office to deliver mail door-to-door rather than at curbside. Its efforts with the Dallas Transit Company produced the aforementioned temporary, inadequate, and ill-fated bus service.[28]

Efforts to keep out surrounding incompatible land use met with only mixed success. The Hamilton Park Apartments, a 106-unit complex, opened in 1961 at the south side of the Schroeder and Bunche junction. They were next to, but not in, Hamilton Park. There was no feasible way at the time to prevent their construction in an area zoned for light industry. For many years the apartments suffered from a high vacancy rate, occasional poor maintenance, and "problems." They served as a small beachhead for Hamilton Park, sixteen households moving from the apartments to single-family homes in the community. Four households moved in the other direction—to the apartments. The cross-migration ceased in 1974. By 1986, Hispanic families occupied 41 percent of the rented units, and four years later 80 percent of the occupied units rented to Hispanic households. The 1961 suit to halt an apartment complex on Willowdell failed, but—as noted in chapter 4—no apartments were built on the site.[29]

The struggle against the cement-batching plant was a success. Many residents remembered the plant, built across Forest Lane to supply material for Hamilton Park and for other construction projects in the area. In 1961 the cement company appealed to the planning and zoning commission to convert its temporary permit into a permanent zoning designation. But the prevailing southerly winds blew cement dust across Forest Lane into Hamilton Park. Residents went to the hearings and spoke against a permanent berth for the plant. They won. As Vincent Rohloff of the DCIA remembered, one of their most ardent supporters was a white man who lived in the area. He had opposed the black community. But he was isolated and he was up against the white elite. In the ten years after the community began to build, he had changed his mind. "He mentioned how he had opposed Hamilton Park," Rohloff said. But the white man declared: "I have reversed my position. These people are out there on Saturdays and Sundays taking care of their homes and yards. I want this development to continue. I'm opposed to the cement company." It was a signal victory for the community and it presaged many more such battles.[30]

The most portentous struggle occurred in the early 1970s. The skirmishing over covenant violations confirmed the elite's withdrawal from the community's internal affairs (see chapter 4). But it also did more, because the ultimate decision not to prosecute resident violators of the deed restrictions left adherence to most of the rules to an individual's conscience. When the restrictions coincided with city housing and zoning codes, city officials were the ultimate enforcers. Aside from calling in official enforcement, the Civic League's recourse lay only in persuasion, not prosecution.

Previous league presidents had exhorted their neighbors to keep up their property, control roaming dogs, and properly place their yard waste for collection. More serious problems than upkeep gradually accumulated as time passed. By late 1971, chain-link fences, prohibited beyond the front building line, had nevertheless sprouted in several front yards. Nonconforming sheds were proliferating in backyards. Despite "numerous complaints from neighbors," a church operated out of a home in violation of the provision that the lots be used for residential purposes only—and a sign, also in violation of the covenant, advertised that church or another "in one of the homes." Hedges and shrubs higher than the permitted two feet blocked motorists' views at intersections.[31]

Willie Smith, president of the league, visited the violators and appealed to them to conform. The violations, Smith believed, were "an encroachment upon this little community that we loved so much and that the intent had been expressed in the documents themselves." In minor matters the league received some cooperation. Cicero Bruton, who planted shrubbery on his lot at the northeast corner of Bellafonte and Tobian, remembered that Smith's brother "just mentioned" the height of the shrubs—"he didn't have to preach to me about it. I agreed with them that that was a hazard—or would have been—if I had let it get too high where they couldn't see." Fences, outbuildings, and shoestring churches were another matter entirely. When Smith asked their owners to conform he was told "'Go fly a kite,' in so many words." Then Smith appealed to the Hoblitzelle Foundation, and was told that the property owners, not the white elite, would have to enforce the covenants.[32]

At the next meeting of the Civic League, Smith urged the organization to sponsor legal action against the violators. His "position was that the restrictions applied to all, one as much as the other, that they were for the protection of one and all, so let's sue and see if we can't get the restrictions enforced." He believed "that if you want to lose your neighborhood and want it to start deteriorating, start letting people do as they please in violation of restrictions that are there for the protection of everyone. You will see a neighborhood deteriorate." But the vote went against him. Smith believed that neighborliness, a disinclination to pit conforming neighbors against those whose violations were not, on the whole, major, explained the decision "more than anything else."[33]

Smith also suggested a reason behind the willingness to wink at covenant violations. The showdown over the violations occurred, he believed, "during the transition in the neighborhood. So many of the original owners had now moved away"—a migration Smith dated from 1967 at the latest. "Then people started to migrate; people started to move. Oak Cliff started to open—better houses, larger houses. Income had increased, and people wanted larger houses, and we started to lose a lot of the good people."[34]

Smith was correct on most counts. Census tracts in the Oak Cliff area south of the Trinity River were, in 1960, predominately white. Tract 89, traditionally African American, was 75.5 percent black, but the rest of Oak Cliff was practically lily white. By 1970, however, the continuing expansion of black housing had burst the boundaries of the settled African-American communities. Five miles southeast of the bluff, Bishop College and its Highland Hills subdivision were magnets pulling people across the long Trinity bridges from South Dallas and other parts of the city. In 1970, fourteen of fifty-five tracts in the east Oak Cliff area and to the south held African-American populations of 80 percent or more. Incomes were up, too. An African-American employed couple earning the median income for blacks in Dallas made $7,749 in 1970, an increase of $4,439, or 2.3 times, since 1959. Prices were up, but the consumer price index rose only from 87.3 to 116.3 during the same period, an increase of 75.1 percent. In other words, income more than doubled, while prices increased substantially less than onefold.[35]

Whether Hamilton Park had lost "a lot of the good people" was a more subjective evaluation. The 1967 city directory revealed that 173, or 23.4 percent, of the original heads of household no longer lived in Hamilton Park (see appendix A). Some had died; others had moved after taking a better job. Not all of the "good people" who wished better housing necessarily needed the inducement of a higher occupational status. Savings, a spouse's improved employment, or other situations could dictate a move away from Hamilton Park. Many "good people" remained and some "good people" moved in. But the original spirit had slackened. Smith said that new arrivals "never had the pride and the feeling of ownership that we all developed. See, we started at Hamilton Park with a house and one tree and maybe five shrubs. We could ride around in Hamilton Park ten years later, and we could see the fruits of our labor . . . trees and beautiful lawns." Many of the later arrivals "had no appreciation for that."[36]

However, those who replaced the pioneers were not necessarily any the less devoted to Hamilton Park. George and Thelma Wells moved to the community in 1963 and in 1971 Mrs. Wells became president of the Civic League. Melroe and Thelma Self, first listed in the city directory in 1977, were active in the community, with Mrs. Self playing an important advisory role in the Buyout (see chapter 9).[37]

There was, besides the reasons Smith listed, a belief that people had the right to develop their own property within very broad limits. This belief was not confined to newcomers. Leaving aside the violators, the belief lay dormant among some original residents until Smith's challenge awakened it. Other pioneers may have agreed with William Edmond. Edmond was active in the league, but believed that a suit against the violators would fail. Besides teaching, Edmond "waited on tables at Preston Hollow Country Club," overhearing the problems of "the big-shot white folks" who "couldn't win" their suits or threatened suits to enforce their deed restrictions. The Civic League could hardly hope to succeed where influential individuals had failed; therefore, the league should not pursue the matter, "at least not with my money."[38]

The Civic League concerned itself with a flurry of other activity, agitating against a business in the shopping center that was a reputed beer parlor, urging better home maintenance on backsliding owners, and working for street improvements. Improvement was most noticeable when the league could work with city officials to enforce ordinances. Smith patrolled Hamilton Park looking for inoperative cars in yards. He turned the addresses over to the city manager, who "would send someone out, and they would ticket all those cars. If those cars did not disappear, then those orange wreckers would come out and pull those cars out." Similar measures worked with heavy trucks. Smith remembered one later resident of Bellafonte who "parked that big truck part on the sidewalk and part on the street." The truck owner declared that "no one was ever going to tell him where to park his truck. So I called the police and told them what he said. The response was, 'We will put a ticket on there every hour, as long as it sits there.' And it disappeared. It sure did."[39]

Smith was not always successful, even with the city ordinances at his back. A. W. Dupree remembered when "a teen-ager driving Daddy's truck" east on Ebony lost control, shot across the junction with Hallum, jumped the curb, and plowed into his house, smashing "a big hole" in it. "Well," he told his family, "we are going to have to let the truck stay in the yard until we get things squared away." Soon Smith spotted the truck. "Willie Fred Smith came out here and told me, 'That truck is creating an eyesore in the neighborhood. It's got to be moved.'" Dupree's spirited response was, "you did not come up here to see if anybody got hurt, or you didn't come up here to see if there was anything you could do to ease my situation. You came up here trying to give me orders. You've just put your life on the line. You just get out of my yard. That truck gets moved when I decide it's going to move, not you." After that, Dupree "wasn't bothered by Fred Smith," but that occasion and others left him with the conviction that "the Civic League's endeavors have just been on surface things." Smith may have had his experience with Dupree in mind when he said, "I did not make a lot of friends as Civic League president."[40]

By the end of Smith's tenure in 1971, the parameters of Civic League activity were set. They involved the maintenance and improvement of the public areas in and around Hamilton Park, including the park, shopping center, and surrounding streets, and the attempted encroachment of business as Dallas's growth surged north around and past the community. The last issue would become more pressing in later years, as would the question of house and lot maintenance within Hamilton Park.

The IOC, the second inclusive association in the community, was founded about 1957. Its functions were two: first, to serve as a frankly political and legal agency; and second, to be an umbrella organization for the disparate groups in the community. As the IOC's long-time president Curtis Smith explained it, the Civic League could not advocate political positions or candidates; the league was a nonprofit educational organization that could handle "civic affairs" but "could not handle other things"—for example, intervention in partisan politics on behalf of the community. "It wasn't supposed to be able to go to court; it wasn't supposed to be anything political."[41]

The IOC's second role—the umbrella function—sought to bring all groups, educational, social and charitable, civic, and religious, together for an exchange of views, political action, and coordination. A flower and garden club, four social clubs, the Civic League, the Dads Club, the PTA, the Baptist and Methodist churches, the Church of Christ—all were active in Hamilton Park. "It was an opportunity to preserve the interests of the community by organized voting," Zan Holmes remarked. "As a matter of fact, we became overorganized, so we came up with the idea that we needed that one group where we could all come together and coordinate our efforts for the good of the community." The IOC included both individual members and representatives from its constituent organizations. As with the Civic League, all residents of Hamilton Park were members, but actively participating individuals paid dues. Active organizations paid, too, but, at least in the case of the Hamilton Park Methodist Church, the financial support went beyond its nominal dues.[42]

The IOC soon organized a voter-registration drive. "Our first concern was to register our people," Zan Holmes said. "We went from house to house. We collected poll taxes at the church [Holmes's Methodist church], and you were expected to be registered to vote. . . . There was a lot of voter education that went on." Holmes maintained that "at one time we literally had the highest turnout of any precinct in . . . Dallas county. We voted that well." The turnout, expressed as a percentage of registered voters, was high. Interviewees who offered a percentage placed it at from 83 to 90 percent.[43]

The IOC was deeply involved in the desegregation of the Hamilton Park School (see chapter 8) and in the rezoning of the land that was purchased by Texas Instruments (TI) to the east of the community, across from the railroad and a creek. This was the property sought both by TI and the real-estate agents attempting to expand Hamilton Park—property ultimately secured for TI.

Meetings between TI representatives and an IOC committee acting as the voice of the community occurred in 1967. The IOC became involved, Smith recalled, because of the strong possibility of "litigation." The IOC and TI discussions were generally amicable, however. Areas of agreement included improved traffic circulation, especially the widening of Forest Lane, the extension of Floyd Road south to Forest Lane, and other projects that were not completed until many years later. Attractive landscaping and generous setbacks for TI buildings were agreed upon. There were some differences in emphasis. Both agreed that Hamilton Park residents would be hired, but the IOC—while acknowledging TI's past "fair employment" record—expected "[t]hat job opportunities at TI for residents of Hamilton Park will increase proportionately as TI is expanded." The IOC also wanted information on job advancement for blacks and urged the company to give more consideration to bids from African-American contractors, especially maintenance firms and vendors. TI "said yes, but nothing was in writing," in response to the urgent requests for hires from Hamilton Park. Other resident concerns, such as TI's using its influence to help obtain street improvements and a community center in Hamilton Park, were beyond the boundaries of the company's business.[44]

TI did come through on its implied promise of jobs for Hamilton Park. At the time, Curtis Smith "felt that if you were qualified and you went up and put in your application, you would be considered. I have not, to this day," he said in 1990, "heard of Texas Instruments being discriminatory in that plant. No one to my knowledge has complained about TI having a need for a person and wouldn't hire him because of his color."[45]

The IOC's most important and persistent activities were its candidate forums and the candidate endorsement lists it published and circulated to each Hamilton Park residence before every major election. They were the largest part of the "voter education" to which Holmes referred. They rose in importance as the IOC's work in the areas of intergroup cooperation and coordination declined.

The IOC organized the candidate forums by telephoning the candidates and asking them to participate. Candidates for mayor and for other city and county offices often responded, as did those running for state representative and senator. John Connally appeared when he ran in the

Democratic gubernatorial primary of 1962. Connally won the primary and the general election. As governor he rode with President John F. Kennedy in the ill-fated motorcade on 22 November 1963. The gunfire that felled the president also wounded him, but he recovered to conduct volatile, highly publicized careers in politics and business. Less well-known outside Texas, fiery, feisty Jim Mattox came to the forums at times in the 1960s and 1970s while he served in the state legislature and in the U.S. Congress.[46]

The forums convened in various locations until the Hamilton Park Methodist Church completed its education building in September 1963. Then for many years the meetings were held there. "We have a big area," Smith said of the building, "and we have those curtains you can move back and make it bigger. We then set up chairs." The IOC insisted on a disciplined format. "We've had as many as four or five candidates running against each other who would come," Smith said. "We'd have each one of them have a little speech of three minutes. Sometimes, if there wasn't too many of them, we would make it five minutes. But we let every one of them speak, and it would be a controlled speaking. We would have somebody with a watch . . . and when each time was up, we'd just politely tell him, 'Your three minutes is up.' Then we'd have a question-and-answer session after everybody had spoken. If somebody wanted to ask a controversial question, whatever, we would do it, and we would make sure it was addressed to a certain person." The candidate could answer, and any opponent who wished could also respond. "We'd let them do that, but we wouldn't let it get into a debate. We'd tell them that in the beginning: 'We're not having a debate tonight.' "[47]

The candidate forums and other information served as the sources for the next phase of pre-election activity, hammering out the IOC endorsement list. The process demanded preparation, determination, and a spirit of compromise. The endorsement meetings usually were less well attended—from fewer than ten to about thirty—than the candidate forums. They were more fractious and lasted into "pretty late hours sometimes." Agreement was not necessarily rapid or easy, because the forums, political television appearances, and other information about a candidate could yield conflicting information. On occasion, the meetings could not reach a consensus, in which case the IOC endorsed no candidate in a particular race. The IOC, according to Smith, sent a message through its endorsements: " 'This is our belief as to who is best for our community. You, as an individual in the community, may not agree.... This is what we believe, based on the information that we received.'" Or, as Pauline Dixon put it, "I believe in working for the total welfare. Now, what do you mean? The total welfare right here is black."[48]

A preference for the Democratic Party supplemented and reinforced the focus on community. To be sure, African Americans had been voting heavily Democratic since 1936, but this was because of the economic benefits of the New Deal's racially inclusive work-relief programs. But the New Deal generally displayed caution where civil rights, as such, were concerned. President Truman's desegregation order to the armed forces in 1948 marked a decisive break with the bigoted white Southern Democratic record of the past. Truman ended the tepid response of the national Democratic Party to civil rights agitation in 1948 with his powerful civil rights plank in the party platform. White Southerners revolted against Truman, forming the "Dixiecrat" party. The doughty president won the election of 1948, isolating the Southern white bigots, who never again would have the power to control the party stance on civil rights. Not that the Southern Democrats gave up. Most returned to the Democratic fold, where they continued to fight desegregation and exercise a moderating influence on national civil rights politics. In their home states, they fought a rearguard action against the civil rights movement for twenty years. Texas's Governor Alan Shivers mobilized the Texas Rangers to keep blacks out of the Mansfield schools in 1956. The Democratic Texas legislature passed ineffectual but symbolic bills against school desegregation in 1957.[49]

But the Southern white Democrats could not prevail. Democratic President John F. Kennedy was pressing for a civil rights bill at the time of his assassination in 1963. His vice-president and successor, Lyndon B. Johnson, masterfully maneuvered three landmark civil rights bills through Congress—the Civil Rights Act of 1964, the Voting Rights Act of 1965, and the Fair Housing Act of 1968. The barriers to black advancement characterized by the dual labor market weakened, in no small measure because of the federal government's pressure.[50]

The Republican years between Truman and Kennedy, by contrast, accomplished little. True, the Eisenhower administration (1953–1961) bracketed an exciting, productive era in civil rights; notably, the Montgomery, Alabama, bus boycott, the lunch-counter sit-ins begun in 1960 at Greensboro, North Carolina, and the rise of Martin Luther King Jr. to national leadership in the movement and to international fame. The federal courts followed the breakthrough Supreme Court *Brown* decision against racially segregated schools with a stream of antisegregation decisions. But the Eisenhower administration itself did little to advance the cause of African-American equality. Dwight D. Eisenhower's presidential virtues were many, but his civil rights attitudes ranged from mild hostility to indifference. The civil rights act of 1957 was proposed mostly because Herbert Brownell, Eisenhower's attorney general, insisted on it. The 1960 civil rights act sprang more from Eisenhower's concern for upholding federal authority than from anxiety over the short-term denial of minority equality. Both pieces of legislation were limited to voting rights and were largely tokens by the time the then Senate majority leader, Lyndon Johnson, finished the compromising that was necessary to their passage. There were Republican civil rights enthusiasts just as there were Democratic bigots, but neither group controlled their party's racial policy nationally. There was little reason, then, for the residents of Hamilton Park to abandon their traditional partisan allegiance.[51]

The close alliance between the Democratic precinct chair and the IOC reinforced the Democratic bias. The precinct, established in 1960 after years of agitation, recognized Hamilton Park's political potency. Originally the precinct contained few voters other than those in the community; therefore, the precinct chair enjoyed exceptional influence in local Democratic councils. She, in Smith's words, "sold this community to the candidates." The precinct chair also had considerable influence with the IOC—so much so that the IOC neither made endorsements for the Republican primaries nor formally endorsed Republicans in the general elections. The IOC recognized "a kind of touchy situation"—a Democratic precinct chair who attended IOC endorsement meetings had "an input" at those meetings and persuaded endorsed candidates to help pay for IOC mailings. "You just don't have a chairman of the Democratic party that's going to support a Republican." Therefore the IOC did not "publicly put the name of a Republican on an endorsement."[52]

Then the IOC circulated its endorsement list to the precinct, at times with help from some of the endorsed candidates, who contributed stamps for the mailings. Smith believed that the list made a difference in Hamilton Park. "The community pretty well follows our endorsement," he said—a concurrence making Hamilton Park famous for its "block voting." Some residents disagreed with Smith's assessment as it applied to them personally. Of the IOC recommendations, one said, "I never would vote for them, because they always supported the wrong politicians—always! Invariably!" Another "looked at" the IOC lists, but "I decided by myself who I voted for on the basis of the issues. I like to do my own homework, and I make my own decisions." The majority of interviewees, however, paid close attention to the IOC slate; it had a considerable influence on them. A member of the IOC declared that some members may not have approved of a particular candidate, but "we in the organization supported the slate, of course, whether we agreed with it or not." Another resident, not an active IOC member, "agreed with most of them most of the time." She praised candidate forums, which "worked beautifully" for people who "wanted to ask questions and get things firsthand." Two others made similar statements about accepting the slate. "Yes, usually, I follow them on that," said one, "and I usually vote the ones that they endorse. Usually, I do, since I feel that they are interested in the neighborhood." The value of the endorsement list for the second interviewee was that the slate "probably helped to determine my decisions on some candidates, because I'm not really a political person that listens to every candidate that comes on TV to see what they have to say."[53]

Whatever their reaction to the IOC's endorsements, the voters in the community marked their ballots for Democrats. In the 1964 presidential balloting they gave Lyndon B. Johnson 1,198 votes to an insignificant 10 for Barry Goldwater, Johnson's Republican opponent. The liberal Democrat Ralph J. Yarborough defeated a youthful George Bush by almost as large a margin, 1,177 to 10, while Democrat John Connally returned to the governorship with 1,164 votes from Hamilton Park to his opponent's 12. Republicans fared a little better in subsequent years but lagged far behind their Democratic opponents. In 1972, George McGovern garnered 1,101 votes in his losing bid for the presidency, the triumphant Richard M. Nixon receiving 46. In 1988, Hamilton Park voters registered their indifference to the presidential campaign by giving the victorious Republican George Bush 16 votes, but only 194 to Democrat Michael Dukakis.[54]

The Civic League and the IOC provided for social as well as civic activities. The IOC's candidate forums, its endorsement meetings, and its monthly gatherings provided opportunities for exchange of personal and community information. The league meetings sometimes included refreshments and a speaker on a topic of civic interest, followed by a question-and-answer session. The league's first picnic, in 1960 at the shopping center, was entirely social. A children's softball game, a teen dance, adult activities such as horseshoe pitching, and food and drink for all filled out the day. In succeeding years the annual league picnics at the

Organizing in Hamilton Park

park included more adult and young-adult activities organized around a softball diamond, tennis courts, and an outdoor basketball pavilion. The picnics, social gatherings emphasizing family-style entertainment, had an overriding civic purpose—to promote community solidarity; nevertheless, the social dimensions of the league and the IOC always were subordinate to their larger civic purposes.[55]

The Civic League and the IOC focus left plenty of room for social organizations and there was no lack of groups to fill the space. The Gold Cup Garden Club, the Hamiltonians, Hamiltonettes, and Hamonites all played important social roles in the community's early years.

The Gold Cup Garden Club began with a group of "ten or twelve" women who met monthly with no other agenda beyond becoming better acquainted as members of the community. All were Christians and the gatherings focused increasingly on the varieties of biblical interpretation among Methodists, Baptists, Episcopalians, and others. "It became so interesting," Doris Robertson recalled. But one member, a Roman Catholic, expressed concern over the wide divergence between the Douay Bible and the Protestant versions. She also expressed reservations about attending Protestant services. Rather than allow the group to splinter or lose a member, its organizers sought a new, inclusive basis. Mrs. Robertson, who was then attending garden club meetings outside Hamilton Park, suggested a similar organization for the community. She further suggested that the group could learn about plants and flowers, beautify the area, and "invite other women in." The group adopted her idea and, when they asked her to select its name, she took Gold Cup Garden Club from an award-winning rose variety.[56]

From its founding in 1962 the garden club engaged in activities that, while serious and constructive, were primarily social rather than civic. Its members continued to meet, monthly, studied plants and flower arranging, and affiliated with Dallas and national organizations. They won flower-arranging awards in citywide contests and the club itself received a special-recognition award in 1988. In 1990 the Gold Cup Garden Club was the only community-based social organization still continuously active, with thirty-five members and a monthly turnout of twenty to twenty-five.[57]

The largest of the social clubs in Hamilton Park, the Hamiltonians, was founded about 1956. A men's group, it was modeled on the Regular Fellows, an old-line social club active in South Dallas. The Hamiltonians sponsored an annual banquet and dance at a large hall or hotel. Picnics, cocktail parties, and other events throughout each year kept members socially active. Sales of raffle tickets to such gatherings helped to raise money for the annual banquet. Some seventy men belonged to the group in its heyday, but moves out of the community, changing interests among its aging members, and a lack of interest in recruiting younger move-ins contributed to its decline. The group ceased to be continuously active in the early 1970s. The Hamiltonettes, established a few years after the men's group, operated both independently and as a women's auxiliary of the Hamiltonians. The wives and girlfriends of the Hamiltonians knew one another, began socializing together, formed their organization, and "went from house to house for cards and parties," as Velma Jackson explained. The Hamiltonettes remained active much longer than the men's group.[58]

Most residents belonged to neither, nor to the other, much smaller, men's social club, the Hamonites. Some interviewees who never belonged or who ended their memberships cited a lack of interest in organized social life or partying, the expense involved, and changing interests. Others were invited, with their spouses, to Hamiltonian functions and thus never felt the need to join. One interviewee objected to the Hamiltonians calling itself a "social and charity club" when the group spent more per year on "social affairs" than it did on charitable activities. Others worked too many hours in the early years to indulge in much organized social life. As A. W. Dupree put it, "my social life was work. All I did was to go to sleep, go to work, go to sleep, go to work, go to sleep, go to work." On Sundays he attended church and on rare days off he might go to a civic meeting.[59]

All this secular activity aside, organized religion played a significant role in the community and in the lives of its members. Three established churches served the community—the Hamilton Park Methodist (later United Methodist) Church, the First Baptist Church of Hamilton Park, and the Hamilton Park Church of Christ. All of them confirmed the importance of organized religion in African-American life, a dimension of black existence sequestered from observation and contact by the larger society. Besides a sense of autonomy, the churches offered redemption from a life of struggle against inequities, a moral discipline, and a rewarding social and charitable activity. The historical importance of having an institution removed from white control had lessened, if it had not entirely disappeared by the time Hamilton Park was founded, but the other aspects of organized religion remained central to the residents of Hamilton Park.[60]

The first church building in Hamilton Park was the Methodist, where its congregation held its initial worship service on 25 January 1959. Before then, however, the eleven charter members held their first worship service on 4 August 1957 at the Hamilton Park School. They followed the service two days later with their first official meeting in the home of Eloise Valley, one of the charter members. The church had the good fortune to be a mission church of the Highland Park Methodist Church, a well-to-do congregation. The pastor, Dr. Marshall T. Steel, was a racial liberal who had participated in the dedication of Hamilton Park. The Rev. Ira B. Loud, a prominent African-American pastor, also played a significant role. Loud persuaded Steel to make the Hamilton Park church a mission project as the Highland Park church had done "in other places throughout the city." The Highland Park board of missions purchased the church property on Schroeder Road immediately north of the shopping center for about $6,000. It granted the Hamilton Park congregation $10,000 toward its first building and loaned it an additional $10,000 for construction, with the Highland Park church paying the interest on the loan.[61]

The church benefited from able leadership as well as from financial help. Loud, of the St. Paul Methodist Church, became the first pastor of the Hamilton Park church. At the time a young theology student at Southern Methodist University, Zan Holmes, was serving his internship at St. Paul. Holmes became the associate pastor. Loud preached some sermons, but he was also responsible for his own congregation, so Holmes, as the younger man phrased it, "was doing all the work." On 29 April 1958 Holmes began his ten-year ministry. The first church school, sixty-eight-children strong, was held at the home of Henry Davis. Davis, a staunch Baptist, had a large house on High Point Circle. "I told them to use the whole house!" he said emphatically. "You know, there was some people some time, you believe me: 'Hey, man, you're a Baptist! What you doin', letting the Methodists in there?' I said, 'They know God, too.' That's what I told them."[62]

Meanwhile, the church grew with the community. In 1960, church women organized an Altar and Flower Guild to care for the linens, vestments, and other materials used during the services and to supply candles and flowers for the altar. The Methodist Men held some of their early meetings with members of the other Hamilton Park denominations, which "did much to solidify the community." In 1963 the church completed its education building and opened a day-care center.[63]

The other large congregation, the Hamilton Park First Baptist Church, held its first meeting at the Lee J. Booty home. The Rev. J. L. Foster, the founding pastor, soon moved the church to the former Anderson Bonner school on Coit Road, across North Central Expressway from Hamilton Park. Later the membership bought property at 8219 Bunche Drive, in the northwest corner of the subdivision. The city directory of 1962 first lists a building at that address. The smallest congregation with its own building, the Hamilton Park Church of Christ, worshipped in a tile-block structure at the south edge of Willowdell Park.[64]

Many residents of Hamilton Park were active in one of the three congregations. But others, not already members of a Methodist, Baptist, or Church of Christ congregation, held to their faiths. Some preferred to remain with churches outside Hamilton Park, even though a transfer would have involved no change of faith. Pauline and Frank Dixon maintained their membership in Zion Hill Baptist Church, even when the church moved—from near North Dallas south, across the Trinity River—to a less-convenient location in Oak Cliff. Others changed churches. Willie F. Smith, raised a Baptist, joined the Hamilton Park Methodist Church with his family because the Methodists had established an active youth program and the Baptist church had not then built on Bunche Drive. But, he said, in 1974, with both children grown, "I went back to my roots." Smith joined the First Baptist Church of Hamilton Park. William Edmond belonged to the Hamilton Park Methodist Church but "got tired of the organized deadness on Sundays," so he joined the Concord Missionary Baptist Church in Oak Cliff.[65]

Several residents were active in extracommunity organizations, including the Amigos, a Dallas interracial social group of the 1960s, the Christian Action Layman's League (unofficially the political arm of the Amigos), and the National Association for the Advancement of Colored People (NAACP). Often they belonged to these groups while participating in the Civic League, the IOC, or a church in the community. They could, in other words, commit to an organization beyond Hamilton Park and at the same time be involved with, for example, local youth activities. They could be heartily concerned about maintaining the community's deed restrictions, getting rid of the cement plant, or paving the alleys. They could be deeply involved in the work of the IOC, its candidate forums, and its endorsement meetings.

Extraordinarily active members of the community such as Doris Robertson were busy with the Civic League, the IOC, the Methodist church, the garden club, and the PTA. Edward and Mary Newhouse limited their intense participation to the Church of Christ yet were highly pleased with life in Hamilton Park.[66] All of these varied roles suggest that people were experiencing the community in many legitimate, if different, ways. Each of their involvements and reactions contributed to the community and it is possible that their experiences in jobs and outside organizational work enriched their participation in Hamilton Park and its groups. Diversity of interests and different levels of involvement, then, did not weaken the community; indeed, the very variety of residents' experiences may have strengthened it.

7

SCHOOL AND COMMUNITY

The Hamilton Park School was a community school. It figured powerfully in a web of relationships stretching within and beyond its trim walls. It symbolized the hopes of the older generation of residents for the younger; it served as meeting place and meeting ground; and it socialized its scholars in an atmosphere of sympathetic discipline. The close involvement of school and community engendered controversy over the curriculum and operation of the school. Parents sometimes expressed their frustration with their children's academic progress or with the comparative poverty of the equipment at the Hamilton Park School by ad hominem attacks on the district administration, principals, or faculty. Others in the community were as quick to defend the school and its staff. In any event, the controversy was an earnest of the community's dedication to education.

The physical, emotional, and intellectual symbiosis of school and community was as fortuitous as the development of Hamilton Park into a tightly bounded enclave. When the City of Dallas annexed Hamilton Park, it thrust a jurisdictional shaft into the sprawling Richardson Independent School District (RISD). Back then, the RISD served a farming, processing, and commercial town of 1,289, plus scattered settlements along graveled lanes and narrow blacktop roads. Smug white subdivisions in a few years would sprawl among the interstices between gravel and blacktop. The scene was still bucolic over much of the thirty-eight-square-mile RISD during that drizzly, October 1953 dedication of Hamilton Park. On 4 January 1954, the RISD board moved to begin negotiations with the DCIA to transfer Hamilton Park to the Dallas Independent School District (DISD).[1]

The RISD effort could be interpreted as a racist response calculated to avoid schooling the children of Hamilton Park. Yet any black subdivision of a certain 173 acres but potentially of unlimited size, would be treated quite differently from the small, semirural, postemancipation African-American settlement nearby. There, the RISD provided the frame Anderson Bonner School for the primary grades. It sent the secondary students, junior-high and high schoolers, to the DISD's Booker T. Washington High School—a common practice for segregated districts with small black populations. Racism was not, however, the sole motive, as became evident when the RISD's attempt to transfer Hamilton Park to the DISD failed. Faced with building a full-order, grades-one-through-twelve school, the RISD entered negotiations with the DCIA to buy some twenty acres at the northern edge of the original tract, north of Towns Street between Oberlin Drive and Schroeder Road. When the DCIA refused to sell the property, the RISD board voted, on 7 June 1954, to condemn it. The next month the board racheted up the district's property values 20 percent "in order to sell sufficient bonds to build a school in The Hamilton Park Addition (colored)." The Hamilton Park Elementary and High School opened in September 1955.[2]

The RISD initiatives neatly bracketed the seismic desegregation decisions of the United States Supreme Court, later known as *Brown I* and *Brown II*. For years the Court nibbled at the "separate but equal" prescription formulated in the *Plessy v. Ferguson* decision of 1896. The "separate but equal" formula of black-white racial segregation in civic settings came under steady assault in public education. Judicial attacks were limited to the most blatant, hypocritical denials of equal education that did not at the same time threaten separation in the primary and secondary grades. When the NAACP decided to test the validity of the entire "separate but equal" conception, it set in motion the *Brown* cases. On 17 May 1954, a unanimous Court found that "separate" education was "inherently unequal," in violation of the equal protection clause of the Fourteenth Amendment. *Brown II*, of 31 May 1955, urged timely compliance with the mandate to end the use of race as a criterion for pupil assignment. The second decision placed desegregation under the direction of the federal district courts.[3]

In 1955, however, those connected with the RISD, whether parents, teachers, students, or administrators, imagined the *Brown* decision to be symbolic of a commitment to equal education rather than a firm declaration for immediate desegregation. The several discussions between Crossman of the DCIA and RISD officials were aimed at the district's providing a superior if segregated education for the children of Hamilton Park. It may have been Crossman who suggested the closing of the Anderson Bonner School and the cessation of busing RISD students to Dallas as partial compensation for the expenses involved in constructing the Hamilton Park School. As for *Brown*, Crossman was a racial liberal only in the Dallas setting of the early 1950s, a landscape of black subordination and white domination in public life. However shifting and ultimately fragile those arrangements were, it would have been inconceivable for Crossman to issue a constitutional challenge to them in the midst of parleys with the RISD over Hamilton Park. Had he done so, the response of the RISD would almost certainly have been an abrupt refusal, coupled with an antagonism that would have clouded the negotiations.[4]

Nor were parents, absorbed in the minutiae of their move to the new subdivision, concerned with participating in an imminent revolution against racial separation. The immediate concern of the first arrivals was not the racial exclusiveness and presumptive inferiority of the Anderson Bonner School, but safe student access to it, by bus or a paved sidewalk. With the opening of the Hamilton Park School, parents strove for quality education for their children within the new building. Although the school soon established reputations in scholarship and sports, parents chafed under what they believed were inadequate materials, supplies, and programs for their children; at times they thought there was overcrowding. Not until the closing of the high school loomed in the late 1960s did parents propose to integrate the junior-high and elementary grades by expanding the Hamilton Park School boundaries to include white children.[5]

It was scarcely surprising that the youngsters who would attend Hamilton Park accepted segregated education. Young people in and around Hamilton Park rarely, if ever, associated with whites; they were protected from abrasive interracial contacts. "Here we were shielded from poverty," Donald Payton said, "and we were partially shielded from racism." Regarding whites, Theresa Patrick remarked, "I knew they existed, I knew they were out there." That was all. "For the most part we were isolated." Richard Bonner lived in the established black neighborhood west of Hamilton Park and attended the old school. The Anderson Bonner School "was just like a home away from home. Everybody knew everybody." The school was "just out in the country there—fresh air. It was just like another family." The principal "was like a mother away from home." The building, frame with a detached auditorium, "was not a modern place, but a fun place to be and learn." Hamilton Park School was newer, larger, and more diverse, but Bonner found the same supportive environment there.[6]

The Hamilton Park School represented fresh opportunities for black administrators, faculty, and staff. The Anderson Bonner School, with perhaps sixteen employees including the principal and the maintenance staff, gave way to a much larger plant. By 1966, the Hamilton Park School employed an administration, faculty, and staff, not including maintenance, of fifty-five. The RISD hired some teachers from Hamilton Park who had previously ranged far afield to find work. Vivian T. Starks had taught for two years at a junior high school in Bryan; then for several years she was a supervisor of teachers in Fairfield, about half the distance from her home. Next she took a supervisor's job at Corsicana, which at the time was beyond the southern fringe of Dallas. She told the superintendent at Corsicana that if she received an offer from a district nearer her home, she would resign from Corsicana and accept it. The arrangement was possible because supervisors began their work well in advance of the opening of school. After she returned home following her first stint at Corsicana, the RISD superintendent offered her a job at Hamilton Park School. In September 1958 she began teaching high-school math, soon switched to English, and after three years became the counselor. Mary E. Garnett taught English in Lodi, in east Texas, for two years; then for seventeen years she taught in Malakoff, an old coal-mining town south and east of Dallas. In 1956 she and her husband bought a house in Hamilton Park, each of them continuing to teach elsewhere. Tired of the expense and bother of maintaining two residences, she decided to further her ambition to move to Dallas by applying to the RISD. She was hired to teach English, beginning in 1959.[7]

None of this denies that Hamilton Park parents, students, faculty, and administration wished for an open, desegregated society based on equality of opportunity. At the same time they were realists who lived in the world as it was and who perceived the advantages of a properly-conducted community school. Students fondly recalled their years there. Richard Bonner remembered how the teachers stressed fairness. "We were known as the poor people" who lived west of North Central Expressway in "old farm-type houses" that contrasted with the new, ranch-style homes in Hamilton Park. Vivian Starks would not allow such invidious comparisons to pass uncorrected. She told Hamilton Park students who called their classmates from old White Rock poor "that 'these guys are not poor people at all. As a matter of fact, they're landowners, and they're going to be wealthy one day.'" When the White Rock contingent on the football team became upset over the "preferential treatment" given to a player from Hamilton Park, coach James O. Griffin dealt with the problem, "and everything was smooth after that."[8]

Stressing fairness and justice did not equate with teacher toleration of slack student performance. Sheila Allen's fourth-grade teacher, especially, "had great expectations for Afro-American children, and she took such time in preparing us for" adulthood. "She expected that our society would change a lot, and it was her job" to develop the necessary understanding and skills so that her pupils "could reckon with those changes and make the best of what those changes would bring to us. She always encouraged self-esteem and confidence in us as black children." Theresa Patrick's teachers behaved "as though they were out to prove that we were good and that we were capable" of breaking out of the "traditional black careers," such as, for women, teaching and nursing. "'Go for it! Do it! You can do that!' Those were the phrases you heard" in the classrooms of Hamilton Park. "If you wanted to be a physician, then you could be a physician; if you wanted to be an architect, you could do that. It just depended on what you wanted to do and how you applied yourself." Donald Payton "understood at an early age that education was the key"; thus, "school was a very serious thing with me. I never liked the feeling of being one of the kids in school without his homework; that was always a real shallow, empty feeling, that there were twenty-two or twenty-three kids who had their homework, but you didn't." If a lack of understanding prevented a student's completing an assignment, however, "you could go by and visit your teacher" at home. "If you had problems with the homework, you could go by after school."[9]

Teachers confirmed that their students worked hard. "Very seldom they were unprepared," Vivian Starks said. "They didn't take that chance," even in courses demanding enough for college and university freshmen. Mary Garnett insisted on completed course work from every student. On one occasion she disciplined a senior who thought that "he could get by" without turning in a paper for English class because of his achievements in sports. She, acting as senior sponsor, dismissed him from the baccalaureate service because he had not passed English. "That was on a Sunday evening. On Monday morning he brought that paper so he would be able to march and get his diploma." The occasion illustrated Mrs. Garnett's adherence to standards, but the action, dismissal from baccalaureate, was scarcely typical. "I think that's the only time I pulled somebody out of the line in thirty-nine years. That's not bad—once in thirty-nine years."[10]

Students performed well, in great measure, because their parents expected them to work hard and to succeed in school. Most teachers knew that if a student failed to perform up to his or her ability, or became a discipline problem, they could appeal to the parents' family pride and ambition for the student's success. Vivian Starks sometimes sent notes home with students whose academic performance was below par, although parents usually informed themselves about their children's academic progress. In one instance, however, a parent waited until open house to inquire about her daughter's work, only to discover that it was unsatisfactory. "She was so angry," at first, but the parent's anger passed and the daughter later "did well" in her university studies. "I never felt that I could not go to a parent," was Mary Garnett's assessment of the familial relationships. "If you were not doing your work, I'd tell you, 'I'll be by your house this evening. Tell your mother I'll be by then.' You could not get by with anything in Mrs. Garnett's class, because if you didn't do it for her, you were going to have to do it for your parents, and they were going to give you trouble. See, it has just been in later years that parents feel like you shouldn't even fool with things like that."[11]

Parents affirmed their commitment to education and to their children's success. Ola Lee Allen, whose six children attended the school, had a "good relationship" and frequent conferences with teachers. Velma Jackson encouraged firmness in a teacher who was reluctant to discipline her son. When Freddie Ervine inquired why her son's grade in one course had dropped below an A, the teacher blamed peer pressure. "The teacher called me and said my son wanted to be accepted and he didn't want to be smart. The other boys wouldn't like you if you were too smart." Both Mary Newhouse and Mildred Patrick were comfortable in their dealings with principals and other administrators. Robert E. Price, whose wife taught at Hamilton Park from time to time and whose three children attended there, saw the situation from both sides. He believed that the teachers "were not there for the money, but . . . because they loved teaching."[12]

Dolores Price tutored, without charge, the grade schoolers who came to her house on Saturdays. The "family-oriented" teachers, Price said, "spent a lot of time" with disadvantaged children. The Price family, like the families of other teachers, helped students whose parents were struggling financially, providing them with clothing and school lunches. As a parent, Price found the teachers to be "candid, and they would be fair" in their assessments of student performance. "You could approach the teacher on a good level, in a family way, to know how your kid was doing." The principals lived with innumerable pressures, and of course had human failings, but they were "part of the total community. You saw them at church; you saw them at the football game; you saw them at the school; you saw them at the store." They were approachable, and were "good role models"—people whose personal lives were "above reproach." Superintendent Joseph Jones "J. J." Pearce was no desk-bound administrator but one who "would visit the school" and "was in tune with the students."[13]

The students enjoyed a rich extracurricular life. At the elementary-school level most of the diversions were not directly related to academics. Affiliated groups played important roles. The Cub Scouts camped, hiked, and went on field trips. The Junior Red Cross helped supply "needy" people with "health products" at Christmastime. Physical education classes, parties during the Christmas period and at Valentine's Day and Easter, and school programs all complemented the classroom work. Students in the fifth and sixth grades published a monthly newsletter describing activities in each room of the grade school.[14]

The high school, embracing grades seven through twelve, sponsored a wide range of extracurricular activities. Some of the most dynamic were related to classroom work or future careers. The Office Helpers Club provided practical experience in office operations; the Future Homemakers of America promoted domestic and community interests; the Jets provided "those students who are particularly interested in math, some insight into the field of engineering"; the New Mechanics Club fostered industrial arts, and the Dramatics Club provided an outlet for acting talent. Through the Future Teachers of America, aspiring teachers learned something of their art and craft and of the "development and purposes of our free public schools." The Student Council, the National Junior Honor Society, and the Senior Honor Society developed scholarship and leadership and a Y Teen chapter and a Boy Scout troop were affiliated with the school. Debate and other forensics, student plays, the Miss Hamilton Park High School Pageant, and the *Dallas Morning News* Spelling Bee for seventh and eighth graders provided further outlets for student abilities.[15]

Many young people immersed in the Hamilton Park environment emerged to attend colleges and universities. Statistics on student performance compiled from RISD files contain discrepancies and are not comparative; nevertheless, they demonstrate a strong commitment to higher education. Records from the 1960s show that the percentage of graduates entering colleges and universities ranged from slightly more than 51 percent in 1964 to 66 percent in 1966 (or, the alternative figures, 62 percent in 1964 to 83 percent in 1966). Of the 1960 graduates who attended colleges and universities, 62 percent were enrolled for the 1963/64 year. Of college-bound 1961 graduates, 75 percent were continuing their higher education; in the 1962 group of matriculants, 82 percent were enrolled. Four graduates who were attending North Texas State University during the fall of 1965 had grade point averages below those garnered at Hamilton Park, not an unusual experience for high-school graduates, but all were earning averages above seventy, or minimum C.[16]

Productive as the academic side of life was, sports created by far the most general excitement in the community. The Hamilton Park Bobcats fielded formidable teams in their segregated high-school leagues. Although basketball and track and field had their following among students, faculty, parents, and other residents, football was the standout attraction. Every Saturday night during the football season—the traditional Friday night was reserved for white teams—almost everybody who was able packed the stands at the district stadium at Greenville Avenue, north and east of the community. As one former resident remarked, "if anybody ever wanted to rob Hamilton Park, you should come to Hamilton Park on the night of a football game." Parents, all tired from working one or two jobs, tired from house and yard work, yelled for their children and the neighbor's kids while the cheerleaders bounced and the Bobcat band played. One fan who worked long hours was Cicero Bruton. Asked whether he attended the football games, he exclaimed, "Oh, listen! Whenever they played! If they lost every week, we were going to be there." Most residents "followed them everywhere they would go." Parents with mortgages, car payments, and all the other family financial demands dug deep into pockets and purses to buy hot dogs and soft drinks, knowing that the net proceeds would go toward new band uniforms.[17]

And not only parents. Albertus Edley, though childless, sometimes joined the Saturday night exodus from Hamilton Park. J. B. and Dorothy Simpson, though having no children, "went to a few of the games." Vivian Starks attended the games because teachers "had to work the gates most of the time." But neither having no children of her own nor having a night off from game-night duties prevented her from attending. "Then when I didn't have to work the gates, I was there anyway. I enjoyed it. I was hollering louder than the cheerleaders." Mary Garnett, another teacher without children of her own, also went to the games whether or not she had duties assigned. "I don't know of any that I missed," she said.[18]

Bobcat football nurtured some talented athletes. Some advanced to the college and professional level, most notably Carl "Spider" Lockhart, a 1962 graduate who played football at North Texas State University in Denton, some forty-five miles from Hamilton Park. A standout defensive back on one of the first integrated teams in Texas, he survived financially because of help from the university and others. When Irene Mitchell, a Hamilton Park pioneer, commuted to North Texas for her degree in home economics and education, she often gave Lockhart a ride, sharing her breakfast and lunch with him. She "talked to him a lot, hoping I was helping him to get through," and remembered how "he was always such a nice young man." Lockhart went on to an outstanding career with the New York Giants in the National Football League.[19]

Other young men, although not superstars, benefitted from their Bobcat experiences. Leroy Brewster quarterbacked the Bobcats to the state championship in 1961, then played football at Oklahoma State University and Arkansas AM&N College. "He was a legend out here in Hamilton Park," his widow, Charlotte Brewster, remembered. When the Brewsters were house hunting in 1975 they rented, and later bought, a house on Willowdell Drive. They did not then intend to remain there permanently, but it was a good "stopping point" because Leroy Brewster "liked it out here. He knew everybody, and everybody knew him. And he was respected out here." Richard Bonner, a linebacker on the 1961 championship team, credited his approach to life to the "positive" attitudes learned on the football field. After he arrived on the campus of the predominantly black Prairie View A&M University, he taught himself the rudiments of golf. He impressed the golf coach. "I told him I was from Dallas and that I'd been playing all my life." Soon Bonner was on a golf scholarship and on a championship team. "We won the conference every year, so we played in the nationals." His talent and temperament paid off. "I just walked on and got my golf scholarship and traveled all the southern states and the northeastern states playing golf. That was a heck of an experience."[20]

The atmosphere was sustained for some even after the high school closed in 1969. Everson Walls, who played his high-school football at the RISD's Berkner, then played at Grambling University, became a walk-on defensive back for the Dallas Cowboys in 1981. He developed into an all-pro cornerback and team leader. Released by the Cowboys in 1990, Walls signed with the New York Giants.

Success for Hamilton Park youngsters was not confined to sports. Referring to an all-school reunion, Theresa Patrick remembered that, among the several hundred participants, "85 percent of them are professional people" who owed much of their success to teachers at Hamilton Park. "When we all got together for that reunion, it was just phenomenal to see the IBM engineers, the AT&T vice-presidents, the doctors, the architects, the attorneys." A long-time faculty member and administrator confirmed Patrick's observation. Describing Hamilton Park graduates, he said "we have doctors . . . we had one young man that started at Hamilton Park and finished at Lake Highlands, and he went to the Air Force Academy. We have them working in pharmaceutical plants as chemists; we have them as teachers and in the private business realm. One young man owns his own business and sells Mercedes."[21]

In this sheltered world of Hamilton Park childhood and adolescence, close bonds developed as classmates moved through the school. The environment encouraged the usual schoolboy and schoolgirl crushes and the more serious romances of adolescence. Some of these affections deepened into engagements and marriages. "Most of my friends married girls they had dated, had crushes on from about the seventh grade," Donald Payton said. "I'm glad to say that a lot of those couples are still together. I had some friends who got their first Valentine's cards in about the fifth grade and in the fifth grade decided that this was the girl they were going to marry." Hamilton Park was not so isolated that its young people did not select marriage partners from outside the community, yet Payton's observation has validity. Several of the interviewees had at least one child who married within the community: Irene and Marion Mitchell, Willie F. Smith, Charles E. Smith, Freddie M. Nance, and Ola Lee and Freddie Allen.[22]

As the close attention that many parents gave to every dimension of school life suggests, parents, and also childless residents, were deeply involved with schooling. Their own educational and occupational level fostered an intense interest in education and a concomitant ambition for the youth of Hamilton Park. According to a school study published early in 1966, there were "214 teachers, office clerks, postal clerks, doctors, and nurses" of "1275 registered voters"—close to the total adult population. The survey found that 28 percent of Hamilton Park fathers were college graduates; another 22 percent had "an education above the eighth grade." Thirty-two percent of the mothers had graduated from high school. Fourteen percent had "some college training." The percentages for primary and secondary educational attainment were roughly the same as those of other African Americans across Greater Dallas. The number of college graduates or college-educated parents in Hamilton Park was substantially higher than the Greater Dallas norms.[23]

Much of the parental involvement expressed itself through formal organizations. The Parent-Teacher Association (PTA) was the most important vehicle for the parents' expression of attachment to the school. For the last seven years of the high school's existence the upper grades had a separate PTA, but the two groups were not considered distinct in the minds of most parents and will be considered as one organization. The PTA, as did all PTAs, had a general interest in the welfare of children and youth, and, especially, close cooperation between parents and teachers for the better education of the young. But better education meant more than parent-teacher conferences, "open houses" at the school, and meetings once or twice a month. Members of the PTA served as homeroom mothers and fathers, sponsored a college night for high schoolers, organized talent shows for the elementary and high schools, assisted with trips and tours, held bake sales after school or to coincide with PTA meetings, gave two modest scholarships each year to deserving graduating seniors, and operated a small school-supply store. The PTA's major event was the annual carnival, held usually in the spring, when its members transformed the school into a festive illusion with such diversions as pin-the-tail-on-the-donkey, bobbing for apples, and a haunted house. The older students enjoyed a sock hop, dancing so enthusiastically that "afterward all the mamas would have to then scrub socks by hand before putting them in the washer."[24]

All the labor was volunteered and all the materials came from donations or the PTA treasury. Doris Robertson remembered that, besides other volunteer work, she "would spend endless hours in my kitchen baking and donating the items to the sale." The proceeds from the carnival, the bake sales, and the other fund-raisers went to the scholarships and to lunches and clothing for disadvantaged children. It also went for "extras" at the school, including "fans, electric water coolers, an organ, and Christmas packages for the pupils."[25]

The PTA, predominantly a women's organization, had its male counterpart in the Dads Club. The Hamilton Park Dads Club, an affiliate of the parent Dallas-area organization, served as a booster group for the football team. The club often rented buses for important out-of-town games to enable parents, other adults, and cheerleaders to go with the players and also sponsored football banquets. The club followed other athletic programs as well; nor did its involvement end with sports. It "bought books for the school library," occasionally purchased eyeglasses or other necessities for children from financially strapped families, joined the PTA "in purchasing an ice water fountain for the school cafeteria," and operated a Junior Achievement program. The Dads Club raised money with its "tremendous carnival" in the fall, timed to accommodate the PTA's spring event. Then the club converted the school gymnasium into a showy scene that "was almost like a midway at a fair," featuring games and prizes.[26]

The Band Parents organized in 1956. With Principal Felix L. Jones and the first band director, the Band Parents supported the school's instrumental music program, primarily by raising funds to purchase band uniforms. The white-trousered, red-jacketed Bobcat band marched in uniforms costing $1,100 in 1958—a considerable sum for hardworking parents to raise. But the Band Parents did more. The group continued to purchase uniforms, gave a banquet for band members, parents, and teachers during May 1965, and chartered buses for a band trip during the 1965/66 school year, among other activities. Proceeds from sales at concession stands during football and basketball games were the Band Parents' major revenue source.[27]

The RISD cooperated with the adult organizations at the same time that it tried to maintain and expand a creditable school. Hamilton Park's burgeoning enrollment posed a problem for a district attempting to cope with the mushrooming of subdivisions within its domain. The Hamilton Park grade-school enrollment almost tripled in a decade, from 232 in 1955/56 to 599 in 1965/66. The number of high-school graduates, twenty-two in 1962, increased to sixty-four just six years later. To keep pace with student growth the RISD added teachers and additional space. The district contracted for additional classrooms in 1956, two years after it let the original contract. For the next seven years it built still more classrooms, a cafeteria, an auditorium, a shop, and other improvements, contracting to air-condition the building in 1964. The improvements did not always cope with the conditions, but they appear to be comparable with the improvements made to other district schools.[28]

There was another side to the community-school relationship, however—one that the existing levels of student satisfaction, faculty and staff dedication, parental involvement, and physical-plant improvement could not overcome. Dissatisfaction with the school existed throughout the community, among adults who had no other motive than to achieve better education for the children of Hamilton Park. For some residents, dedicated teaching did not equal effective classroom performance. Charles E. Smith contended that "some of the instruction wasn't up to par." Ocie Turner believed some high-school teachers were not as "educated as they should have been"; indeed, two teachers confessed to him "that they weren't really qualified to be in the high school." Turner laughingly recalled that "they called it 'bootlegging' education," because, even though they may have been technically qualified, they lacked both teaching skills and adequate materials. Besides, the emphasis appeared to be outside the classroom. "It seemed to me that what was going on up there was mostly sports, football."[29]

As Turner suggested, some residents believed that a portion of the teaching deficiencies could be traced to the district's hiring practices and its undemanding curriculum. Ruby Watson recalled that a child who lived near her house had enrolled in a private school while away from Hamilton Park. When the family returned, "they were going to transfer her because the public school was convenient. But when she was issued books, for the coming year's instruction, they were books that she had already completed at the private school." The family "had no alternative but to return the daughter to private school." Other residents found materials and equipment sorely lacking and laid the blame at the door of a racist administration. "The science lab was ridiculous," said Robert Cook, whose interest in the RISD included running for the school board and serving on the district's first biracial committee. "By my being a biology major and a chemistry minor, I knew what test tubes you needed to run a good school science lab." As he remembered it, the laboratory had only "three Bunsen burners in the whole place." At Hamilton Park, "there really wasn't anything there that I felt that our kids needed to work with. By the same token, I could go up to any [other] Richardson school, and they had adequate supplies and had adequate everything."[30]

Joseph Williams agreed. The outspoken physician praised the teachers but condemned the facilities. The school "was really a joke"; the library was only "a room called the library"—so poorly outfitted that "my children's classmates crowded into my living room and den in order to be able to use the *Encyclopedia Britannica*." Williams "had more laboratory ware in my garage and shop than they had in the whole chemistry lab at school. There just wasn't a damn thing there." Mary Garnett saw the situation from the inside. On occasion, the veteran English teacher would find fault with the library or discover that a white friend who taught at Richardson High School had teacher's editions of texts or other material that Mrs. Garnett did not have. "But she would share it with me." Later, she spent her own money to buy books that the district did not supply.[31]

The high school, too, lacked some of the programs featured at the white high schools. Charles Smith deplored the lack of "computer programs at the Hamilton Park School—not even any talk about them—but some of the other schools did have them." The schooling at Hamilton Park "was not satisfactory because the children did not have access to the astronomy and other courses that were being offered in Richardson," Sadye Gee said. "What they did get was tokenism rather than anything else." The district's response was that all programs had to be funded on a per-capita basis. James Griffin, Hamilton Park's mathematics teacher, administrator, and award-winning coach, explained that "funds are allocated based on the size of the student population of the school." Because of the relatively small size of the high school, "kids were asking for things that we could not provide because we did not have enough students to do it. For instance, if a kid wanted to, say, take computers . . . we would not have had enough money allocated to buy them."[32]

Residents faulted not only the central administration but also the administrators at Hamilton Park. Williams believed the first principal to be far too timid and accommodating toward the district office. Williams was one of a group attempting to persuade the principal to ask for more equipment, but the principal "couldn't do a damn thing." At last the group "told him what to go and ask for." The request "was just a matter of some audio-visual equipment and things of that sort. He went and they gave it to him, and he damn near fainted. He just damn near fainted with fright." Criticism continued after 1960, when Felix Jones became the principal of the grade school and Emmanuel V. Goss became the principal of the high school, as well as overall head of the school. It was voiced individually and through the Christian Action Layman's League (CALL), a group originally formed to deal with housing discrimination in North Dallas around the TI and Collins Radio plants. CALL's school committee was primarily concerned with integration problems, but it also involved itself with conditions at the school.[33]

Both as an individual and through the committee, Laurice Stevenson deplored the appearance and maintenance of the school building. A committed Hamilton Park activist, Stevenson complained about not "keeping the grass cut" and about "water flowing in when it rained and dripping all down in the front door." When he pointed out dirty areas to Goss, the principal countered that neither time nor funds permitted any improvement in maintenance. Stevenson denounced the draconian discipline at the school, including a man with a paddle stationed in the hallways to keep order. His objection to a convicted felon teaching at the school resulted in the felon's reassignment. Other residents voiced similar discontents. On 24 September 1968, a CALL delegation of twelve to fourteen people appeared at the grade school, visited three classes, examined other rooms, and asked questions about facilities. Either then or two days later, a smaller group of four Hamilton Park residents and five whites visited the high school, examined various rooms, and expressed concern about crowded hallways during class changes. Apparently both visits were conducted with candor and courtesy all around. Both groups thanked school officials on leaving.[34]

Some of the disaffection with the school could be traced to unhappiness with Goss himself. The principal was accused of being domineering, arbitrary, and capricious toward his teachers. CALL meetings rang with cries for his dismissal. One CALL member accused Goss of favoring the white teachers who had by then been transferred to Hamilton Park, but Vivian Starks recalled that "Mr. Goss was very unfair" to one white teacher. When teacher Starks and Goss had a confrontation, she went to Superintendent Pearce, who backed her. Mary Garnett also felt the lash of Goss's tongue when, during an interview, "he cut me very low on something that I felt that I had always been very careful about, and that was my appearance." Thelma Wells, who substitute taught at Hamilton Park High in 1964, remembered no flaws in Goss's "character" but vehemently disagreed with "his leadership style." Whatever Mrs. Wells did to discipline her students "to try to get law and order, he would call me on the carpet. To me he was afraid of his shadow. So, he was a disciplinarian maybe for the teachers, but he was afraid of parents, and he was afraid of the board." At least two other complaints darkened the Goss administration. The principal sometimes required teachers to attend teas or functions at churches where they were not members, because "he was trying to be a community man." It was also said that Goss was "completely ruled by his wife," who held a veto over the plans for school functions and who ignored the protocol of securing permission from the main office to walk through the building or enter classrooms.[35]

The upshot of Goss's alleged transgressions was a meeting, held at Mrs. Garnett's house and attended by some of the teachers, to discuss the question of the principal's relations with his faculty. As a result of that meeting—probably held during spring 1968—teachers sent a letter of complaint to Superintendent Pearce. One of Goss's responses to that letter and to other disagreements with his faculty was to tell Mrs. Garnett and a few other teachers not to report to work for the 1968 fall term. Employees of the district, they arrived to teach, anyway. In a top-level shakeup, Griffin became the principal and Goss was kicked upstairs to the central administration for the final year of Hamilton Park High's existence, 1968/69. Goss accused Griffin, Mrs. Starks, and his secretary of supporting the rebel teachers and charged Mrs. Starks with "feeding Mr. Stevenson [the CALL activist] information and I believe, backing him in his fight against our school. Many of the statements I hear him make could only come from her." Both Stevenson and Mrs. Starks absolutely denied any such collusion. Goss, hurt by his failure to win over the community and his faculty, and dismayed at the loss of his job, was overwrought. He left the district at the end of the academic year.[36]

Goss's relationships with faculty, staff, and parents certainly left much to be desired; yet four circumstances soften the indictment against the beleaguered principal. First, the administration of the Hamilton Park School was never free from criticism and probably would not have been even with a Solomon at its helm. That was because so many parents so fervently desired a fine education for their children; they would have found fault with almost any level of administrative aptitude, teaching competence, or physical facilities. Goss recognized the situation. "It is true that some Hamilton Park patrons levy a great deal of harsh criticism against our school program, its staff and policies," he wrote less than three years before he left the principalship. The criticism, Goss maintained, was "no sign that these few people disrespect us; rather, it is a reflection of their genuine concern and interest in our community." Zan Holmes agreed that one source of the problem was "the issue of equity. Those parents were determined to have the very best for their children, so they were concerned about the programs in the schools"—a concern leading to "controversy from time to time over the principals that they had up at Hamilton Park." The parents "were strong and very highly opinionated parents . . . who wanted to have a lot of input into what happened at the schools and how they were run. Sometimes that clashed with the position of the principal."[37]

Another practically insuperable problem was the relative lack of parental support and community involvement in the school, including supplementary financial contributions. That reality appears to run counter to the recitals of community activism and dynamism, but in fact it does not. The proportion of eligible parents actively engaged in the support of the school through the PTA, Dads Club, or Band Parents cannot be accurately measured, but probably was 40 percent at most. The realities of the dual labor market and the financial demands on Hamilton Park families meant that many fathers worked at two jobs or had some income-producing sideline activity in addition to their regular employment. Many mothers, too, worked outside the home. Work and the other obligations of living stole time, energy, and money from any other outside activity. As Goss noted in 1966, "many parents work or hold down two or more jobs"; therefore "the communication between the school and parents may not be as regular as it could normally be, and it also means that parent participation . . . is at a minimum." Griffin voiced similar concerns. "We were trying to do different things to give them the best education possible," he said of faculty efforts to help the students, "but I knew that for them to get the best education, you had to have parent participation." Concerning faculty-sponsored activities to raise money for the school, some parents "participated with us, but we were many times the generator of ideas." In "other" Richardson schools, by contrast, "the P.T.A. had people who had time to give to that kind of development."[38]

Griffin placed his finger on the other problem of weary and distracted Hamilton Park parents: their relative lack of disposable income. Hamilton Park households enjoyed a median family income of less than $6,500 in 1959; the Richardson family median was $8,520. In 1969, Hamilton Park's mean family income was less than $10,500; the Richardson mean was $14,015. Such income disparity within the affluent Richardson district meant that the Hamilton Park School received short shrift from private funding. This happened despite the carnivals, the bake sales, and the concession stands. The money was just not there. "At the average school," Griffin asserted, "—and I can say this after having set up the volunteer program in the Richardson School District—for the whole district—parents participate, and they put on special projects to buy things for, let's say, Stults Road Elementary School. If my parents at Hamilton

Park would not put on special projects to help us get the extra equipment we needed, the funds that we got from the school district would not be enough." Griffin went on to say that, during his final years as director of the volunteer program, he went "to many a school P.T.A. meeting . . . and they would say, 'Well, the P.T.A. is going to give the school ten thousand dollars this year to buy extra equipment or whatever the principal needs to insure that the educational standards of the school are retained.'" At Hamilton Park, no such level of funding existed until the school was reduced to the primary grades, then integrated by means of the acclaimed Pacesetter program that brought in the children of well-to-do whites.[39]

The third virtually intractable problem, after continual criticism and the level of parent involvement, was a circumstance common to most public high schools of the era: highly variable student success. The district, school, and community pointed with pride to the professionals, business people, and sports legends who graduated from Hamilton Park. Yet, as elsewhere, there were discipline problems, low levels of academic achievement, and students who failed to capitalize on their abilities. Some of these difficulties were no doubt traceable to school and home environments, but some were also the result of individual young people refusing to apply themselves to their work or to accept responsibility for their actions. One complaining parent "got upset with me about his son," Griffin remembered, "because his son had some problems. We found out the problem wasn't with us; the problem was him!" A high-school study committee acknowledged the differences in "intelligence and aptitudes" among students and in "parental attitudes and cultural backgrounds." Sincere efforts to "minimize" these differences did not always succeed. The RISD's own numbers indicated that, while a majority of Hamilton Park graduates attended college and a majority of those attending graduated, a significant minority neither matriculated nor graduated. This could be traced to a lack of academic talent or deficient ambition. In the case of those who enrolled in higher education, the problems resulted from those two shortcomings and sometimes from an inability to cope with the freedom of university life. As Vivian Starks said of one Hamilton Park graduate who attended a prestigious university, he "was smart" but he "didn't do anything." Such students were the despair of parents and teachers everywhere, not just in Hamilton Park.[40]

Fourth and finally, the physical plant at Hamilton Park continued to improve during the Goss era. Some of the improvement came about the time of the 1964 Civil Rights Act. The district administration carefully followed the debates over the act and, after its passage, began considering its legal implications. It may have been a coincidence that the RISD decided to air-condition the Hamilton Park School during the same year. By early 1967 in any event, the RISD claimed that the Hamilton Park High School was the equal of, and in some cases superior to, all the others in the district in curriculum, texts, visitation, athletics, budgets, library materials, teacher incentives, and student access to services. To some Hamilton Park activists such claims were demonstrations of the old saw about lies, damn lies, and statistics. The intractable problem of the high school's small size remained; and as Robert Cook stated it, "we know there is no such thing as 'separate but equal.'" Nevertheless, the building and its facilities did improve.[41]

RISD officials may not have appreciated all the criticism and monitoring of the Hamilton Park School, but they did, at times, respond to it. "It was a fine school," George Brewer remarked, "but I think it helped a lot for us to get concerned and express ourselves as we did. I think Richardson did better by us as a result of our inquiry and our input, kind of complaining, if you will." In Cook's judgment, despite some inadequacies, the RISD did "try to correct some things in the fifteen-to-twenty-year run before we actually got a solid court decision. I'm not saying that they didn't try to rectify some things, because, I mean, we were complaining every day. Every day there was somebody up there complaining." Griffin asserted that Superintendent Pearce "wanted to give Richardson an outstanding school district" and "did a lot of things for Hamilton Park that people don't talk about." But the former coach and principal conceded that sometimes citizen pressure moved Pearce and the district. On one occasion, an individual persuaded the superintendent to action. When Pearce "made the decision for us to have that track down at the end of that campus and to fix that campus up down there and put a field house down there, I don't know but one guy in the whole Hamilton Park community who was complaining about it. He went up and talked about it, and they did it." The district could have refused to build the track, but "Dr. Pearce ordered it done, and it was done—I mean quickly." With a nod to the success of citizen activism, Griffin added, "I'd been trying to get one for years!" Cook's explanation for the district's and Pearce's timely concessions was curt. "One thing about the administration at RISD," he remarked, "is that they were never stupid."[42]

In various ways the residents of Hamilton Park expressed their devotion to the community school. Not all of their approaches were easy for school officials to accept. Whatever their individual stances, viewpoints, or methods, collectively the residents pressed for quality education within the compass of a segregated society. Their focus was on improving the school as it was—not on desegregating it. But through the years the framework of official segregation weakened and sagged, and in the 1960s it collapsed. Then all of the patrons of the RISD, not only those in Hamilton Park, faced fresh issues and developed new agendas.

8

THE SCHOOL TRANSFORMED

The RISD responded to the pressures of desegregation when it closed Hamilton Park High School in 1969, leaving a truncated junior high. Declining to expand the boundaries of the junior high to include white students, the district closed it in 1970. It was then that a community pivot slipped its socket. Five years later, an ingenious enrichment-magnet program saved the primary grades from extinction when white parents responded by eagerly busing or driving their children to Hamilton Park. But it was no longer a community school.

The RISD administration's critical turn away from segregation came with the Civil Rights Act of 1964, which was more immediately important to it than either the landmark *Brown* decision of 1954 or several subsequent Texas government efforts to thwart integration. The 1964 act thrust the RISD into the vortex of school desegregation, a complex and emotional issue intermixed with the rising African-American insistence on absolute equality, full justice, and the final destruction of all barriers to racial advance. Stupefyingly destructive urban riots, turmoil on university campuses, street demonstrations against a variety of circumstances, including the war in Vietnam and, occasionally, integration itself, were the volatile compound of a fascinating if frightening era. Studies of the school desegregation issue are prone to resolve the conflicts they portray by seizing the moral high ground and judging legislation, federal departments, federal judges, school district boards and officials, students, teachers, and parents by an absolute standard that sometimes verges on the self-righteous, whether or not the viewpoint favors or disfavors particular decisions or actions, or the ultimate desegregation result.[1]

What may be said with certainty is that segregation, in schools and elsewhere, never should have happened in a country committed to individual liberty and civil equality. Once outlawed, it should have been discontinued as quickly as local conditions, as opposed to local opinions or prejudices, permitted. The powerful white majority was responsible for segregation. It was responsible, in particular districts, for the token desegregation, calculated delays of integration, or outright intransigence that led the federal bureaucracy and courts to take an increasingly militant stand against segregationist activity. At their most extreme, Supreme Court desegregation decisions imposed enormous financial burdens on school districts, wrenched young children from their neighborhoods for distant schooling on behalf of a national integrationist policy of debatable wisdom, helped to make a shambles of some urban districts, and earned the contempt of many citizens for "liberal," court-imposed solutions to social problems in general and racial problems in particular. But it must not be forgotten that diehard white opposition was the fulcrum on which the far-reaching federal integrationist policy was raised.

The RISD responded positively to the civil rights sea change because of its relative wealth, small African-American population, progressive nature, and determination to live within the law. The Civil Rights Act of 1964 outlawed segregation or discrimination in public places and lodged broad enforcement powers with the U.S. attorney general. The RISD board reacted in August 1964 with a decision to accept the applications of black students living outside Hamilton Park on the existing attendance-zone basis, without discrimination. There was no formal vote or announcement. In this matter, as in others to follow, the RISD was not entirely open or candid, but its racial sleight-of-hand was less manipulative than that of some other Texas districts and certainly less scheming than those of many throughout the South. The district was also more aware than some others of the far-reaching implications of the earnest federal commitment to the death of segregation. Early on, RISD officials recognized a possible legal difficulty inherent in the Hamilton Park School's all-black student population. They were prepared to meet any challenge to the all-black districting of Hamilton Park with "the position that this is 'total integration.'"[2]

The regulations required by the Civil Rights Act of 1964 and issued by the Department of Health, Education, and Welfare (HEW) in 1965 forced the RISD to formalize its unrecorded decision. The "HEW Guidelines" were in essence racially neutral, although they contained portents for the future, such as a call for faculty and staff integration, a requirement not found in the 1964 act. The RISD readily complied with the guidelines' requirement that racial attendance zones "be abandoned entirely" in favor of zone lines "drawn to follow the natural boundaries or perimeters of compact areas surrounding particular schools." In June, the board of trustees moved to establish zones without regard to "race, color, or national origin" and to make student assignments on the basis of those attendance zones. The Hamilton Park zone involved only the subdivision and the small, older settlement of upper White Rock, from whence came Richard Bonner and other nonresident students. The zone could have been faulted for continuing what the guidelines termed a "dual or segregated" system. There was a defense for it, however. By 1965, the Hamilton Park community was virtually certain to remain an enclave, and the black residents to the west had sent their children to the school since its opening. Hamilton Park was the school closest to those black students and was accessible through underpasses beneath the intervening expressway. In August, the commissioner of education notified the RISD that its plan was "adequate to accomplish the purposes of" the 1964 legislation.[3]

But the RISD would take little comfort from the 1965 letter. That was because the race consciousness embedded deep in American society surfaced in all sorts of ways, including urban riots and white segregationist opposition to the integration of many school districts. In response, official policy quickly moved beyond racial neutrality, embracing increasingly strident demands for racial integration. In 1965, however, the school situation in Richardson was calm. The 1965/66 school year passed uneventfully, with 17,500 students enrolled during the fall. African Americans totaled 1,150, all but 41 of them at Hamilton Park. HEW was nevertheless determined to press all school districts harder, including officially desegregated districts such as Richardson. HEW's much more stringent 1966 guidelines abandoned the requirement for natural school attendance zones and instead demanded an end to "zone boundaries or feeder patterns designed to perpetuate or promote segregation, or to limit desegregation or maintain what is essentially a dual school structure." This and other requirements and suggestions in the new guidelines led to the racial balancing proscribed by the racially-neutral Civil Rights Act that HEW administered.[4]

The new requirements marked the end of Richardson's desegregation calm and the beginning of its rocky, nine-year road to the Pacesetter program. From the beginning, the RISD board, administration, and legal counsel adopted a defensive strategy emphasizing compliance with the Civil Rights Act and the original HEW guidelines. On 19 May 1966, on the advice of RISD attorneys to make some additional show of compliance toward HEW, Superintendent Pearce conferred with Zan Holmes about the qualities that would be required of any white teachers who moved into Hamilton Park and of those blacks who agreed to teach in white schools. Evidence that the closing of Hamilton Park High was already under consideration is found in Pearce's handwritten "Continue H.P.H.S.????" and two comments beneath the question.[5]

The RISD also staunchly resisted any change in the Hamilton Park attendance zone. An HEW official broached the possibility of sending the white children living near Hamilton Park to its junior and senior high schools at least as early as December 1966. During the following month a conference between HEW and RISD representatives struck a tentative deal: closing the high school in 1968/69 and integrating the district faculty beginning in the fall of 1967. One HEW participant foreshadowed the Pacesetter program of the next decade when he "asked if the district had ever given consideration to making Hamilton Park a special school (meaning bus in students from all over to attend special classes)." The RISD did not, of course, respond favorably at the time. To consider only the high school, there was a practical problem involved in the RISD's lack of enthusiasm for expanding the high-school boundaries to take in white students. At the January conference, Pearce "volunteered the statement that growth alone would force RISD to probably close Hamilton Park High School within a couple of years." A high-school plant too small for its anticipated African-American population scarcely would have been a prime site for the increased enrollment that integration would bring. That defense against desegregation was pragmatic, but there was also a racial reason for the RISD's refusal.[6]

The racial motive became clear after the senior school was scheduled to close and Hamilton Park parents and residents asked the district to retain the junior high segment, grades seven through nine; there would be ample room for white children after the departure of the black tenth, eleventh, and twelfth graders. The district, in internally circulated memoranda, began assembling evidence to show that the Hamilton Park School was a roughneck environment. It is difficult to believe that an undated memorandum on comparative vandalism of late 1968 or early 1969 had any other purpose than to cast doubt on the wisdom of sending white children of any grade level into the all-black school. According to the memorandum, the worst white school in the district from the standpoint of vandalism suffered six incidents, totaling $2,191 in damage, from September 1967 to October 1968. During the same period there were twenty-one incidents at Hamilton Park costing $10,527 to repair. The total vandalism damage in the district was $37,371, therefore vandalism at Hamilton Park accounted for more than 35 percent of the total. The memorandum could be faulted for its assumptions—for instance, laying a September 1967 fire to vandalism—but its message was obvious.[7]

Another memorandum suggested that the Hamilton Park environment was not only rough, but was threatening to whites. The memorandum detailed the experiences of a white teacher of social studies during the high school's final year, 1968/69. The teacher told of a member of the Hamilton Park community who threatened her with losing her job; she also spoke of "numerous instances" when students would open her classroom door and "shout 'black power' accompanied by the upraised clenched fist"—a militant slogan and gesture of the era. The same teacher reported that someone threw bricks at her car when she was leaving an open house at the school. A white English teacher reported that a male dropout, despite her remonstrances, entered her classroom to speak with a female student. When she attempted to eject him, "a scene" ensued—a scene not conducive to scholarship. If white teachers were shown so little respect, how would white students fare? That was the unwritten but unmistakable question.[8]

The decision to close the high school resulted from a compromise with HEW. The spring 1967 agreement with the federal agency ended the first phase of the struggle leading to Pacesetter, a phase that began in April and May 1966, when the district stood on the doctrine of local control and refused to sign a new HEW form mandating increased student and faculty desegregation. The RISD's stand was popular with the white majority in the district, but it failed because the federal courts accepted HEW's move beyond racial neutrality and insisted that race itself be an index of desegregation. HEW tried to mollify the RISD and persuade it to sign the new form, arguing that it was not the indefinitely binding "harsh contract" that the district believed. The district's then attorney, Henry D. Akin, responded, "I thought, and still think, to put it in the vernacular," that the HEW contention "is B.S." The federal government was, after all, obligated to control the expenditure of federal aid to school districts. HEW proceeded carefully, nevertheless, because the RISD contended that it received few or no federal funds that HEW could withhold to force compliance and because of rising congressional opposition to HEW's aggressive desegregation policy. Moreover, the federal agency found an acceptable alternative to desegregating all of the Hamilton Park School. The racial imbalance in the RISD could be lessened by closing the high school and dispersing its students and faculty among the other two high schools. The district also sought a compromise, because the Hamilton Park High School was doomed anyway. Moreover, the RISD was increasingly isolated, first by the Texas Education Agency, which sided with HEW, and second by court decisions accepting the HEW guidelines as a new judicial standard imposed upon all school districts. In the spring 1967 the two sides agreed on a settlement closing the high school after the 1968/69 school year and quieting the HEW threat of a noncompliance hearing.[9]

For the residents of Hamilton Park, the struggle between the RISD and HEW was a sideshow; what mattered was the loss of the high school. "It was a shock, man," Streetman Watson exclaimed. With the closing of the high school, the adult activities revolving about it collapsed. "You'd go to school functions with people," Watson reminisced. "Then when the kids split and went to different schools, you didn't have any common meeting ground. It tore the community up." The closing dismayed the students. "I just never thought that it would happen," Theresa Patrick said. During her senior year (1968/69) it was clear enough that hers was the last graduating class, "but because it was our community and because it was our school," the RISD should have better communicated the legal and practical necessities of the closing. Ms. Patrick believed that the shutdown left Hamilton Park "disjointed," and that a "competitive spirit" developed among community youth divided among high schools—a spirit replacing "the loyalties that we once had." Sheila Allen, a fifth grader in 1968/69, "was very very disappointed, because we had looked so forward to getting up there in what we called 'the high-school end' and follow in our siblings' foot steps." When, during fall 1970, she entered the seventh grade at Richardson Junior High School, she felt "hostility and anger because I did not get to live and be schooled in the same area, with the same teachers, as my brothers and sisters had."[10]

To its credit the RISD developed a "plan for improving the educational program of the senior high students at Hamilton Park," and the board approved it on 8 April 1968. The plan called for dividing students between the other two high schools and provided for the full participation of Hamilton Park students in the activities of their future classes. That is, a Hamilton Park student would "be considered a member of the class which they will join in September of 1969 for the purpose of elections, voting and trying out for student organizations." The plan provided for the complete integration of all activities at the host schools, transportation of Hamilton Park students as necessary, and the integration of the Hamilton Park High School faculty beginning in September 1969. Simultaneously an informal group of blacks and whites met in churches and homes in an attempt to ease any ill feelings or misunderstandings. Goss participated in some of the meetings although they were not connected with the RISD. Many of those attending during at least one meeting were also members of the CALL school committee. Henry Davis, who participated in several of the meetings, was not a member of CALL, and it is probable that the activist integrationist group was no more a sponsor of the informal meetings than was the RISD or any other organization. The meetings dealt forthrightly with several issues, including integrated schooling and neighborhoods, interracial socializing, and the bugbear of interracial dating and marriage.[11]

These conciliatory efforts, and especially the superior range of course work at the large high schools, helped to clear the air and to reconcile Hamilton Park residents to their loss. There was also some concern about the adverse influences on young children when children of all public school ages mingled on the same campus, a concern mitigated with the closing of the high school. Robert Cook "felt good when they closed the school. Of course, we lost our football team, which everybody was proud of, you know, Hamilton Park football and basketball, and I understand all that." But "in the interest of progress" it was a better solution for the high-school students who were bused out to the larger schools and for the younger children who remained at Hamilton Park. The district's careful preparation also meant that, for the most part, the Hamilton Park high schoolers had no more than the usual problems involved in transferring.[12]

The second series of moves toward Pacesetter began about a year after the settlement between the RISD and HEW. The events of this phase demonstrated that the RISD would not voluntarily integrate the Hamilton Park School, a result frustrating to Hamilton Park residents. The community was rife with anxious rumors about closing the school altogether—rumors that integrating it would help to dispel. Integration would also raise the quality of the school's offering to parity with others in the district by bringing in white children, whose needs the RISD presumably would meet. In March 1968, the Hamilton Park Interorganizational Committee (IOC) began the second phase when it proposed altering the school's attendance boundaries to achieve desegregation. The 242

The School Transformed

junior-high students, it declared, were too few to secure a full range of programs. In addition, the faculty should be desegregated. On 8 April, the IOC forwarded a second recommendation for the "total" integration of faculty and students in the RISD.[13]

In June, Ben D. McCarley, the president of the board, dispatched a polite brush-off to Curtis Smith, the IOC president. Two months later, Smith complained to McCarley that the IOC had received no real response to its proposals; either the board should "upgrade" the junior high by expanding its attendance zone or it should close the school. Whatever happened to the junior high, the board should leave the elementary school "at its present site and integrate the student body and faculty." Smith went on to vent the frustrations of the Hamilton Park residents. "Good citizens require a good education," he declared. "We will not settle for a substandard school in Hamilton Park any longer. We recognize that the rest of the school district may not be totally satisfied with our solution," but all parties had to accept equitable burdens.[14]

The district ignored Smith's plea for prompt action, but it paid marginally more attention to CALL, which shared the IOC's objectives. The CALL school committee of some ten members, black and white, included a few Hamilton Park residents. The black members, mature and responsible people, were angry over desegregation delays and what they perceived to be trifling with the Hamilton Park School, as well as with the personality and actions of Principal Goss. The blacks were seen by a law-enforcement agency, almost certainly the Richardson police department, not as mature, but as potentially dangerous. For a time in 1968, operatives pretending to be interested in CALL's objectives attended the CALL school committee meetings and reported on the statements of various members. Such surveillance of an aggressively desegregationist group is symptomatic of official nervousness in the rhetorically supercharged, riot-prone atmosphere of the late 1960s, rather than of the radicalism of the CALL school committee.[15]

During the course of several meetings from July through November, members of the committee threatened marches, demonstrations, media publicity, and enlisting the aid of groups outside the RISD to press for integration. The purpose of all the suggested activity was equal African-American participation in society, not its destruction. At first the CALL group discussed retaining the high school and expanding its boundaries to bring in whites but soon surrendered that idea. Some members came to accept closing the school as a means of getting rid of Goss. The CALL group was well aware of the IOC's efforts to improve the junior high and elementary schools and soon its focus shifted to embrace the IOC agenda. After considerable discussion, CALL presented a petition to the RISD board on 25 November 1968.[16]

The petition drew from Smith's August letter and from the statements of several CALL members. It requested the desegregation of the junior high school and bringing both the junior high and elementary schools to parity with others in the RISD. It also asked the board to appoint a biracial committee to investigate the school and recommend any necessary changes. A crowd of 650 listened while 20 people spoke to the petition on 2 December. The board responded by conceding the lesser request but denying the greater, in motions and supporting statements prepared beforehand. It accepted a motion to request the Southern Association of Colleges and Schools to appoint a biracial committee to study the Hamilton Park school in the context of the district and recommend any necessary changes. A later, court-ordered closing of the junior high obviated the committee's mild recommendations. The second motion also carried. With it, the board resolved to maintain the existing boundaries of the Hamilton Park School, to bus no students into or out of the Hamilton Park zone "for the purpose of integration," and to continue all other district policies on the basis of equality.[17]

The second motion made it obvious that the board would not voluntarily desegregate the Hamilton Park School. A board member defended the policy by saying "that any arbitrary change in our present attendance boundary lines for the purpose of arbitrarily bringing white and black students together in a forced integration situation would not be in accordance with the Civil Rights Act of 1964." But by late 1968, those assertions were horse-and-buggy constitutional views, first because HEW had already abandoned racial neutrality and attacked Hamilton Park's all-black student body and faculty, and second because court decisions had rendered any racially concentrated school constitutionally suspect.[18]

Moreover, the statement begged the question of the district administration's aversion to desegregating the school and the related question of white reaction to any change in school zones. The district had generated memoranda demonstrating that Hamilton Park was a high-vandalism area hostile to white teachers. As for the district's white patrons, Akin, the board attorney at the time, guessed "that they probably would have complied" if they were placed in a newly expanded Hamilton Park zone for purposes of integration. "There might have been some that might have moved for that reason, but probably somewhere else in Richardson. I don't remember any hysteria about it." Of course, there was no hysteria because there was no officially proposed expansion of the Hamilton Park zone. John Roberts, then the assistant superintendent for instruction, was more doubtful of the success of any boundary change. Both the board and the administration had the "strong belief," he thought, that any attendance zone changes requiring "white students to attend the Hamilton Park School and be in the minority" would not succeed because the white students "just would not go. I think that probably was an accurate assessment at that time." Therefore, "I think that probably their feeling was that they had to find ways to successfully have the black students that lived within the Hamilton Park community ... be rerouted to other schools within the district. That is, of course, eventually what happened." The second phase, then, ended at an impasse. Hamilton Park residents had demonstrated to the board their awareness and concerns, but they lacked the critical mass to overcome the majority's hostility to integration by means of bringing white students to Hamilton Park.[19]

With HEW momentarily quiescent and the district adamant, the courts seized the lead in marking the third phase of the move toward Pacesetter. Indeed, the Supreme Court had already spoken in the *Green* decision of May 1968, months before the emotional board meeting in Richardson. In *Green,* the Court, exasperated with integration delays, discovered in *Brown II* "the affirmative duty" of Southern school boards to convert at once from dual racial school systems to unitary systems. "The burden on a school board today is to come forward with a plan that promises realistically ... to work *now.*" The test of unitary status and of realism was statistical proof of blacks and whites sitting together in classrooms in a proportion roughly reflecting the racial ratio of students in the district. *Green* thus sealed the fate of Hamilton Park's all-black school. In the summer of 1970, HEW and the Department of Justice (DOJ) conducted a joint sweep through the South to bring all the remaining laggard school districts into line. The RISD was not one of the most recalcitrant districts, but the sweep caught it up with thirty-seven other Texas districts that were statistically flawed. The RISD, in fact, wanted a solution to its stymie as badly as did HEW and the DOJ. Meeting in Austin, the state capital, on 28 July 1970, RISD officials and federal representatives agreed to seek "clarification" of Hamilton Park's status "once and for all by the courts."[20]

The third phase of the RISD's struggle with desegregation continued on the local level: district judge William M. Taylor Jr., a conservative

Lyndon Johnson appointee, received the case on 19 August. Hearings on 20 and 24 August produced a stalemate. Akin filed the existing RISD plan and the government's attorneys filed an HEW plan calling for pairing Hamilton Park elementary with the Stults Road School, southeast in nearby Northwood Estates. HEW, in addition, wanted to close the Hamilton Park junior high, dispersing its students among three other junior highs. Judge Taylor seized upon the junior-high closing to fashion a compromise. His order closed the junior high, a move he said the RISD "more or less agreed to." He rejected the pairing of elementary students in favor of "protecting" Hamilton Park parents and students by keeping the elementary pupils at the neighborhood school. Akin agreed, saying there was no objection to transporting older students but that "these little kiddos" should not be bused. Taylor limited his criticism of the RISD, "a fine school district," to its highly segregated faculty and staff. The rest of the order included the standard fare of school desegregation cases. A majority-to-minority transfer policy and nondiscriminatory programs were required, as well as a biracial committee and elaborate systems of notification to parents and reports to the court.[21]

Both the federal government and the school district did well by Taylor's order. Closing the junior high was in fact a favor to the RISD, which could plead a court order rather than face the unpalatable choices of shutting down the school itself and outraging Hamilton Park or desegregating it and kindling the wrath of the white majority. The DOJ was denied its plan, but it savored a victory of sorts. Statistics were critical during the post-*Green* years, and the RISD's desegregation statistics improved after 1970. Integrating about 280 junior-high students into three other schools decreased the number of black children at the Hamilton Park School, as well as the percentage of all RISD black students there. The qualified victory for the DOJ was no more than that for the RISD. Hamilton Park remained a segregated school, vulnerable to continued legal action. Hamilton Park residents who fought to retain a viable community school were the losers in a contest perceived as a DOJ-RISD struggle. The closing of the junior high was the death knell for the school-oriented adult groups, the Band Parents and the Dads Club. But the loss of the parent groups was merely an incident in the loss of community influence over public-school issues that federal involvement entailed. The command of *Green*—that blacks not bear the burden of desegregation—availed Hamilton Park parents and children nothing. It was more expe-

The School Transformed

dient for the RISD and the DOJ to obey *Green*'s demands for quick action and statistical improvement.[22]

The junior-high students themselves were utterly lost sight of in the midst of institutional self-absorption in goals and maneuvers. The RISD, perhaps because of the very success of its high-school integration, made no similar plans for integrating the junior-high students, beyond allocating them to the three formerly white schools and providing them with buses. The reception accorded them depended, in the main, on the administrative attitude at each host school, as the administration conveyed that attitude to teachers and students. For Sheila Allen, the environment at Richardson Junior High School varied from alien to hostile. The principal was unfriendly to blacks, often attempting to segregate African-American students at pep rallies or other nonacademic events. He generally "made no effort to make this thing work."[23]

At the lowest level of dissonance, Ms. Allen remembered, "the cultures clashed, the priorities clashed, the mores clashed." In her junior-high years, "we black girls didn't wear pantyhose or stockings.... We just wore bobby socks... because in our culture, you know, girls who wore stockings were 'loose' girls.... So it was taboo." But at Richardson Junior High, "the white girls were not only wearing stockings, but they were wearing make-up and hairdos. They were courting guys that were older." The Hamilton Park contingent also had learned not to "talk back" to their teachers, but found the white students freely commenting, discussing, and arguing with teachers during class. On the other hand, the black students were accustomed to talking "loud," by the standards of some whites. Ms. Allen's group rebelled one day in a home economics class when a visiting white mother chastised them, in a "hostile and mean" way, for loud talking just before the beginning of class; she told them they should be more "ladylike." Ms. Allen and her classmates, "as usual, stood together, and we let her have it." The confrontation degenerated into "a real ugly scene."[24]

Verbal abuse was one thing; physical attacks were another. For some time, and almost daily, white students would wait for the black students in the morning and in the afternoon. As soon as the buses rolled to a stop, the whites would attack the blacks and fight them into the building. In the afternoon, whites would be waiting for a return engagement from the building to the buses. If that were not enough, white high schoolers "would come down and make their bid to fight," often enough that the Richardson police regularly patrolled the campus to deter fighting. Ms. Allen recalled one occasion in the gym when she outclassed "a big ol' white girl" on the basketball court and the white girl "beat me in my back to the point that she knocked me down on the floor," to the accompaniment of "obscenities" and "calling me 'nigger' and stuff like that." Though small and rail-thin, Ms. Allen picked herself up from the floor and administered a thrashing to her white assailant. There were times, of course, when blacks threw the first punch or staged walkouts. In any event, the school administration did little to improve the situation until things "had gotten to the boiling point."[25]

Worse than the cultural differences, the words, and the fights was the feeling of isolation. "We were just outcasts. We were misfits, and we were just being tolerated." Ms. Allen needed no better illustration of the differential treatment than one "windy spring day" when the papers of some careless scholars had blown around the campus. That day, the bus arrived late, and the driver assumed that the Hamilton Park students had strewn the grounds with their papers. The driver, himself African American, told the waiting youngsters, "y'all not going to get on this bus until y'all go and pick up that paper." When the students refused, the driver snorted, "find your own way home," and drove off. By then the school was closed and locked. Abandoned, and too uncomfortable to ask for assistance at nearby white homes, the group elected to walk south from central Richardson, a journey of perhaps three miles. The students "cut through pastures and fields" and crossed Interstate 635, the Lyndon B. Johnson Freeway, at rush hour. "I think about it and shudder," Ms. Allen said. She was wearing a heavy back-brace and shoes that, while adequate for school, were scarcely made for hiking. Her parents "were frantic" by the time she arrived home about 6:30. The next day, a furious Ola Allen telephoned the principal about her daughter's travail. The incident was not repeated.[26]

The youngsters at Richardson junior high survived their experiences, as youngsters will. Sheila Allen went on to become a "nationally recognized" track star and top scholar at East Texas State University and at Sam Houston State University, where she graduated. Later she earned a law degree from the main campus of the University of Texas at Austin, establishing her own practice in Dallas. Her junior-high memories do not, however, reflect well on the RISD of that era.[27]

The fourth and final phase of the moves toward Pacesetter occurred in the context of court-driven and DOJ-driven integration and of RISD

The School Transformed

experience, as they had developed to 1974. The Supreme Court's *Swann* decision of April 1971 explicitly condoned busing as a device of desegregation. By accepting the reasoning of previous decisions, it dealt a final blow to the language of the Civil Rights Act barring "any official or court of the United States" from requiring racial balance, or requiring busing "to achieve" it. On the executive front, President Richard M. Nixon was against busing but unable to halt the thrust toward desegregation. From mid-1973, Nixon diverted his energies to the Watergate scandal that would result in his resignation during August 1974.[28]

Perceptions also had changed at the RISD during the years after the Hamilton Park junior high closed in 1970. As Henry Akin said, after *Swann* "there was a different ball game. What we did in 1970, according to *Swann*, wasn't enough." In other words, it was no secret that Hamilton Park's sole one-race elementary school could be considered out of compliance. Akin assumed that the only reason why the DOJ waited as long as it did after *Swann* to file on the RISD was that the Richardson district presented a relatively minor problem. "Assuming for the purpose of argument that it was bad or wrong," he said, "it wasn't as gross a case as many others, and they just had limited manpower and limited funds." Another problem with Hamilton Park elementary, from the district point of view, was its level of academic achievement. John Roberts, then the assistant superintendent in charge of instruction, recalled "that there were constantly a number of things that were done to try to improve the performance level of the boys and girls that attended school there." The RISD's success in significantly raising the "achievement level was certainly less than fantastic. In fact," he concluded, the situation "was frequently very disappointing to the instructional central staff people." The reasons for the disappointment could include the lowering of aspirations involved in the closing of the high school and the junior high. Whatever the reason, the academic performance of the school stood in unhappy contrast to its former reputation, making the district open to some alteration of its circumstances, even if it did not exactly welcome any further change.[29]

It was in these national and local contexts that the DOJ filed suit on 23 May 1974 for the desegregation of the Hamilton Park School. The DOJ position was that almost any segregated school situation was invalid if it resulted from past or present discrimination within the district. Steven H. Gurwin, the DOJ's lead attorney, accused the RISD of following a segregative policy of school location and construction. Gurwin cited *Swann* and more recent fifth-circuit opinions to demonstrate that a one-race school could be justified only if school authorities were not responsible for it and if there were no "reasonable alternatives." Nor could the school be closed, throwing the burden of desegregation on the African-American children. The authorities were culpable, there were reasonable alternatives, and the school could be kept open. Gurwin suggested either "pairing"—that is, exchanging some students with the Spring Valley School—or "clustering," a three-way exchange among Hamilton Park and the Spring Valley and Dobie schools to the northwest.[30]

Attorney Akin addressed the law and the judge in his effort to turn back the DOJ's contentions. He argued that the RISD had nothing to do with the planning or development of the Hamilton Park subdivision or with its racial composition. As Akin pointed out years later, the area around Hamilton Park was practically undeveloped. Except for other African-American housing, there were "no residences in that area." He distinguished Hamilton Park from the fifth-circuit cases, which "involved complicated zoning situations and . . . a number of one-race schools." The RISD fit "the criteria enunciated by *Swann* on all 'fours' to allow the continued existence" of Hamilton Park elementary in an attendance zone. The zone was not "gerrymandered or artificially created" but "bounded" by highways, a busy Forest Lane, and "deep creeks," among other barriers. The DOJ had practically conceded that, except for Hamilton Park, the district was "being operated on a fully integrated basis." Akin deftly complimented Taylor when he suggested that the judge's 1970 decision had anticipated *Swann* in its assurance of a nondiscriminatory system.[31]

Gurwin disputed Akin's last two arguments. The barriers around Hamilton Park were not formidable; indeed, the high and junior-high students crossed them every school day. The barriers argument was "the weak link" in his presentation, Akin admitted, but it was not the major problem for Gurwin. To the DOJ attorney, it was critical that the segregation of the Hamilton Park School existed in a system that had never been unitary. The RISD would continue to be a proscribed dual system until the school was racially mixed. Judge Taylor did not accept Gurwin's rebuttal, but instead took up Akin's flattering suggestion that his 1970 decision established a unitary system meeting the test of *Swann*. Neither pairing nor clustering and the attendant busing would "accomplish any effective or realistically stable desegregation." Taylor was "of the view that this one school on the basis of its history and what the facts are is no indication of any kind of discrimination." There would be no order to the RISD to develop a new plan.³²

Taylor denied the government's motion on 2 August. The DOJ appeal resulted in the fifth circuit's reversal of his decision on 22 April 1975—a reversal reaffirming its aggressive desegregation stance. The heart of the fifth-circuit opinion was that, while the creation of the Hamilton Park School as a one-race school might have been justified, for a decade all black students within the Richardson district attended the school without regard to the proximity to their residences of white schools; therefore, the district had indeed promoted a dual system. Hamilton Park's segregation would end with the opening of the 1975/76 school year.

Within sixty days of the reversal, the RISD was to file a plan with the district court "to achieve the result required." The board appealed to the Supreme Court, although Akin, despite his "hopes," "felt the odds were bad." At the same time, the district began its desegregation planning. "We weren't just trying to take up the time of the courts," Akin remembered, "we were serious in our positions, but it also bought us some time to get ready for what we expected the eventuality to become."³³

The RISD confronted a situation compounded from three elements. First, busing for whites had come to Richardson. Realistically, it was doubtful whether the Supreme Court would hear the case, and as Akin said, "I wasn't surprised when they denied cert"—that is, declined to accept the appeal. Second, the Hamilton Park School could not be closed. The residents of Hamilton Park had made clear their concern over the continuing rumors about closure of the school. On 28 June 1974, Doris Robertson sent a petition to Taylor while he was considering the government's case against the RISD. The petition declared the school to be "an important facet in the social and civic fabric of the Hamilton Park Community." The 882 signers wanted any desegregation programs to be "practicable" and "fair" without closure of the school to "normal classes." The PTA obtained the signatures through a community effort that included a mass meeting at the school auditorium, door-to-door solicitations, and radio station "bulletin board" announcements. Mrs. Robertson, the PTA president, warned the board on 19 May 1975 that, if the school were closed, Hamilton Park parents "will not take it sitting down." Her assertion was no idle threat. The PTA was prepared to go to the federal courts, where recent decisions had virtually guaranteed a victory against the RISD.³⁴

Several issues formed the third parameter. They included white opposition to busing designed to achieve integration; potential inconvenience to both black and white students and families; the further decline of Hamilton Park School's community affiliation because of student transportation in and out; and the likely resegregation of the southern portion of the RISD because of "white flight" from busing, resulting either in the failure of integration or an expansion of busing to pursue white students throughout the district. The Stults Road and Dobie schools, mentioned in several plans for pairing or clustering, already had reached black populations of 18 percent (Stults Road) and almost 11 percent (Dobie). Dobie had suffered an 88 percent student turnover from the previous year, by far the highest in the district. Such instability boded ill for the usual pairing or clustering.[35]

The innovative Pacesetter enrichment program, filed on 20 June, was the RISD's answer to its dilemma. Refined to "almost the very last minute," the idea emerged from suggestions (including a letter to John Roberts from a former neighbor), meetings between school officials and RISD residents (the biracial committee among them), and from marathon staff sessions. Attorney Akin participated in many meetings and gave the program its name. Pacesetter combined a regular elementary curriculum with "specialized educational, cultural, and physical education programs," which would "at least" include a reading center, training for students displaying artistic and literary talent, foreign-language teaching, classes in the "creative and performing arts," with rooms for private lessons, and an early-childhood program. Mathematics and science curricula were among other possibilities. The Hamilton Park School was "unique in its adaptability to the Pacesetter concept," having a large auditorium, standard-size gymnasium, and extensive outdoor physical education equipment. The teachers would be the cream of Richardson's crop—a minimum of 80 percent would have master's degrees—and each teacher would have an aide. Other specialized staff would include a full-time "nurse, psychologist, counselor, educational diagnostician."[36]

The RISD had defined its program, but it wanted to have up to two years to meet its racial quotas despite the courts' impatience with desegregation delays. Its task, then, was to sell the program and the long-term deadline to Taylor over Gurwin's probable objections. The district's "Proposed Arrangements" made a dual thrust toward those objectives. First, the RISD presented its hope for an extended time limit. The administration and board believed that Pacesetter would "draw, within probably

The School Transformed 155

the next two years, a number of white students . . . which will equal and eventually exceed the number of black students attending Hamilton Park." The projected enrollment at Hamilton Park for 1975/76 was some 250, implicitly an easy number to match or exceed, if the RISD were granted sufficient time. Second, the district promised to *sell* Pacesetter: "An active recruitment and advertising campaign" was to be "instituted and maintained to ensure this result."[37]

The district's presentation embedded Pacesetter in three alternate, partial-pairing plans. The administration and board approved these pairing schemes, but without enthusiasm. Retaining them, once Pacesetter was also approved, was designed only to draw the government's fire away from Pacesetter. "It was my feeling from a legal standpoint . . . that we ought to present some other things," Akin recalled. Predictably, Gurwin's response of 7 July riddled the three partial-pairing plans because all fell short of complete desegregation. But the decoys did not deter Gurwin from attacking Pacesetter. The federal attorney admitted the advantages of Pacesetter's retaining Hamilton Park children in their attendance zone while bringing in whites; however, he deplored the RISD's lack of a quick "assurance" of rapid desegregation (their asking for two years). The Pacesetter proposal violated the injunction of *Green* to write a plan that would "work now," as well as the fifth circuit's mandate to begin effective desegregation during fall 1975.[38]

Publication of the RISD plans produced several more plans and suggestions. On 11 and 12 July, Judge Taylor held unusual, informal sessions during which he allowed interested parties to testify and be questioned. School officials stood by their plans, and Gurwin by his. Hamilton Park residents pointed to the busing of their junior-high and high-school children and asked white parents to share the burden of future desegregation.[39]

Taylor studied the plans and on 15 July opted for Pacesetter. He hoped that it would appeal to residents of the RISD, in which Hamilton Park was the only school able to accommodate the full enrichment program. The judge's opposition to "forced busing" also influenced his decision; Pacesetter, he declared, "comes nearer guaranteeing stability of your neighborhood residential patterns." On the other hand, Taylor would not countenance any delay. He responded to Gurwin's misgivings by allowing the RISD a mere two weeks to enroll at least 250 nonblack volunteers for Pacesetter. The two-week deadline (to 1 August) was a radical reduction from the district's bargaining-chip offer of two years.

"I thought we might get maybe six months," Akin commented, "and I started out with two years, and I never expected to end up with two weeks." The volunteers for Pacesetter, once accepted, could not transfer to another school, except under extraordinary circumstances. In the event that the Richardson officials failed to meet his requirements, Taylor leaned toward implementing Gurwin's plans for pairing or clustering, or a plan to enlarge Hamilton Park's attendance zone.[40]

School officials responded to their 1 August deadline with a thoroughgoing publicity blitz. Superintendent Pearce sent an explanatory letter to all parents and the district established a "Pacesetter Hot Line"; neighborhood meetings were arranged for 22–24 July. Roberts, the chief assembler of the program, and other staff members stressed program quality, an extended-day option, and their decision to keep Pacesetter, probably, should the Supreme Court overturn the fifth-circuit decision. The *Richardson Daily News* supplied excellent editorial and news support. Roberts worried about reaching the racial-quota goal, but Pacesetter was well received. The program made its quota in all six grades by noon, 1 August.[41]

It was already warm on the morning of 20 August 1975, when the yellow buses braked in front of the Hamilton Park School, their accordion doors snapped open, and white children spilled out to begin their first full day. The voluntary busing of white kids into the depths of a black community in Texas made the national news; reporters and television cameras seemed to be everywhere. The media circus heightened the natural anxiety of RISD officials. Griffin, who became the coprincipal with the beginning of Pacesetter, admitted a week later to the Richardson Noon Lions Club that he "had butterflies" on the opening day, but that the children were enthusiastic. "See, the secret to it was," he recalled many years after, "the kids were having a ball. The kids started liking each other the first day, and that's the key." In addition, "everybody in the communities—in all the communities—were trying to make [it] work, and everybody bent over backwards." Because of school desegregation difficulties elsewhere, however, "we had newspaper people looking over our shoulder every day, and they were trying to make us say that things were going on wrong that were not going on wrong." Nor was media interest quickly stilled. While the school prepared for its Christmas program, "one day NBC had a person come out of their Atlanta office for an interview." Television cameras "were on me all day . . . I got to go to California during the Christmas holidays, and I walked into this friend's home, and they said, 'We just saw you on television!' They were telling me about it, but I never saw it."[42]

Pacesetter was an educational success from the beginning. Both the Robertsons and the Akins sent daughters to the program. Wendy Robertson, the Hamilton Park daughter of a black postal employee, and Mary Akin, the daughter of a prosperous white attorney, were enthusiastic about their Pacesetter experiences. And so were their parents. Hamilton Park interviewees whose grandchildren enrolled in the program were pleased with Pacesetter. Pacesetter also revivified the PTA and volunteerism at the school. At the open house held the day before school began, the indefatigable Doris Robertson urged PTA membership on the new parents. "Everything is going really well," she said. "We're getting lots of new members signed up and everyone seems to be very enthusiastic." The PTA expanded its small store of pre-Pacesetter days into "a complete supply store," operated by volunteer parents, with prepackaged supplies for students in every grade. Mrs. Robertson herself became a computer-training volunteer; Freddie Nance, a teacher's aide before Pacesetter, stayed on to help operate the supply store.[43]

Responses outside the community helped to reinforce the educational image of Pacesetter. The Supreme Court's October refusal to review the primary-school desegregation case assured the survival of Pacesetter, provided the program lived up to its advance billing in the eyes of other educators. It did. An independent study of the first year concluded that "the weight of evidence supports the academic and emotional effectiveness of the Pacesetter program." Volunteer students were working a grade above their grade levels, and the 84.5 percent return rate of volunteers was "unusually high." In 1986, the U. S. Department of Education selected Hamilton Park for an award of excellence, an honor shared that year by only five other public and private schools in the Dallas area and by but 271 others nationwide. In 1991, the RISD completed a $2 million renovation of the original building and its additions, removing the vestiges of a plant designed in part for high schoolers and adding new classrooms and other spaces to improve the program for its pupils, prekindergarten through sixth grade.[44]

Community enthusiasm, educational excellence, and national recognition did not down criticism of the Hamilton Park School any more than did the improvement efforts of bygone years. The complaints revolved around the loss of the traditionally close relationship between school and community. Joseph Williams argued that the program was never intended to benefit Hamilton Park children solely or primarily. Pacesetter, he maintained, "was really not for blacks." The school had to be kept open, and "some preference" had to be given "to blacks who were in the area, but the intent was never to provide that type of education for blacks." Pacesetter, instead, was "the best thing that ever happened for affluent Richardson, because those parents come in the morning in their Jaguars and Mercedes," and leave the children. The parents devote their days to adult activities, while the children remain in school in the extended-day program. "Then the parents come back and get them about 6:00 P.M. — best thing that ever happened for affluent Richardson, and they realize it."[45]

Williams's analysis, however, must be viewed from the perspective of 1975. Roberts's problem in 1975 was to appease his white former neighbor and others like him who would happily send their children to Hamilton Park, provided they could receive a "quality education." At the same time, the program had to enrich the education of the "three hundred students who were already there and who were a total cross-section of boys and girls who lived in that attendance area." The RISD's challenge, as Roberts put it, "was that we had to provide a program that was so good that it would attract the white students . . . but would also be a program that would be exceptionally good for those that were already . . . attending the school." From the community perspective, however, Williams's remarks have merit. The high-quality program would not have been created for the Hamilton Park School alone; the community school was destroyed as a conception, transformed, and opened to others in order to save it.[46]

Judge Taylor's order that the school could be no more than 50 percent black created problems for Hamilton Park parents who assumed that, because they lived there, their children would be enrolled in the nearest school. In the early years of the program it fell to coprincipal Griffin to disabuse parents of that idea. If they had recently moved to the community, or if they had sent their children on majority-to-minority transfers and "now wanted to come back," they usually could not be accommodated. Griffin "had to sit there and say 'no' because . . . we had to stick with the court order." He remembered that it was not pleasant to tell a parent, "I know you're a Hamilton Park resident, but because of the court order and because of where your child finished school last year, we do not have an opening." Soon "we had waiting lists for the Hamilton Park kids; we had waiting lists from kids from across the school district who wanted to come." The waiting lists became so lengthy that one pregnant and prescient Hamilton Park resident was said to have registered her unborn child. Another court-mandated problem was that the Hamilton Park School, though in a black community and with a 50 percent African-American enrollment, had to reflect in its faculty makeup the approximate racial distribution of the district at large. Robert Cook remembered the RISD approaching the biracial committee to approve a fourth black teacher for Hamilton Park "because it would have put them a little over the limit." Cook thought that the court-imposed limit was ridiculous. "I would say, 'If it's a black school and it's in a black community, why can't we have more black teachers?'" Griffin agreed. "I think it's a hard law," he said, regretting that more African Americans could not teach at Hamilton Park.[47]

With the passing of years and the continuing turnover in the community as well as in administrative and teaching posts in the RISD, other problems surfaced. One of these was the assignment of a relatively high proportion of black children at Hamilton Park and throughout the district to remedial classes without fully informing their parents of the implications of the placement. That difficulty was corrected in 1991, but the issue of appointing a black principal or coprincipal was unresolved.[48]

One of Pacesetter's several ironies, then, is nostalgia for a time when an African-American community wielded considerable influence over its school. Theresa Patrick has spoken to other teachers about the changes at Hamilton Park, "and if it were to go back to an all-black school, we would be there in a New York minute. We're looking forward to the day that we can retire like that—teaching an all-black school in the community." But that day is unlikely to arrive. Another irony of Pacesetter is that the government attorney, the PTA, and the Civic League preferred traditional pairing or clustering plans to Pacesetter, despite Pacesetter's promise of educational excellence. Whether those plans would have been superior to Pacesetter cannot be known, but it is not unreasonable to be skeptical of any other outcome. Pairing or clustering would have undermined Hamilton Park's community identity as surely as Pacesetter did. Finally, the success of Pacesetter depended in part on its location in a once-segregated school with elaborate facilities, including an auditorium and gymnasium. Without this inheritance from the discredited "dual system," Pacesetter would have been a diminished program.[49]

Nationwide, school desegregation struggles continued for many years after the *Brown* decision of 1954, in districts as dissimilar as "thumb prints," as a DOJ official once characterized them.[50] It is, therefore, difficult if not impossible to place Richardson in any meaningful comparison nationally, regionally, or across Texas. Clearly, its record of desegregation after the Civil Rights Act of 1964 is superior to those of many other districts in Dixie, in part because a comparative handful of African-American students in the RISD lived outside of Hamilton Park. The 1969 closing of the high school responded partly to federal pressure but also to the realities of maintaining a small, isolated high school in an affluent district with large high schools having sophisticated programs. The district handled the closure in a prudent, enlightened manner. Unhappily, the same judgment cannot be passed on its management of the junior-high closing; neither the administration nor the board gave any serious consideration to expanding the Hamilton Park boundaries to bring in white students, although hindsight strongly suggests that even a successfully-integrated junior high would not have saved the district from trouble with the DOJ over its all-black grade school in the same building. What was unfortunate was the RISD's failure to smooth the path of the Hamilton Park junior-high students into their host schools. Richardson Junior High School was a snake pit for the Hamilton Park youngsters unfortunate enough to be assigned to its attendance zone.

As for the Pacesetter option, its arrival marked the final destruction of a community school where the rafters once rang to cheers for the Bobcats and the music of the sock hops. But the federal courts cared little, in 1975, for any sentiment or tradition surrounding one small primary school. Pacesetter, on the other hand, capitalized very well on a remarkable set of conditions. It does not diminish Roberts's innovation to see it in the context of precedent in an affluent district relatively unruffled by racial conflict. The idea of busing white children into Hamilton Park, though resisted when presented only in terms of transportation to achieve racial balance, was nothing new. An HEW official had suggested it in 1967. The IOC and CALL integration plans in 1968 had stirred the public discussion of busing, as had the court cases of 1970 and 1974. In 1975, a teacher at Hamilton Park had suggested to Judge Taylor a "Specialized School Concept," similar to Pacesetter except for Pacesetter's traditional core elementary program. Roberts and the RISD staff crafted Pacesetter unaware of any previous specific proposal, but they did not have to be aware, given an atmosphere laden with ideas for educational improvement.[51] When at last a few hundred white students were asked to ride the buses, it was not merely in fealty to a controversial social ideal but also in response to a shining opportunity. The RISD could afford the costs of promoting Pace-

The School Transformed

setter and of shifting an extra $200,000 to the instructional needs of the program; it could afford to retain the experienced, well-trained teachers required; it could afford to refurbish a former grades-one-through-twelve school practically lying fallow.

Finally, the Hamilton Park School illustrates two general conclusions about the difficult world of desegregation. First, the process was complex, shifting, and laden with emotion. Second, success could never be absolute, for some persons or groups would be discomfited no matter what the outcome. The community suffered from losing some of its close involvement with the school. The Pacesetter solution was preferable, however, to closing the school, or to busing all the primary-grade children out of Hamilton Park for all or part of their elementary school years. In the light of these alternatives, the changes in Hamilton Park were positive.

9

ANOTHER TRANSITION AND THE BUYOUT

During the Buyout, a developer proposed to purchase every piece of private residential property in Hamilton Park for $35 per square foot. The deal fell through with the plunge in Texas real-estate prices that followed the collapse of the "oil patch" boom in 1985. Had it not failed, the smallest lot in Hamilton Park would have grossed about $250,000, an unbelievable sum for a lot and house that cost $9,000 or so in the 1950s, even considering the intervening inflation.[1]

The Buyout itself is unimaginable without an understanding of the changes sweeping over the upper White Rock area of Dallas from 1960 on. North Central Expressway, built only as far as Forest Lane in 1950, stretched north beyond Hamilton Park and into Richardson. The 1961 city directory listed only 20 addresses fronting the expressway for almost two miles, north from Walnut Hill Lane to Forest Lane, the southern boundary of Hamilton Park. By 1965 the number had increased to 40 and by 1970 it had reached 96. Five years later, it stood at 261, and by 1981 the 20 addresses of 20 years before had risen to 786. The North Central traffic count increased phenomenally. In 1955, it was 10,210 at a point near Hamilton Park. By 1960, its count stood at 40,620. In 1970, it had reached 64,150—near the design capacity of the highway. By 1980, 96,000 cars and trucks per day rolled by, scarcely a quarter mile from the west edge of Hamilton Park. Five years later the count was 116,000, an increase suggesting a virtual saturation with vehicles.[2]

The changes wrought by the completion of Interstate 635 (the Lyndon Baines Johnson Freeway) were equally startling. According to the 1969 city directory, the road contained but one address in the arc from Hillcrest Road to Abrams Road, a sweep of some three and one-half miles from the northwest to the southeast of Hamilton Park. In 1975, 230 addresses were listed in the area; in 1985, 440. The traffic counts were even more astonishing: 51,680 vehicles per day in 1970, two years after completion; 127,000 in 1980, and a veritable flood of 170,000 daily in 1985.³

The census told a similar story. Hamilton Park itself held to a fairly constant population, reaching 2,786 in 1960, when the community was nearing buildout. In 1970, the completed community was home to 3,218, including the apartments at its northwest corner. The mature Hamilton Park, again including the apartments, registered 2,670 in 1980. Meanwhile, its North Dallas census tract of approximately ten square miles rocketed from 7,385 to 46,998 in twenty years, despite the loss of about a square mile to other tracts.⁴

The pressures on Hamilton Park reflected these changes. From 1973 through 1988, the Civic League wrestled with some sixteen potential intrusions, developments so close as to constitute a threat. Some of these were minor, such as a zoning change some distance away that would marginally increase congestion in the traffic-choked area. Others were more serious. The apartments at Schroeder Road and Bunche Drive were a source of problems. Though not part of Hamilton Park itself, they were cheek by jowl with it. Charles E. Smith, the Civic League president from 1973 to 1988, recalled that "after three or four years" the apartments bred difficulties. A nearby homeowner complained of "gun play" after a bullet tore through his house. Cleanliness was a constant problem. The lawn of the Baptist church, then across Bunche, was littered with beer cans on Saturday and Sunday mornings. In 1982, speeding on Schroeder Road, partly attributed to "young people" in the apartments, became serious enough for Smith to complain to the district councilman. The police set traps and "caught a lot of the speeders." The troublesome apartments were in less than an ideal location for multifamily housing. Their low, 60 percent occupancy rate was one successful argument against the attempted rezoning in 1976 of land for apartments north of the Baptist church and south of the LBJ access road.⁵

Of all the proposed land-use changes in or near the community, none drew heavier fire from residents than a proposal to open a lumber yard in Hamilton Park. In the eyes of the Texas Western Lumber Company the property was ideal. It was the same wedge-shaped 3.22 acres that nearby homeowners and a development company had fought over in civil court during 1961, when the company won the right to build apartments there. But the company did not build and the land remained vacant. A broad swath of the acreage opened on Forest Lane, busy if still only two lanes wide, between the shopping center on the east and Cottonwood Creek on the west. The screens of the Gemini Twin Drive-In Theater rose west, beyond the creek, between the creek and the North Central access road. North of the theater, a string of commercial buildings reached up the road toward the I-635 interchange. Surely, it would make an excellent location for a sprawling lumber company.

It was indeed an excellent location, except for one thing. The property backed up at its north end on Willowdell Park and the south curve of Willowdell Drive, across the street from houses. When representatives of the lumber company approached the Civic League's Smith about their plans in the late spring of 1978, he took their proposal to his executive committee. On 7 June he replied "that no useful purpose could be served" by a meeting between representatives of the lumber company and the Civic League. The organization was "vehemently opposed" to the project and "no amount of concession" could erase that opposition. Nevertheless, the lumber company forged ahead. Defeated at the planning and zoning commission, it took its request for heavy commercial zoning to the city council.[6]

Smith and the Civic League organized several defenses. Smith wrote a letter to both major newspapers, a letter making two points: first, "spot zoning" threatened Hamilton Park, for twenty-five years a proud and stable community; second, if Hamilton Park could be undermined, no other community was safe. The Civic League also circulated a draft letter for its residents to use as a model when corresponding with officials about the issue, and it circulated a petition against the proposal—a petition signed by "everybody we got to," Smith remembered. "That was unanimous. Nobody wanted the lumber yard." The league retained an attorney who was a member of the Committee of 100, a group of African-American professionals, and received a resolution of support from that organization at the hearing before the city council. It enlisted the aid of the Dallas Black Chamber of Commerce, which presented a resolution and sent a speaker on the community's behalf. Both the committee and the chamber argued against the lumber yard on the ground "that whenever we get a stable black community, then we find that commercial establishments want to move into it," beginning a downward environmental spiral.[7]

The league's most impressive response was to mobilize members of the community to appear at the council chambers on the afternoon of 8 February 1979, renting a city bus that picked residents up at the shopping center. Many other community members made the trip in private cars. Although Smith's "that's the time we practically had all of Hamilton Park there" was an exaggeration to make a point, the turnout was probably more than a hundred protesters. The council rejected the zoning change. Later, the Methodist church bought the property for future expansion.[8]

Other anticipated intrusions were airborne and involved TI, the community's neighbor to the east. TI, a major manufacturer of semiconductors and electronic devices, bore somewhat the same relationship to Hamilton Park as would an amiable 800-pound gorilla to a much smaller creature. TI was a well-disposed neighbor and an employer of Hamilton Park residents, but it also had a great deal of leeway, like the gorilla, in choosing its seating arrangements. In 1982, TI applied for a permit for an "Electro Optics Fabrication Facility" that would emit hydrocarbon exhaust. The Civic League opposed the plan and requested a public hearing. Smith remembered that the league was concerned because a member had detailed information about the damaging effects of the emissions from such a plant, added, as they would be, to contaminants from vehicle exhausts on the heavily traveled roads surrounding the community. The Texas Air Control Board denied the request for a hearing and issued a permit to TI. Subsequent checks showed that the company was staying within the allowable emissions limits. In January 1984, a TI official addressed a league meeting to explain the company's expansion plans, to announce an emissions reduction of 57 percent from levels of the recent past, and to pledge a continuing effort aimed at further reductions.[9]

In September, however, Smith wrote the company, reporting "numerous complaints concerning a *bad odor*," possibly coming from TI. "Some of the neighbors that lived closer [to TI] brought it to our attention," Smith remembered. The company "assured us that it was not coming from their plant" and after a time the odor vanished. Some two years later TI applied to the Federal Aviation Administration for a helistop—a landing and takeoff pad for helicopters ferrying VIPs from and to airports. "We were concerned about the helicopters coming over us, and we just assumed that we'd have helicopters all day and part of the night and just whenever," Smith said. The league approached both TI and Mayor Annette Strauss, who received the company's assurances that no TI aircraft would fly over the community. In January 1987, a TI representative appeared at a Civic League meeting to assure residents that no flights would operate over Hamilton Park and to discuss the company's most recent property-development plans. With an added agreement to limit the hours of operation, the TI plan was approved. The company observed the terms of its license.[10]

Traffic on Forest Lane, the south border of Hamilton Park, although not a physical intrusion, became a headache, if not a waking nightmare. When the community opened in 1954, Forest Lane was a two-lane, blacktop, country road with a rickety bridge over Cottonwood Creek. Traffic mushroomed with the development of intersecting Greenville Avenue, to the east, into a major thoroughfare, the widening of Forest Lane to four lanes from the west to a point between the North Central access road and Cottonwood Creek, and the opening of I-635, not to mention commercial development along Forest Lane itself. Minor improvements to Forest Lane did little to relieve the situation. The Gemini Twin Theater "generated just great traffic jams," Smith recalled. There was a stoplight at the T-junction of Schroeder and Forest, but the theater patrons drove their cars over the path of Schroeder Road traffic, forming a bumper-to-bumper chain that gave no entry to traffic from Schroeder when the Schroeder light turned green. The only solution for a Hamilton Park resident so trapped was to turn around and drive the length of Schroeder to the eastbound I-635 access road, enter the freeway, and from there select an alternate route.[11]

In 1971, Willie Smith, then the president of the Civic League, asked for the widening of Forest from east of North Central east to Greenville. Charles E. Smith's correspondence bristled with later requests to the city, the county, and other citizen groups in efforts to develop a six-lane thoroughfare from North Central to Greenville. A successful bond issue by the county and city-county cooperation resulted in the reconstruction of Forest Lane, beginning in 1980. The related problem of Schroeder Road as the only way in and out of the community continued to be acute. As early as 1972, Thelma L. Wells, at that time the Civic League president, wrote of the need for a street "from the L.B.J. Freeway Frontage Road straight down the east side of Hamilton Park extending to Forest Lane. This additional road will take the increasingly heavy flow of traffic through Hamilton Park from L.B.J. Freeway down . . . Schroeder Road." For several years the city planned to extend Shepherd Road north from Northwood Estates across Forest Lane to connect with an extension of Campanella Drive, then continue Shepherd north to meet with Floyd Road at an I-635 underpass. Ultimately the city built Floyd Road south to Forest Lane, extending Campanella east to meet Floyd. Thirty years after the opening of Hamilton Park, its residents enjoyed a second entrance-and-exit road.[12]

The kaleidoscope of change swirling about Hamilton Park partly explains the Buyout, but developments within the community also illuminate its desirability for commercial redevelopment. Although over the years the city continuously improved Willowdell Park—planting trees and adding picnic tables, trash barrels, a softball diamond, tennis courts, play equipment, a wading pool, and other improvements—many of the facilities came after Hamilton Park's first generation of children had grown too old to enjoy them. The city's widening of Willowdell Drive to add a parking lane at the park's eastern edge and its attempts, not entirely successful, to control the flooding of Cottonwood Creek at the western edge, demonstrate some degree of responsiveness to a steady stream of requests from individual residents and the Civic League. The city did not, however, supply the long-sought enclosed recreation center until just before the Buyout (see chapter 10).[13]

The shopping center at the south entrance to the community also generated its share of grievances. Over the years the center was home to a variety of businesses, including a grocery, barbershop, dry cleaner's, drugstore, beauty parlor, luncheonette, two service stations, and, later, a post office substation and fast-food outlets. Inadequate exterior cleanliness, neatness, lighting, and landscaping formed the gravamen of Civic League complaints. In 1972, Thelma Wells met with the center's merchants, who pledged to improve conditions around their places of business, and with the city sanitation department, which agreed to place litter barrels on public property nearby. She then appealed to the shopping center's manager to improve trash collection, lighting, business signs, and "landscaping" to bring the place up to the area standard. The center's appearance improved after that.[14]

But the improvement was not permanent. By 1977, Charles Smith was writing the operator of a fruit stand in a former filling station about his "negligent" upkeep of the stand. When the operator abandoned the stand it was not refurbished and Smith wrote the owner that it "looks terrible." The owner cleaned and painted the building, but it deteriorated again and continued to be "a problem" until it was demolished and replaced by a fast-food restaurant. In 1981, Smith wrote a manager of the shopping center about the "dirty conditions" around the main building; once again, they improved. The Civic League helped by purchasing two trash barrels and paying to have them emptied. Cleanliness and even safety around the center could not, however, be taken for granted. Myra Christian, whose beauty shop fronted on Schroeder Road, recalled unwelcome partying in the parking lot, trash strewn about, and the center's unkempt, unpaved alley in full view of the Methodist church. In the mid-1980s, the roof of Christian's shop leaked so badly that an inspector from the fire department ordered a complete reroofing. In 1987, an illegal billboard, advertising cigarettes, went up north of the shopping center, next door to the Methodist church, where anyone traveling up or down Schroeder Road could read its message. Eiland Collins and others complained about the sign. Collins, then active in the work of the Methodist church, "didn't think we needed it there, right where we are trying to teach little kids right from wrong." The Civic League worked with the district councilman to have the sign taken down.[15]

Vexing as were the problems of intrusions, traffic, outlets, access, the park, and the shopping center, the issues of house and yard maintenance increasingly claimed the Civic League's time and attention. The perceived decline in upkeep of houses and lots was attributed in part to the greater permissiveness of the 1970s and after, as well as to the inability of aging pioneers to care for their properties as they once had (see chapter 10). But permissiveness and aging scarcely explain most of the problem, for Hamilton Park itself was changing, just as was the world around it. By 1970, of the original 739 computer-listed pioneer heads of household, 478 remained. Widows of pioneers totaled seventeen.[16]

The numbers compare very favorably, if residential persistence and stability are considered virtues, with a group of randomly selected residents of the first eight streets of Spring Valley Park. Spring Valley Park, established for whites only, first appears in the city directory of 1959, at what would become the northwest quadrant of North Central and I-635. In 1970, the selected 161 Spring Valley Park households listed only 38 continuing pioneer heads, a mere 23.6 percent. There were no widows of original residents. Nevertheless, Hamilton Park had experienced change since 1960, when 610 heads of household and but one widow described the community.[17]

Hamilton Park's occupational categories for the gainfully employed (that is, heads of household other than those describing themselves as having no occupation, as retired, or as students) remained remarkably stable over the years. In 1970, 38.4 percent were unskilled manual laborers; in 1960, the number was 40 percent. In 1970, 7.3 percent were in the upper-professional and managerial group, compared with 7.4 percent in 1960. In 1970, 4.4 percent were in the lower-professional and managerial ranks, a slight increase over the 4 percent in 1960. The most significant growth involved the proprietors: 2.8 percent in 1960; 6.1 percent in 1970. Other comparisons, by category, are semiskilled manual labor, 21.4 percent in 1960, 17.6 percent in 1970; domestic and food service, 7.7 percent in 1960, 6.4 percent in 1970; upper-level manual labor, 3.5 percent in 1960, 5.6 percent in 1970; public safety and other service, 0.8 percent in 1960, 1.2 percent in 1970; and lower-nonmanual, 12.5 percent in 1960, 12.8 percent in 1970.[18]

The picture of relative household stability had altered dramatically by 1980. In that year, 394 pioneer heads of household were still in the community—a decline of 84 in a decade. The percentage of pioneer heads dropped from 64.6 to 53.3. The number of widows rose to forty-five. Comparisons with Spring Valley Park hardly are helpful, because the formerly all-white neighborhood had become a turnstile or beachhead community, affected not only by the pressures of commercialization and improved housing elsewhere but also by its lack of easy intercommunication among streets—a positive feature of Hamilton Park. In Spring Valley Park a mere twenty-two of the original household heads remained, or 13.6 percent.[19]

A striking increase in retired household heads marked the graying of Hamilton Park's population. In 1960, one household head was listed as retired; this was a tiny 0.1 percent of all households. By 1970, the percentage of retirees had risen to 2.7; by 1980 it had reached 13.4. Five years later, in the midst of the Buyout, the 1970–1980 trend was intensifying: retiree heads accounted for 30.2 percent of all households. Only 287 of the original heads of household still lived in the community, a fall in five years from 53.3 to 38.8 percent. There was, of course, some compensation in terms of community consciousness in the rising number of widows: 71. In terms of the occupational standing of the gainfully employed, the community's stability continued. The 1980 percentage of unskilled manual laborers, 35.1, was virtually unchanged in 1985 at 35.7. The percentage in the upper-professional and managerial category slipped slightly, from 7.4 to 6.2, but lower-professionals and managers increased from 6.8 percent to 9.6. Other percentages changed little from those of 1980, which were not significantly different from the 1970 percentages. The apparent stability masked a relative decline, because Hamilton Park did not attract the rising generation of affluent blacks. The increase in heads of household reporting no occupation, even though some were no doubt working, was also disquieting. That percentage, 4.2 in 1960, drifted up to 4.7 in 1970; it then rose to 9.8 in 1980 and to 13.3 in 1985.[20]

People who moved from Hamilton Park did not necessarily tie their departures to their immediate economic circumstances. Nor did they abandon Hamilton Park. George Brewer left in 1964 to take a pastorate at the St. Mark's United Methodist Church in Lockhart, some thirty miles south of Austin. When he returned to Dallas, his church provided a parsonage, although he would have considered returning to his Hamilton Park house had he not sold it. In any event, he and his wife maintained their Hamilton Park friendships. Willie Smith, though steadily rising in his field of title work, did not move for strictly economic reasons. As early as the late 1960s and the rapid expansion of African-American housing opportunities in Dallas, he began looking for another house because of the early signs of the decline of the familial atmosphere in Hamilton Park. In response to the question of why he decided to leave, he said, "First and foremost, I think, the family was beginning to break up." In 1969 he bought a lot in nearby Northwood Estates, a newer housing development soon to be racially integrated; still, he was reluctant to move. But in 1972, the Nixon administration ordered a price freeze and Smith decided to build before the administration lifted the freeze and a new round of inflation set in. He moved into his new and substantially larger house in 1973. However, his ties to Hamilton Park remained.[21]

Others moved because they wanted larger houses and the resale value of extensive improvements was problematic. Myra Christian described her house in Northwood Estates as "2,400 square feet, four bedrooms and two and a half baths, living room and dining room, den, big kitchen, morning room, breakfast room, utility on the back . . . double garage in the back." In contrast, "I just had three bedrooms in Hamilton Park, and a little kitchen and a bath and a living room about the size of the breakfast area over here." Adding on to the Hamilton Park house would have robbed the backyard of too much space. Besides, a friend who expanded her house "almost put as much money into the addition as I did in building a whole house." Mrs. Christian continued to work in her beauty parlor in Hamilton Park, severing no ties with the community. Thelma Wells moved in 1979 to a larger house in a scenic section of Dallas's South Oak Cliff area because the family "needed more space. We had improved our house up to what I thought we could get, and I didn't want to overimprove it. . . . We had our three children, we had one bathroom and two bedrooms." The improvements to the Hamilton Park house included "central heat and air; and we had added a den, a utility room," aluminum siding and other improvements—"and it still was not satisfying us."[22]

Whatever the apparent or ascribed reasons for moving, a generation after its opening Hamilton Park no longer seemed adequate to some. Whatever their attachments to the community, residents had to weigh the advantages and disadvantages of remaining where they were, including the economic consequences of adding to a residence in an aging area of mostly small and unpretentious houses, against those of fresh job opportunities and the needs of growing families. There was also the question of status. The desire for a larger home in which to entertain expansively, to display furniture or art objects, to live less confined by small rooms, a restricted floor plan, and nearby neighbors, or to announce a level of economic achievement and security—all these are legitimate, even worthy, aspirations. Such aspirations are components of status. Neighborhood quality is one determinant of an individual's standing; therefore, it would be reasonable to assume that at least some moves to "better" houses and neighborhoods were at least partly motivated by status. As Zan Holmes aptly phrased it, Hamilton Park "was a launching pad for a lot of people. . . . That was the status thing—to be in Hamilton Park. But as our people prospered, and other areas developed where blacks could live, the big status thing then was to be able to leave Hamilton Park."[23]

Of course, not everybody in Hamilton Park expressed status by moving, or worried about expressing status. Many residents improved their homes and stayed, the most common alteration being central air-conditioning added to central heating or, in houses with wall-panel heaters, installation of window air-conditioning units. Many owners repainted exterior walls or trim in colors other than the original, or added siding. One popular structural change was converting the garage into a living room, dining room, or family room, as in the homes of William Edmond, Cicero Bruton, and Edward and Mary Newhouse. The garage conversions were sometimes combined with other alterations. Ona and Roscoe Smith converted their garage into a den, remodeled the kitchen, and added vinyl siding. Lapetta and U. J. Collier added a large, multipurpose room and a bath at the back of their house, doubling its size. Le Verne and Willis Fields added a den, a bedroom, and a bathroom, and also undertook extensive remodeling.[24]

By 1985, during the height of the Buyout frenzy, Hamilton Park had assumed the look of a mature community—an old one, by Dallas standards. There were the houses altered from the developer's floor plans; wide variations from the trim and siding that originally suggested the name, to outsiders, of "Easter egg houses" or "rainbow houses"; widely varied levels of house and yard maintenance; some homes bristling with security "burglar" bars; and trees grown to mature size. All these changes bespoke a different community than the Hamilton Park of thirty years before.[25]

The ten years from 1975 to 1985 witnessed intensive Civic League efforts to maintain, not the older uniformity but remembered standards of community pride, decorum, and maintenance. To that end, the league continued its committee structure, as well as its awards for the most attractive Christmas display and for best-kept lawns during the growing season. It circulated a newsletter with information about the community and exhortations against "deteriorating" housing. About 1980, Charles Smith noted some houses "in dire need of a paint job," and "window and screen repair." He also noted "wrecked automobiles and rubbish in yards." The league continued to sponsor the annual picnic in Willowdell Park. It encouraged residents to become active members at the annual dues rate of $6, an effort resulting in, for example, 241 paid memberships in 1983.[26]

Beyond exhortation and modest awards, the Civic League in extreme cases used coercion. In 1976, Smith supplied the area director of public works in Dallas with a list of "disabled automobiles"—twenty-eight junkers, all but three in front yards. Smith also supplied a list of street locations needing repair. He later described the city's cooperation in repairing streets and tagging, or towing, inoperable cars as "good." "When we sent them a list, they would clear it up for us." Poorly maintained houses became a problem as early as 1977. In that year Smith wrote to two absentee landlords about the condition of their property; one was deteriorating; the other, Smith charged, "is being used for an auto repair shop and parking lot." When Smith and others complained to the city, the district's council member replied that the poorly maintained house was "still substandard" despite spasmodic efforts to improve it, and its owner had been cited to appear in court "for violations of the housing code." Three inspections of the alleged illegal garage concluded that the resident "was working on his own cars, and he said that he did not ever work on cars belonging to others." The house eventually was improved but the auto-repair problem continued, "until, finally, the guy moved. That's the only thing that solved it."[27]

Other complaints highlight the Civic League's clearinghouse function. Members fed up with potholed streets, noise, or unsafe conditions brought their problems to league meetings. "That way not only would the president and the officers know," but the complainants would "know the community is aware and that it is concerned." Besides, "we always found we got better response when it was through an organization rather than through an individual lodging a complaint."[28]

A concern aired at the league's November 1983 meeting illustrates the sort of matter dealt with. Members complained about a loudspeaker on Galva Drive on the community's west side. A woman had been moved to found a church in her home and to share her nightly theological insights with her near neighbors, and some not so near, via the loudspeaker. "I could here it up here," Smith said of his house on the east side, over the low, north-south ridge dividing Galva from his house on Bellafonte Drive. Nearer neighbors were treated to a higher volume. "Every evening . . . we would get a free sermon. Well, not necessarily free. It was uninvited, I would say," Ruby Watson remembered. Her "neighbors all drove around and pinpointed it." Whether because of complaints from neighbors, trouble with the city, or the failure of Hamilton Park residents to flock to the raised religious banner, the offending sermons "finally ceased."[29]

By 1983, residents' concerns about increasing crime resulted in the league's promoting a Crime Watch program. On 14 May 1984 a police captain spoke to a league meeting about the crime problem and urged the marking of all personal property. In 1986, when two officers appeared at a league meeting, they offered a monthly computer printout of crime in the community, which they declared was a relatively low-crime area. The officers stressed the importance of home security. The police assurances that Hamilton Park was a low-crime area were only partly reassuring. "But, you know, if it's a low crime area, you'd rather have a no crime area," Smith said. Assaults, burglaries, and thefts led the monthly lists, with domestic quarrels also appearing (see chapter 10).[30]

The struggles against declining standards of maintenance, property use, and behavior, rising concern about criminal activity, and the accelerating property turnover strongly suggested that Hamilton Park was not the desirable residential community it once was. The suggestion would have been there, even had the community remained the "island" that it was in the late 1950s and early 1960s. But it had not. Increasingly crowded by commercial developments and busy roadways and losing pioneer residents to death or people moving out, the community was isolated by incompatible land uses as well as penetrated by air and noise pollution. Little wonder, then, that the Buyout generated so much interest, not to mention the lure of that minimum of $250,000 for every lot in Hamilton Park.

The Buyout was the result of not only the internal and external changes swirling around Hamilton Park but of the soaring land values of the early 1980s, when skyrocketing oil prices and voracious development seemed to herald a financially illimitable future. Even before the oil-patch boom of the 1980s, however, there had been rumors of a corporate, perhaps a TI, interest in the property. TI's interest was unlikely, given the company's substantial acreage and its policy of plant deconcentration, not to mention the high prices for land in Hamilton Park.[31]

A block party for residents during summer 1984 in the northeast corner of the community may have been the catalyst for developer and real-estate agent interest. The two residents who organized the party, small children when they moved to Hamilton Park, spoke to their parents and the other long-term residents about the need for care when selling their property. The remarks were brief and were not intended to promote concerted sales, nor to be the centerpiece of the party, but a reporter present emphasized them. Whether or not because of the publicity following the block party, a real-estate agent called Charles Smith "and said he was going to offer $75,000 to $80,000 for the homes." Smith "told him that the homes are worth much more than that—the property was—because of the location." The same or another agent may have leafleted the community or portions of it with a similar deal. In any case, Smith considered the offer "an insult." At about the same time, Willie Johnson said, "I was offered $125,000 from a real estate person" for her corner lot on Galva but "I just laughed at them and turned it down." Despite the rejections, the real-estate agent who contacted Smith told him, "I guess some people are going to sell."[32]

Smith took the issue to the executive committee of the Civic League, which decided to act in a deliberate, prudent manner. The committee made two fundamental decisions. First, it decided to work through an attorney rather than deal with developers directly. To that end, Smith appointed a "legal counsel committee" to request a résumé and an interview. The committee selected Reuben M. Ginsberg from among the candidates because of his experience in real estate and specifically because of his involvement in the Buyout of a small, semirural, incorporated area surrounded by nearby Richardson. The executive committee and later the Hamilton Park property owners ratified the choice.[33]

The second decision was to form a homeowners' association open to all the residential property owners. The homeowners' group would be represented by the attorney and would promote the twin notions of all property owners selling for a uniform price per square foot and of all property owners selling out at the same time. An executive board committee solicited $25 from each property owner who could be located. Not all of them contributed, but so many did that in November 1987, after the white heat of the Buyout had cooled and many of the attorney's fees and related expenses had been paid, the treasurer reported a balance of $5,606.47. The homeowners' group and the Civic League shared an identity, as suggested by the official name of the homeowners' group: the Hamilton Park Civic League Home Owners Association. Smith served as president of both groups. Except for a few association-called meetings at the school auditorium, the two groups met simultaneously, alternating between the Baptist and Methodist churches. At either type of meeting, Le Verne Fields, the Civic League secretary, kept the minutes. The only association officer not filling the same job in the Civic League was the treasurer, Pauline Dixon. The arrangement validated Smith's statement that the homeowners' association "was just a mind thing. It was just for the separation of the finances only."[34]

The homeowners' association surveyed property owners to ascertain how many would be willing to sell out and to have the homeowners' attorney represent them in the transaction. The group received some 450 positive replies by 21 January 1985. The response was far from unanimous, given the 742 lots in Hamilton Park, and 733 owners. Well before 21 January, Smith knew that the related ideas of one attorney representing all property owners and all property owners selling together at a fixed price would be difficult to sustain with near unanimity. In a circular letter to homeowners dated 15 October 1984 he had warned against residents becoming "excited," "emotionally charged," and swept along by "overnight committees" and "panic groups." He urged "calm heads and organized planning." Smith said that the panic groups were a few, relatively small clusters of property owners who had already decided that their lots were worth more than whatever a Civic League–mandated organization could secure for the mine run of properties in the community. He characterized their attitude as "if you sell, we'll hold out."[35]

For the time being, however, most residents were willing to allow the homeowners' association and Reuben Ginsberg to take the lead in fixing a standard price per square foot and finding a developer. When Ginsberg informed the property owners that he was ready to solicit bids from developers, the homeowners' meeting of 19 February 1985 had to pick a price. By a rising vote, the property owners settled on a minimum price of $35 per square foot. As experience and hindsight would show, the price was prohibitively high, yet it was not irrationally or arbitrarily chosen.[36]

Any statement about the relatively high price of the lots must consider that the property owners knew, or should have known, the range of prices in the Hamilton Park area. In a newspaper article some two weeks before the 19 February meeting, Thelma Self, a second-generation Hamilton Park resident as well as an independent real-estate agent active in the Buyout, was quoted as saying that houses sold for $50,000 to $60,000, or some $6 or $7 per square foot for the average-size lot. These were residential prices, of course. All of Hamilton Park, she continued, "would sell for the right price, and the only way to get a right price is to sell to a commercial developer." Mrs. Self said that bidding should begin at $25 a foot. Before the vote on the asking price, she responded to a question about market prices, saying that current prices for property along North Central Expressway, I-635, and Forest Lane ranged from $27 to $60 per square foot. But these prices were for properties fronting on the expressway, the freeway, or on heavily traveled, commercialized Forest Lane. Residential Hamilton Park enjoyed openings to the freeway access road, to Forest Lane, and to Floyd Road, but only eight house lots adjoined Forest Lane at Schroeder. It should have been evident to the property owners, therefore, that their properties were less valuable than those in prime positions. Mrs. Self had given a *range* of prices, and the top price of $60 a foot should have been understood as the maximum for strategic land under highly speculative, boom conditions.[37]

A member of the Civic League had already declared at the same meeting that $35 a foot would bring $262,500 for a lot of 7,500 square feet. After listening to all the information, the property owners voted for that amount, voting at the same time to approve the wording of Ginsberg's circular letter to developers. The decision for a high price may be justified in two ways. First, although the oil-patch boom would soon collapse, its impending demise was not as evident in February 1985 as it would be a few months later. Therefore, a belief that February prices would soon be exceeded and $35 come to seem a bargain was not so outlandish. Second, the price of $35 was not necessarily decided by market conditions. It was, instead, the price at which most property owners were willing to face the disruptions, expenses, and anxieties of forsaking an old, settled community with all its attachments and seeking a new neighborhood.[38]

The majority, of course, agreed with the twin principles of the homeowners' association: presenting a united front and selling for the uniform price of $35 a square foot. Interviewees who favored the idea of a common effort did not comment fully on their support, but its sources are evident. A uniform price would help create cohesion, reduce the rumors of high-priced spot buying of individual properties, lessen the chances of holdout owners achieving higher prices, and comport with the City of Dallas policy requiring a high percentage of property owners in a residential neighborhood to agree to sell before the planning and zoning commission assented to a change in land use. At the least, a uniform price should have produced neighborliness, but, as will be seen, it did not always do so. Interviewees were definite, however, about the potential benefits of selling out at $35 a foot. Pearline Proctor "thought I could have taken care of myself the rest of my life on that if I managed right." William Edmond believed in trying for "the best deal you can, but if $35 is the best deal you can get, you ought to get it." Albertus Edley was without "sentimental values. I was looking at the market and a big profit" that would have fulfilled his dream of a "big home."[39]

Property owners who believed that $35 a foot was a barely sufficient or an insufficient price should have been sobered by the response to Ginsberg's letter to developers. The attorney's circular explained that development around Hamilton Park had undermined its value as "a single-family neighborhood." Ginsberg stated his belief that if "a majority" sold to a developer, "all the other owners would follow suit" and that it was "very likely" that the RISD, the city, and the churches would sell their property as well. Ginsberg offered to write a contract between the developer and each owner, but issued two warnings. The owners, he suggested, could vary in "needs, desires, and objectives." His second caution dealt directly with the issues of unanimity and price. "If you are unwilling to consider the acquisition of the entire subdivision" at a minimum of $35 per foot, he wrote, "please feel free to disregard this information, since I will not consider any proposals for less than such amount."[40]

On 26 February 1985, Ginsberg sent the letter to thirty-one developers, including such major players of the boom era as Cadillac Fairview, Folsom Investments, Lincoln Property Company, H. Ross Perot, the Vantage Companies, and the Trammel Crow Company. The silence of the response to $35 a foot was deafening, although at the 16 April meeting, Smith and Mrs. Self reported that some developers had expressed an interest but had made "only small bids." Smith remembered that the limited interest was in effect "no response. Then we just figured it wouldn't go . . . because we were asking a minimum of $35."[41]

That was when William E. Hamilton, the principal of the Hamilton Financial Group, met the minimum offer. Hamilton, in letters dated 25 April, offered to purchase the community at $35 a square foot, a price grossing the owners of the smallest lots about $250,000. Negotiations followed about details of the terms between Hamilton and Ginsberg, with Ginsberg taking matters to the executive board of the homeowners' association, then reporting to Hamilton on any changes in his initial letter that would be required before the attorney and the executive board would accept them. Ginsberg's letters exhibited candor and caution. He advised Smith that no homeowner should make any irrevocable financial commitment based on the sale. During the negotiations with Hamilton, he warned the developer that he would have to approve any letters of intent to sell in advance of their distribution to the homeowners, or he would oppose them. He left no doubt that Hamilton would have to, at some future time, reveal the company or individual that he represented. Hamilton's later refusal to do so was the rock on which the Buyout broke. On the other hand, Ginsberg suggested that if a rephrasing of the proposed contract severely limited the purchaser's right to reject the sale of any or all lots, then a high percentage of homeowners probably would sign a letter of intent, "although," he added carefully, "I do not know this to be the case."[42]

On 23 May, Hamilton met with the 700-plus property owners, the interested, and the curious who jammed the school auditorium. The real-estate investor outlined the terms of the sale but refused to name the party or parties behind him. "We represent a developer who is not Dallas based and whose identity won't be revealed until contracts are ready to be signed," he informed the crowd. After the meeting he told the media that the offer of $35 was "extreme," because many current sales in the area were made at $24. He did not know the developer's plans, he said, but they would have to involve "a high-rise office development to justify the price." From then until March 1986, the Buyout drew increasing numbers of property owners into the net. By 4 August 1985, 523 of 733 owners had signed letters of intent to sell. Ultimately, Ginsberg had in hand 586 contracts out of 736 parcels, the number varying because of ownership changes. Hamilton received another twenty-nine contracts from property owners who were working with real-estate agents or attorneys other than Ginsberg. The 615 contracts represented 83.6 percent of the property owners, or more than the 80 percent required under a city policy designed to protect residential neighborhoods from raiding redevelopers who wished to rezone small packages of choice lots.[43]

The final contract terms were close to those that Hamilton had announced at the beginning. He agreed to buy all the lots offered, although he could refuse to buy them all because of defective titles to any of the properties. For ninety days after the closing, each property owner had the option to purchase the house for $10 and eleven months to remove it at the owner's risk and expense without damage to the lot or its trees and shrubs. A lot owner could lease the property back from Hamilton for ten months by paying $1 a month, assuming all risks and repairs, and exposing the new owner to no liability. Among the conditions was the buyer's right to decide if he were offered enough lots to make development feasible; another was the buyer's obligation to make an earnest-money deposit with the title company of 5 percent of the entire purchase price. When Hamilton accepted the properties, or when he assigned the contract to a third party, he had to reveal the name and financial standing of his backer to Smith and Ginsberg.[44]

While Hamilton, his attorney, Ginsberg, and the homeowners' association struggled with successive drafts of the letter of intent and the contract, emotions reached hurricane force. Rumors flew. At the February 1985 meeting, Smith had responded to a question about "spot buying" by urging all homeowners to "stick together as a group" and sell out in one package to prevent spot buying. The next month Smith put down a rumor that the Southland Corporation, then the parent company of the 7-Eleven convenience stores, was buying the north end of the community, from Campanella to Bunche.[45]

Smith, an island of calm in the storm of rumor, could pacify people at the meetings of the homeowners/Civic League. He "was very relaxing, and he didn't get upset. He was in control, and he would let people talk. Then he would tell them the way it is." But neither Smith nor anyone else could down the emotionalism surging through the community. Some property owners, convinced that the Buyout was on the near horizon, made only the most necessary home repairs and had stopped doing the meticulous yard work that was the hallmark of the early Hamilton Park. In April 1985, Smith warned against neighborhood neglect and pointed out that the purchase could be delayed for a year or longer. He remembered that "a lot of people then began to think that they were gone, so started letting the property go and not doing anything to keep it up. We knew that this wasn't the way it should be because the deal hadn't been consummated yet." Other emotions revolved around leaving the community, even among those willing to go. "It was nerve-wracking, to think that you were going to uproot," Ona Smith said. Looking at other houses, so many that "I can almost pass a house and tell what the floor plan is like," was a "very emotional" experience. "I guess you would have to be involved in something like that to realize what it takes. It disrupts your life." The media contributed to the "constant pressure. You had to live with that."[46]

Real-estate agents, anxious for relocation sales or for representing the sale of Hamilton Park property, bombarded owners with newsletters, flyers, personal visits, and statements to homeowners' meetings. A few agents, as well as a few property owners, held seminars on financial subjects such as selling and buying real estate, investing, and personal money management. Some of these were legitimate business activities. The seminar sponsored by Margaret Stevenson, a Hamilton Park pioneer, and the real-estate newsletters from resident Thelma Self and from Hendry & Associates were useful, factual, and free from exaggeration. Other presentations, while not unlawful, departed from the best ethical standard. One flyer flaunting capital letters urged property owners to join the "Hamilton Park Residents Relocation Program" for $149 a year for a "one year family membership." The benefits of this "relocation club" were those offered elsewhere without charge: access to house listings, a broker's assistance, and a financial-planning seminar. Other inducements included a drawing for a "free full length mink coat" and reduced prices on fur coats and jewelry. Some agents allegedly persuaded residents to whom they showed houses to sign contracts contingent upon the sale of their Hamilton Park property, itself a legitimate arrangement, but tied the contingent sale to the agent's handling both properties. That would have earned the agent 6 percent of the price of both transactions—a comfortable sum. As Thelma Self told a meeting of homeowners, it was cheaper to have Ginsberg handle the sale of their Hamilton Park property than to retain an agent at the standard 6 percent commission.[47]

It helped to have a detached, even cynical view of the entire proceeding. "It was totally chaotic; it was like a circus," Sadye Gee remembered.

Another Transition and the Buyout

"The realtors were just like little hound dogs, just running here, there, and everywhere. I ignored them all." Of the real-estate agents' efforts, she said, "I received U.S. mail, I received flyers, I received telephone calls galore—all encouraging us to select them as our financial planner, planning ahead, relocating our home for us, and all of that combined. We even had seminars. Seminars were held on how to plan your future and your money. And," she added with a laugh, "what money?"[48]

Freddie Nance "never did really believe it that we were going to sell." The efforts of the real-estate agents, she thought, were the "biggest bunch of malarkey. I wouldn't even come to the door when I saw them coming." Curtis Smith thought little of the Buyout at first but attended some meetings later, signing the letter of intent and the contract. The issues of the Buyout "didn't bother me very much"; he and his wife had purchased a retirement home. For Curtis Smith, the major advantage of the Buyout, had it "materialized," was that it would have solved the problem of the disposition of his Hamilton Park house. He would have invested the bulk of his proceeds. Vivian Starks signed a contract for a town house in San Francisco, but made certain that it was a contingency contract. She got her money back when the Buyout collapsed.[49]

Not surprisingly, the question of the fairness of Hamilton's offer of $35 a square foot kindled some of the deepest emotions, especially because at least some of the holdout owners believed the community, or part of it, to be worth more. Laurice Stevenson believed that, if property generally was worth $35, some strategically located lots nearer Forest Lane were undervalued at that price. A belief that $35 was inadequate was often mixed with other concerns. Stevenson also believed that Hamilton should have been more open and candid with the homeowners. Sadye Gee was unimpressed by the prospect of money because of a strong attachment to the community. "I came here to be buried from this spot," she declared. "It's easier to be poor than it is to have some money to be managed by somebody else." Lapetta Collier was not interested in selling because she feared a surge in house prices when hundreds of Hamilton Park homeowners threw themselves on the real-estate market at once. Besides, "at our age it wasn't feasible to take up house payments again." The Colliers had just completed additions to their home and there was an illness in the family. Moreover, they knew a man who had sold some property for which he received a partial payment; the new owner could not continue payments on his debt. The man's property was returned, but he owed taxes on it and found it unsalable. The Colliers wanted no part of any similar transaction. Freddie Allen objected to what he believed was the coercive atmosphere and herd mentality of the mass meetings.[50]

Lurking not so far beneath the surface of some of the skepticism and refusals to deal was a knowledge of the history of savvy but unprincipled whites bilking blacks out of real estate or other valuable property. "I was reminded of the Depression years in East Texas, when they found oil on the blacks' property, and they would dangle cash . . . maybe $700 in cash: 'This is what we'll give you if you will sign these papers,'" said Sadye Gee. "There are oil wells pumping in the front yards of many of the residents in Tyler, I know, and the people get no money whatsoever. I remembered that." Marion Mitchell recalled how a white-owned corporation purchasing land from African-American owners in Dallas retained "another buyer to front for them in buying it." Hamilton was white, the parties he may have been representing were presumed white, and, for that matter, the community's attorney was white.[51]

There was no doubt that arguments over price stirred the deepest emotions. When the Colliers' refusal to agree to sell became known, Lapetta Collier remembered, "one man told my husband he was stupid, that that would be more money than he ever had in his life." Rumors about spot, speculative sales flew through the community. "And even we were accused of having sold," Mrs. Gee said. Albertus Edley remembered a lot of "bickering" over all the issues raised, but especially about price. There were "a lot of discussions, and friendships were lost." The disagreements helped to encourage the tentative organization of an alternate homeowners' group, the Hamilton Park Development Association. The group held a few meetings in 1985 and drew up "articles of agreement." Its members soon discovered, however, that its operating expenses would be high; shortly thereafter "it fizzled out."[52]

Some of the media and real-estate agents poured oil on the flames of emotion. The extensive newspaper coverage was generally well balanced, but television interviews with residents focused on the question of an individual's selling or not selling, giving the impression that some sort of sale would take place. The interviews, shown all over the city, intensified the excitement. "When you'd see your friends, or go visit somewhere, they were asking you a lot of questions," Ona Smith recalled. "That can be a lot of wear and tear on a body." While some real-estate agents behaved professionally, others held out unrealistic hopes for higher prices. One of the agents passing out business cards at the initial meeting with Hamilton said he believed the offer of $35 to be too low. Among the flurry of letters from agents was one urging property owners to "market all properties as a package, at a tremendously higher price." A justification for that statement was that there was "nowhere in the area that property can be purchased for $35 per square foot"—an assertion that flew in the face of all other price quotations. "The developer has come to the residents with what he wants to pay for the land," the letter continued, ignoring the fact that the residents, not Hamilton, had set the price.[53]

The reality of the collapse of oil-boom prices set in soon enough. As early as the June 1985 Civic League meeting, Vivian Starks, a *Wall Street Journal* subscriber, noted that the economy was "going down every day." By the contract's execution date of 6 January 1986 there was in fact no closing, in part because of the increasingly unjustifiable price of $35, in part because Hamilton had not then secured all of the properties he deemed desirable or essential. At the Civic League meeting of 28 January, he asked for a thirty-day extension of the contract, but refused to name the developer he represented, which the spirit of the contract, if not its letter, required him to do. A majority of the property owners voted to grant the extension on Hamilton's terms. They required him, however, to reveal the potential purchaser at the expiration of the extension. Hamilton in effect had practically a two-month extension, because the league skipped its February meeting, "pending decision on contracts." At the 18 March meeting, Ginsberg told the property owners that Hamilton refused to name his backers and the deal was off.[54]

Speculation then centered on whether the property owners had made the correct decision by forcing Hamilton's hand. A substantial minority disagreed, on the grounds that it made no difference who the developers were, as long as they were willing to put up the escrow money and go to closing for the properties. On the other hand, the Buyout had run on for more than a year, Hamilton's first proposal dated from May 1985, and prices had skidded since then. Given the precariousness of the situation, a bona fide buyer could have saved it by revealing his identity. Perhaps the refusal to reveal was the best way for Hamilton to end an untenable arrangement.[55]

Speculation was also rife about the developer behind Hamilton, if indeed there was one. Richard Bonner heard that Canadian buyers were interested but that "something happened in Canada or something happened here with our economy," other than the end of the oil-patch boom, "that just shut it down." Another possibility was the ever-present

TI. Then there were those who believed that Hamilton was representing no one but himself, in the hope that he would assemble a package attractive to a large developer.[56]

It is equally possible that he did have a developer lined up and was assured a participation in the redevelopment of Hamilton Park, provided he could commit the necessary property. That situation would help explain his frustration. He said that the properties he failed to secure "were scattered all over and would not have allowed us to close off a single street." Of course the developers could have replatted some streets, but at an expense piled on top of a price per foot that appeared less and less palatable. A few holdout lots were, therefore, strategically essential to Hamilton's redevelopment plan. Had the boom times continued, or had the homeowners' price been at the market price instead of well above it, a few holdouts could have received more for their key properties, despite all the pieties about selling together at a uniform price. But the boom collapsed, and the price was too high to bear the weight of still more expensive parcels. It is also very likely that, had the deal gone through, those holdouts who owned nonstrategic property would have been left in their houses indefinitely, contemplating the destruction of their community. They would also, probably, have suffered the paradoxical plight of crowding from new commercial development while living in virtually unsalable houses. Few homeseekers would want to buy residences so situated, and developers would be uninterested in purchasing at commercial prices until they had developable properties committed, their financing lined up, and preliminary plans made. Depending on circumstances, any additional redevelopment could have required years, perhaps decades, to mature.[57]

What is certain is that the Buyout failed. The failure was in no way the fault of Ginsberg, who represented Hamilton Park fairly and fully. The attorney frequently appeared before Civic League meetings, answering questions carefully and completely. His clients understood that. At the end of the Buyout trail, after he had announced Hamilton's refusal to name his developer, the property owners gave Ginsberg a standing ovation.[58]

Naturally, there was disappointment among those who hoped to sell. Pearline Proctor would have missed her neighbors but hoped they could relocate close to one another. Others, including Ocie Turner, had houses, or at least neighborhoods, picked out. Still others were ready to leave a community, however historic, that was in decline. Richard Bonner, the owner of two houses in Hamilton Park and the joint owner of a third, spoke to that sentiment. "Being in history is fine," he said, "but being wealthy, I think, is better."[59]

The Buyout would never have occurred had it not been for changes within Hamilton Park, and especially the rampant commercial growth around it. Its failure was symptomatic of a late boom phenomenon— hopes for high land prices maturing at the peak of a speculative frenzy. In retrospect, the price of $35 a square foot was too high. But the price was never intended to reflect the market; rather, it was set to encourage a high percentage of property owners to commit to a sale. The price was intended to cover the considerable costs of relocation, the purchase of a new home and its maintenance, operation, and taxes, all the while leaving, perhaps, a little nest egg. Circumstances could have merged the market price and the asking price, but they did not. Instead, the Buyout left each property owner to wrestle with difficult questions, including each owner's view of the past, and the future, of Hamilton Park.

10

A MATURE COMMUNITY AND ITS MEANING

Physical change and emotional currents swept over Hamilton Park in the 1980s, but in at least one matter nothing changed: the community continued to vote Democratic and to support the Democratic Party. In 1980, the Interorganizational Council (IOC) asked for financial support to send Esther Lee Harris, the precinct chair, to the Democratic National Convention in New York. The party renominated Jimmy Carter and his vice-president, Walter Mondale. Four years later, the IOC again endorsed the Democratic slate, but again had no luck with its leading candidates: Ronald Reagan and George Bush swamped Mondale and the first major-party woman vice-presidential candidate, Geraldine Ferraro. The Mondale-Ferraro ticket did, of course, carry Hamilton Park. Lloyd Doggett, the Democratic candidate for the U.S. Senate, fell before Phil Gramm, although he, too, won in Hamilton Park.[1]

Hamilton Park voters sometimes fared better in local or state elections, as when, in 1987, the community supported Annette Strauss, the victorious mayoral candidate. In 1990, Hamilton Park delivered 938 votes for Ann Richards, the successful gubernatorial candidate, compared with 121 for her Republican opponent.[2]

As the varied votes suggest, the Hamilton Park of the Buyout and post-Buyout era was by no means trapped in stagnation or decline. "We've always squealed, and we've gotten the grease," Charles Smith said. The continued improvement of Willowdell Park, culminating in the construction of the Willie B. Johnson Recreation Center, is a case in point.[3]

The Civic League had pressured the city to build a recreation center in the park for years. The city included a center for Willowdell Park in a successful 1978 bond package, but two years later the park board had not acted, claiming that inflation had rendered the planned center impossible to build. Charles Smith implored the board to act, to provide a place for teenagers, older residents, and "young families with small school age children" to spend time in constructive activities; to reach community centers in other parks, Hamilton Park residents had to carpool, and in any case, they were treated "as out-siders" when they arrived.[4]

A year later, the city added to the bond provision; then in 1983 accepted a low bid of $488,000 for two buildings: one, a covered gymnasium; the other, a multiuse building. The city organized a groundbreaking ceremony at the site, on the higher ground at the park's north end. Thirty-eight people, including three reporters and three photographers, dignitaries from the city and the park board, and community leaders watched as Willie B. Johnson turned over the first shovelful of earth. The sixty-nine-year-old matriarch was within sight of one of her community goals—a recreation center for Hamilton Park.[5]

While the center was building, the Civic League began a campaign, including a petition drive, to name the center for Mrs. Johnson. Working the late shift at Parkland Hospital during Hamilton Park's early years gave the licensed vocational nurse time during the day for community programs. She retired from nursing but her zest for involvement was undiminished. Charles Smith wrote, when nominating her for an unrelated honor, of twelve separate activities in which she was involved, many of them continuous and coincidental. One of the achievements Smith cited—securing a left-turn lane and signal at newly widened Forest Lane to enable eastbound traffic to turn north on Schroeder Road—typified Mrs. Johnson's determination. She remembered that "we'd have to stand there sometimes ten or fifteen minutes to come off Forest Lane to get into Hamilton Park." So she telephoned, then "went downtown two or three times before I got that light. I'd go to their meetings. . . . I asked questions." Her efforts paid off. "She is persistent," Smith said, "and she just worried the city traffic department until we got a turn signal." She was involved with people, too, as one who "seems to attract people to her because she's always concerned. . . . She's the kind of person that will get you some help if there is any way in the world possible to get it—she'll get it for you."[6]

Mrs. Johnson was a tireless advocate for a community center, an indication of her concern for the people of Hamilton Park. "Her crusade is known to many at City Hall," Sadye Gee wrote in 1983. She had urged "city officials since she became a resident of Hamilton Park almost thirty years ago, to erect a recreation building on the park to save the children of the community." In March 1984, the Civic League forwarded its request to name the center for Mrs. Johnson. The park staff submitted the request to its board, which approved it and passed it along to the city council. The council unanimously added its approval on 24 October 1984. On 2 December, the parks and recreation department held an hour-long dedication ceremony, followed by a reception. Mrs. Johnson was the center of attention in a ceremony that included a recitation of the Pledge of Allegiance by the third-grade class of the Hamilton Park School. The youngsters she had taken to other parks because Willowdell lacked a recreation center had long since grown to adulthood.[7]

The center quickly became a focus of community life, providing meeting rooms for the Civic League and the local chapter of the American Association of Retired Persons (AARP), sponsoring a dance for Ethiopian relief, organizing bus trips to the State Fair of Texas and to the Louisiana Downs racetrack, and overseeing the annual Juneteenth celebration. Juneteenth, originally a Texas festival, recalled 19 June 1865, the date when federal troops at Galveston issued an order enforcing the Emancipation Proclamation in Texas. In 1987, Mrs. Johnson, the grand marshal, rode at the head of the Willie B. Johnson Recreation Center Juneteenth parade.[8]

The Civic League maintained its traditional activities, although with a slowly declining membership in the years following the Buyout. It attracted "very few" younger people, but continued to report code violations to the city and to work with elected officials to control that perennial problem, the flooding of Cottonwood Creek. The summer lawn-beautification awards also continued. An indication of the organization's graying was its abandonment of the annual picnic in favor of an adults-only reception, beginning in 1988.[9]

Denominational changes in Hamilton Park reflected in part the massive growth around the community. Hamilton Park First Baptist Church grew over the years to 2,500 members, too many for the Bunche Drive sanctuary to accommodate, even after a substantial reconstruction. In 1986, the church moved to a large building in Richardson, the former First Baptist Church of Richardson, while another Baptist congregation took over the Bunche structure. The congregation retained its name, Hamilton Park First Baptist Church, but its physical association with the community was lost. Earlier, the Church of Christ moved from its small, tile-block building to another North Dallas location. The church grew from some fifty to "over a thousand members." "Most of the people are not from Hamilton Park."[10]

Of the original congregations, in 1990 only the Hamilton Park United Methodist Church remained. In 1979 it launched a three-year construction program, in addition to purchasing the more than three acres to the west of its site, the arena for the fight over the lumber yard (see chapter 9). In 1980, it opened its new sanctuary. The next year it established Harambee House, "an activity center for older adults," in a satellite building. As its membership grew, so did its activities and committee structure. Its day-care center was licensed to supervise one hundred children. The Helping Hand Committee organized to assist needy persons on a short-term basis. Its expanding role was another indication of demographic change. At first confined to assisting church members, it widened its outreach to include first Hamilton Park and then all areas sharing the community's zip code. Some donations in later years went to charity organizations working in Dallas and beyond. But the church changed no more radically than its membership. Of the 1,602 members whose street addresses were available in 1991, only 319 lived in Hamilton Park.[11]

Change occurred within the community. The 1990 census recorded 117 single-parent families, more than the 86 of 1980 and more than a two-thirds increase over the 70 female heads of household recorded in the 1970 census. By contrast, Spring Valley Park's 20 of 1970, rose to 36 in 1980, then dropped to 14 in 1990.[12] The 1990 percentages confirmed the difference: 9.4 percent of Hamilton Park's households were female-headed, 5.9 percent of Spring Valley's.

At the same time, the number of pioneer heads of household had eroded from 1985's 287 to 199. The count of widows of pioneer household heads rose from 71 to 77 in the intervening five years. However, Hamilton Park remained cohesive by comparison with Spring Valley Park, where but 18 pioneers and 2 pioneer widows lived. Hamilton Park was becoming a geriatric community—an expected development given its relatively large number of aging pioneers. Retirees headed 38.6 percent of the households. The percentages of pioneers were 26.9 for Hamilton Park, a fading 11.1 for Spring Valley Park.[13]

Not surprisingly, echoes of the Buyout reverberated through the changing community. In 1989, property owners received a contingent offer of $30 per square foot, provided enough of them showed interest, but nothing came of it. In 1991, Thelma Self, a real-estate agent who was active in the Buyout, asked property owners for an expression of willingness to sell. A sufficient number of interested owners, she wrote, would prompt a search for a buyer at a price of between $18 and $24. Nothing conclusive developed from Mrs. Self's feeler.[14]

Property values also echoed the Buyout. In 1990, the mean value of Hamilton Park residential property was $56,731. Forty-two comparable properties in Spring Valley Park had a mean value of $58,125. The great difference was in the value of the lots. In Hamilton Park, where a developer had sought the land, the lots were almost always assessed at $34,000, whereas a typical Spring Valley lot was listed at less than half that taxable value.[15]

A development coincident with the Buyout demonstrated how the Buyout could have moved rapidly to a settlement, and how it could have eventually collapsed. It involved the "Fields houses," seven homes on the west side of Schroeder between Willowdell and the junction with Bunche. The houses, owned by members of a prominent black family and some relatives, predated Hamilton Park and were not part of the community, but four of them faced the west side of the school campus across Schroeder. They were the site of an effort to introduce a clutch of mini-warehouses in 1977, an effort that failed in the face of the Civic League's determined opposition.[16]

In 1985, a developer asked to rezone the Fields property to permit the construction of a luxury, high-rise hotel. As part of a package the corporation arranged with the city, access to the hotel grounds would be gained via Churchill Way from the west. The city would seek state funds to bridge North Central Expressway, bringing Churchill Way into the area. Schroeder Road, increasingly a north-south thoroughfare, would be closed north of Campanella Drive, and south of Churchill Way, extended. The north end of the south portion of Schroeder would be reshaped into a cul-de-sac. Schroeder would then become strictly a residential street from the cul-de-sac south to the Methodist church and shopping center. Residents and businesses to the north would be able to use the northern part of Schroeder-Churchill, or other streets in Hamilton Park, for ingress and egress. The plan would have clipped off 3.47 little-used acres at the north end of Willowdell Park and incorporated them into the new arrangement. The property was purchased and the houses moved. Then the deal collapsed. The Fields family members were paid, of course, but the property itself lay undeveloped and unsalable for several years.[17]

Through all the changes, Hamilton Park remained, pressed closely by the commercial-industrial world around it. The ever-present TI continued to be a source of concern for some pioneer residents. They wondered aloud about TI's industrial emissions and their relation to high rates of kidney failure and cancer in the community, as well as to paint damage and a strange, white film on automobiles. There was, to be sure, no evidence whatever of TI's complicity in any of it. Moreover, TI continued to be a good neighbor, conforming to all its agreements with the community as well as generously providing critical right-of-way for the extension of Campanella Drive to Floyd Road. It continued to keep Hamilton Park residents informed of its plans; it responded to another problem when a string of self-storage units and a chain-link fence blocked an informal entrance to the community over Hallum Street. Then some persistent drivers crossed a field that TI owned, dropping mud and debris in the alley behind Hallum. Residents of the immediate area complained to TI and the company put up a fence, leaving a space wide enough for a person to walk through but too narrow for a vehicle. Some problems with other commercial neighbors had no solution. On the west side of the community, a nearby office tower cast brilliant reflections into several Hamilton Park homes, unwelcome reminders of the sea of change around the residential island.[18]

Pioneer residents continued to deplore many of the transformations within Hamilton Park, problems involving property deterioration, a decline in standards of behavior and political interest, and crime. The latter included theft, burglary, the random violence of drive-by shootings, and drug use, an acknowledged breeder of violence and crime. Falling standards of property maintenance concerned many interviewees. Some blamed the situation on a growing number of newer, less-interested, less-involved owners, or renters and indifferent landlords. "I think the neighborhood is now going downhill because of the rent houses," said one. Originally, another remarked, those who "moved out here were . . . glad to have a clean place to go, a clean neighborhood. They took pride in their lawns and everything. But when the second owners come along, or the third owners, or when it starts to be rent property, then it goes down." A third complained about "a lot of" unkempt houses and yards. "I guess the original owners sold to somebody else who is not that interested. We have a lot of rent houses." The perception that there were a large number of rental properties was historically correct, but perhaps was overdrawn, considering Hamilton Park's later, relatively close-in location making it desirable rental property. In 1960, there were but 7 renter heads of household in the community. The number soared in the 1960s to 52, but climbed slowly in the 1970s to 61. Then it leapt again in the 1980s, reaching 95 renters in 1990. Even then, the renters lived in but 13.2 percent of the total occupied units. The Hamilton Park situation of 1990 compares favorably with that of Spring Valley Park, where rental houses were 56 of 234 occupied units, or 23.9 percent. Nevertheless, the situation had changed radically from the 1950s, when all pioneer residents were required to be homeowners.[19]

The aging of the pioneer population also was seen as affecting upkeep. A widow remarked, "I guess, too, we're older. I don't have a husband now to do my yard." Another pioneer added, "The older we get, a lot of times we don't keep up property, and I think I'm one of them. We let things run down." Another pioneer, speaking of the first generation, said, "People are tired, and nobody takes care of one thing. They're not altogether sick, but they're just by themselves, quite a few of them, and they are just kind of tired." In the 1980s, the city conducted code-violation "sweeps" through many neighborhoods, including, in 1986, Hamilton Park. Charles Smith believed that the sweeps "made a difference" in the overall maintenance in the community.[20]

Others linked community problems to more recent beliefs in personal irresponsibility. Several complaints about "residents and visitors," at two addresses causing "a nuisance, especially in the evenings and on weekends, with loud music, profanity, drinking, etc." did not involve renters but property owners and their guests. One pioneer vigorously denounced "all this running up and down the alleys . . . noise going all night long . . . four or five cars being worked on. They're not doing it with the automobile radios shut off. Every damn radio was turned on as loud as you can get." Another interviewee recalled the front doorbell ringing after midnight. Concealing a pistol, the householder opened the door and confronted a young man who asked for $5. The young man, known to the householder, was told to "get moving." The third command to leave was reinforced by a display of the pistol. Then "that little monkey jumped off my porch, and he ran up the street." A third pioneer censured "the attitudes" of neighbors who lacked "respect for themselves" and who failed to develop "their children's respect for others. You look at all that[,] and think about that young dude out there, fifteen or sixteen, sitting on a car and drinking a can of beer. I can't handle it. He's got a home to drink the beer in, and I think that's where he ought to drink it. You can't say anything because the daddy was sitting out there that evening and doing the same darn thing." In the opinion of this interviewee, "I don't think the house maintenance has run down as much as the personal responsibilities have."[21]

The rising incidence of crimes against property worried the original residents, especially when contrasted with the halcyon days of early Hamilton Park. "Our garage door stayed open," said one. "We never let the garage door down unless we were going out of town." Asked if it would be possible in 1990 to leave the garage door open, the pioneer replied, "I wouldn't dare leave it open. We had our lawn equipment in a storage shed in the back. It was locked." Thieves used a bolt cutter on the heavy, locked chain, then stole the lawn-care items and bicycles. "Now that's the difference. We used to leave it in the garage with the door open, in plain view. It was locked and out of view and still stolen." Many interviewees knew of similar incidents, including house burglaries. "Now, if I wanted to go into my back yard, I almost have to put my burglar alarm on," said one. The contrast with the early days was painful: "We were a neighborhood. I could have been a block or two blocks away with my front door open, my screen not locked, and all I had to do was to tell a neighbor, 'I'll be back in a few minutes. I'm going over on Campanella, and I'll be back in thirty minutes. The house is open if you need anything.' Nobody else was going to come in the house. It was just that safe." A third pioneer resident maintained that it was now impossible to leave doors unlocked because there were "too many 'kooks' out there, just waiting for you to . . . leave your doors open, your car doors unlocked, and things of that nature. So, yes, it is a lot different than it was thirty years ago. I know that. That's why I got [a] security [system]."[22]

Other long-time residents worried about their personal safety. "I walk about four miles every morning," said one, "and I confess that I'm very concerned out there because it is very dark. I meet quite a number of people around by the park area. With some of them, I just turn around and come back because you don't know what the situation might be. That's how it has changed since the beginning." An interviewee who owned a house in Hamilton Park told of a drive-by shooting while angrily displaying pieces of broken wrought iron. A bullet from a gun in the passing car had snapped off the wrought iron from the front security door on the house and shattered the safety glass behind. Luckily, the bullet did not penetrate the wooden door in back of the security door and the occupants of the house were unharmed. "Of course," another pioneer remarked, "now we've got so many crack houses out here and those kind of things that it's not safe on some of the streets to walk around. I used to go up to the school and walk in the evening, but I'm almost scared to be out now."[23]

As the last comment suggests, many interviewees linked crime, especially crime against persons, to drug use and sales. The problem had become severe enough by the autumn of 1989 that Eiland Collins believed that something had to be done. Collins, elected president of the Civic League in 1987, organized a march against drugs. He had the support of the churches and other Civic League members. In November, some two hundred youths and adults carrying hand-lettered signs marched for two miles through the community, then held a rally at the Willie B. Johnson center. "We've looked the other way [with regard to drugs] for too long," Collins told the press. "Generally we didn't want to believe our children were involved . . . but now we have to." Collins added, referring to the Civic League meetings, "we have a meeting every third Tuesday, and I say the same thing over and over." A former football player and a man not easily intimidated, Collins acknowledged a fear of drug dealers throughout the community. Partly because of fear, the rally had only limited effect, and later planned marches were cancelled when no one appeared. Collins also attempted to start a "non-profit organization that will teach drug education." But the man in charge of the program "said he got threatened, so he stopped." The antidrug crusaders then decided to work through the Methodist church.[24]

A decline in voter participation suggested a decreasing interest in extracommunity concerns. Charles Smith's repeated exhortations in Civic League meetings to "please let's vote" and to return "to [heavier] voting" responded to the decline. Smith had good reason to goad his audience. In 1964, a voting-age population of about 1,800 cast 1,208 votes in the Johnson-Goldwater race—a 67 percent turnout. The 1972 Nixon-McGovern campaign produced 1,147 votes, a decline to 62 percent of the potential 1,844, but still a good showing by national standards. In 1988, however, the Bush-Dukakis contest motivated a mere 210 voters— a feeble 12 percent of the potential 1,689.[25]

Whites and Hispanics moving into the community was a change that almost all long-time resident interviewees noted but viewed with mild interest or indifference. White heads of household probably lived in Hamilton Park at least as early as 1960, despite the efforts of Associated Construction to keep the community African American. In that year, thirteen householders identified themselves as other than black.

By 1970, one census block containing fifty-four people was but 77 percent "Negro"; five others ranged from 87 to 99 percent. The 1990 census recorded two Native Americans, forty-five Hispanics, and twenty-five whites among Hamilton Park's 2,186 residents. Only one interviewee was concerned enough to raise objections when the white move-ins began. Though fully understanding the ironies of his position, this pioneer urged the community to buy houses and resell them to blacks, in order to keep whites out. The basis for the opposition was not an objection to a racially mixed neighborhood, but rather a fear of racial conflict. The argument was rejected. Opponents said, "Well, we can't afford to do that, because too many people might move and then we own a whole lot of property out here and we can't pay for it, and we can't find a buyer."[26]

Some interviewees saw, not a decline in the community, but rather a general social situation reflected in Hamilton Park. One pioneer said that increased crime was "not only here, but probably all over town." Another commented, "I just think that this is part of society in general." A third referred to his "little grandson" as an example of a rising generation not required to do heavy labor but who expect to acquire material goods without working, a dilemma in Hamilton Park and elsewhere. The third pioneer had ceased attempting to reform the community but continued to work with his grandson. "So I took him different places, and I'd tell them, 'I got a grandson here who doesn't want to work.' They would say, 'What? And he's still living! Come here, son, let me look at you. If I'd have told my daddy that sometime, he'd have stomped me right on the spot....' I think he understands now that he's got to work if he wants to make it in life." As one of the interviewees argued, social change was harder for the pioneer residents to accept, because the community was once so law-abiding.[27]

Doubtless some nostalgia mists the memories of the early Hamilton Park, "the most serene, pristine environment that you would want to see." The Civic League's third annual banquet and reception featured a skit that went over well perhaps because it recalled a time of youth and relative innocence; its topic was "how we were years ago." To wax nostalgic is pleasant and positive, but it may obscure for some a Hamilton Park that, while a superior place to live, was less than "pristine." Back in 1962, Henry Davis, the retiring president of the Civic League, complained of high-speed car driving and racing, cars being driven in Willowdell Park, and roaming dogs. He urged better support for the league among those who "have been slack."[28] The unpaved alleys, floods in the park and at the junction of Schroeder Road and Forest Lane, the occasional youthful scrape, and the rare break-ins may appear tame in retrospect, but they were difficulties that residents had to cope with. The vandalism at the Hamilton Park School and the struggles with breaches of cleanliness and decorum in and around the shopping center were painful reminders that an improved community environment did not always induce correct behavior.

Yet the pioneer interviewees who still lived in Hamilton Park overwhelmingly expressed satisfaction with their lives. Their statements sometimes included expressions of contentment and nostalgia, to be sure, but they also cherished the Hamilton Park of later years. "It's like a family," said Ona Smith, speaking for many of them. "You feel that safety net that surrounds you, even though we have new neighbors that have moved in and a couple of others that have moved away. But most of them, they blend in very well. I guess they, too, had the dream." She recalled a young resident who spoke during one of the Buyout meetings. He wasn't interested in selling because he had moved to Hamilton Park to fulfill "his dream. . . . So . . . I guess it still has that attraction. There's something about it that you just like to be part of. Most people have good memories of Hamilton Park."[29]

A Hamilton Park pioneer of 1990 could look back over a kaleidoscope of interwoven city, community, and national events covering forty years. The South Dallas bombings of 1950 and 1951 catalyzing the search for the solution to the African-American housing problem, the St. John Baptist Church choir singing "Plenty of Room" at the 1953 dedication of Hamilton Park, the breakthrough Supreme Court *Brown* decision of 1954, the civil rights acts of 1964, 1965, and 1968, defining a revolution in the legal situation of blacks in America, all were part of the swirl of events. Hamilton Park participated in the momentous shifts in schooling of the 1960s, although the closing of the high school in 1969 and the junior high a year later were decisions taken elsewhere. The Pacesetter program of 1975 and after proved that racial integration could function effectively in a primary school in the midst of an affluent district, but integration's antithesis was declining parental and community control.

Hamilton Park never required a Saul Alinsky–type of intervention from an outsider to supply cohesion, self-esteem, and organizational expression. John W. Rice of the Dallas Negro Chamber of Commerce helped community activists with founding the Civic League, but his brief assistance was in no way comparable to the Alinsky-style immersion in a directionless community. The residents of Hamilton Park knew what they wanted and quickly mastered the techniques of presenting their concerns. They needed no help from anyone in establishing the Interorganizational Council.[30]

Through the years, the leading secular community organizations remained the Civic League and the IOC. The IOC, working in tandem with the Democratic Party precinct chair, brought candidates to forums, overwhelmingly endorsed Democrats, and urged Hamilton Park residents to vote. The Civic League fought encroachments such as the lumber yard and waged a ceaseless campaign against potholes and poorly maintained property. Through the homeowners' association, it maneuvered along the difficult course of the Buyout, persuading more than 80 percent of property owners to agree to a sale. The collapse of the Buyout was no fault of the league, but rather a symptom of the dramatic plunge in oil-patch real-estate values during the mid-1980s. The league and the IOC, then, were practically identical in their "indigenous" leadership, their outlook, and their methods to the conservative neighborhood organizations that Robert Fisher contrasted to more radical, adversarial groups. Marxist formulas of community organization, such as organization as an expression of a drive for territorial control, or for the empowerment of politically or economically isolated blacks, or for the exclusion of outsiders from the community, have almost no relevance to Hamilton Park.[31]

The large number of property owners willing to sell and the many expressions of fondness for Hamilton Park create an apparent paradox. How could people who love their community be willing to leave it for a payment that was generous enough but less than munificent? The answer lies in part in the incalculable but sometimes contradictory impact of sudden wealth, or relative wealth, on the human psyche. More fundamentally, however, it lies in a rational recognition of change in human affairs and the necessities of adaption to change. Barbara Darden responded to the dilemma by recognizing a situation that required a response. "Something is never forever," she said, "and in your life you're supposed to be able and willing to take changes." Commercial development almost always supplanted residential, "unless you want to stay next door to a business." Most people, "when you get to a certain age," should not be isolated by commerce but should move in order to "be around a group of other people."[32]

Change in Hamilton Park, or even the community's obliteration, did not mean that it had no significance in the lives of its residents or in the larger worlds of urban development, race relations, or African-American advancement. "Hamilton Park had all the right answers for me at the right time," Cicero Bruton said. "It came along at a time when my family—my wife and I—were young and ready to meet a challenge like this, and we welcomed the challenge with our arms out." Or, as Robert Price put it, "Hamilton Park offered us a way of life, a noble way of life, that we could look back on." Continuing material progress meant, however, that many youngsters who grew up in the community found greater satisfaction elsewhere. Price speculated that "if they had come back and made their homes in Hamilton Park . . . maybe Hamilton Park would have been better." The community, nevertheless, played its vital role in launching those "doctors, CPAs, schoolteachers."[33]

Through it all, Hamilton Park remained a "defended neighborhood" —one having a location of comprehensible size, sharing a common culture, and with a self-identity grounded in institutions and activities. Its role as a residential community with a high degree of autonomy was clearly defined. But the concept of a defended neighborhood did not deny the possibility of profound, uncontrollable changes undermining the very community to which its residents were committed. The problematic future of Hamilton Park is a case in point. Many interviewees appeared reconciled to its ultimate dissolution. Gentrification, although always a possibility, seemed unlikely, because of the many small houses and small lots, uncongenial to anything but a thorough replatting and rebuilding.[34]

Thomas Hayman, whose company built almost all the houses in Hamilton Park, in 1989 was a keen observer of physical change and values in Dallas. "The very bottom line is that Hamilton Park will not exist too long. That's not my saying anything against Hamilton Park. They are being encroached upon by the commercial elements. It's going to get to the point where they will be able to be better off selling than staying." The daughter of an interviewee heard a similar statement expressed more cynically by a real-estate agent. "She said that the plan was to snuff us out, just let us rot from inside." Such a development would not, as Bruton and Price pointed out, negate the historical value of Hamilton Park.[35]

The currently fashionable conception of community, the "community of limited liability," is widely accepted because it fits a contemporary view of human beings distanced from purely neighborhood concerns, inexorably drawn into a larger web of overarching institutions and decisions. They merge into other "communities" based, not on locale but on shared interests and activities. It would be unrealistic to deny that citizen involvement in ever-expanding activities has increased in the twentieth century. It would fly in the face of everyday experience to argue that American adults do not spend significant amounts of time deeply engaged in activities far removed from their residential communities.[36]

The "community of limited liability" idea, then, arises, as good theories should, from the assimilation of verifiable experience. Yet there is a difficulty with the phrase *community of limited liability:* it is a truism. Historically, every community, save those so coercive as to undermine the very ideas of shared values and common concerns, has allowed its members to vary their participation in strictly local matters. This was the case in the English and Massachusetts Bay communities so revered by some historians, and with every community since. The identification of a geographical "community of limited liability" in the 1950s may have been a revolutionary way of reordering thinking about metropolitan areas, but that possibility scarcely qualifies the phrase itself as insightful.[37] The untested assumption behind the "community of limited liability" is that the citizen must reduce involvement in place-based community to the extent that his or her commitment to outside activities increases. Its premise is that human physical and intellectual activity has closely constricted limits; that life is, indeed, a zero-sum game. In other words, if the citizen expands his or her role outside the community, it necessarily follows that his or her active devotion to the community will decrease. If Hamilton Park demonstrates anything, it is that this premise is not valid.

Many interviewees, involved to a greater or lesser extent with their community, were also committed elsewhere. A. W. Dupree Jr. and Robert E. Price, among others, were active Masons. Willie B. Johnson and Ona B. Smith were not alone in Hamilton Park in their work with the NAACP; Ocie Turner, to mention but one, was an active member of the AARP chapter;[38] several others belonged to churches miles away from Hamilton Park. The meaning of such diverse commitments is this: that we must not underestimate the flexibility and reach of the human mind and the human spirit. There are physical limitations, of course. Within those limits, as many residents of Hamilton Park demonstrated, the human mind is a wonderful creation able to reach beyond community *and* to be immersed in it, at one and the same time.

APPENDIX A

THE CITY DIRECTORIES AND THE CONTROL NEIGHBORHOOD

The city directories used in this book to derive quantitative information about the residents of Hamilton Park and the control neighborhood, Spring Valley Park, are located in the Texas and Dallas Archives of the Dallas Public Library. They are the Polk directories, once produced by a variety of firms but increasingly published nationwide under the imprint of R. L. Polk & Co. The Dallas Polk directories include two sections pertinent to this study. One, the alphabetical section, contains all the enumerated persons and businesses in the city. The other, the street section, lists all streets in the city alphabetically, together with all the building numbers on each street, from the lowest to the highest, in vertical columns. The name of the householder appears beside each house number.

The city directory street lists were photocopied (a practice that the library no longer permits), those for Hamilton Park beginning with 1955 and those for Spring Valley Park beginning with 1960, and after, at five-year intervals or at the publication date following the fifth year if no directory was published for that year. For example, no directory was published in 1990 so the 1991 directory was used. The alphabetical section was scanned to find the householder, then to record the listed information about that householder.

All houses and households in Hamilton Park were included. The categories of information were the householder's numerical order among the householders at that address, gender (invariably male unless an unmarried female declared herself to be the household head), marital status, the year moved in, the area of Dallas previously occupied if it were possible to locate the area, and the initial reason for the move-in if one could be surmised. The householder's occupation also was recorded, again recorded at the next five-year interval and at the following five-year intervals. Any rise, fall, or continuation in occupational status was noted. The move-out year, occupation at move-out, and any change or continuation of occupational status was recorded. Finally, the householder was traced to a new location in Dallas if possible. If householders moved out within any five-year interval, both the street and alphabetical listings were used to record all information about all householders living at any address during that interval. All information was coded, corrected, and analyzed using an SSPS package.

The information gathered for Spring Valley Park residents was essentially the same. No effort was made to record the areas from which or to which they moved, except that any removes to the suburb of Richardson, a popular destination, were noted. The information was processed in the same way as for Hamilton Park.

There are some difficulties with the city directories. They did not list a new householder for about a year after the householder actually moved in. For example, a move-in occurring in 1954 would be listed in the 1955 directory. Because the directory enumerations occur mostly annually, any move-ins or move-outs within the year or biennium were missed, lowering the recorded rate of mobility to and from the two locations. Enumerators only rarely recorded addresses in error, but they frequently misspelled names, especially in Hamilton Park. Therefore in some cases a judgment had to be made about whether a householder was indeed the same person as one listed previously. In such instances a comparison of occupational and other information was helpful, if not always conclusive. In cases in which several related or unrelated persons occupied a house, each one stating that he or she was the head of the household in succeeding years, judgments about move-ins and move-outs were made on the basis of the best available information.

Marital status was not always easily determined. The directory enumerators depended upon information supplied by respondents, which was usually accurate, but not invariably. A brief marriage at the address in question created a presumption of divorce, especially if a person with the same name and occupation was listed elsewhere in Dallas in the same or the next year's directory. This was true whether or not the female listed herself as a widow. A woman's listing as a widow was suspect if she changed her last name. Conversely, a long marriage created a presumption in favor of separation by death, especially if no contradictory information was discovered. Similar tests were applied to a married male householder whose wife was no longer listed. In all cases of a change in marital status, the year of change was determined and the missing parties searched for, if necessary, in the directory of the following year.

Time and funding imposed constraints on the use of the city directories. A few spot checks indicated that a higher percentage of departing residents could be located in Dallas if they were followed through two years subsequent to the move-out rather than just one. Similar follow-ups would have resolved a few more ambiguities about marital status, but the additional tasks, imposed on a lone scholar sifting through hundreds of cases, were not worth the effort.

The control subdivision, Spring Valley Park, was chosen from among several begun for whites in the same general area as Hamilton Park. Established about three years after Hamilton Park, Spring Valley Park was less affluent than the other nearby white subdivisions. Its easternmost streets were favored because the size of Spring Valley houses and lots increased as construction moved west from a point near the northwest corner of the future intersection of Interstate 635 (LBJ Freeway) and the North Central Expressway (Hamilton Park is in the southeast quadrant of the same intersection). The investigation of the control neighborhood had to be both feasible and reliable; therefore, 161 numbers were computer-selected from a table of random numbers to reduce the burden of tracing the householders in the 298 houses located in the study area. That area is a wedge-shaped tract expanding northwest from the junction of Coit and Alpha Roads, containing portions of eight streets and most of the modest houses in Spring Valley Park. The case numbers were assigned to streets and houses by a count beginning with the lowest house number on the easternmost street and ending with the highest house number on the westernmost street.

Some difficulties with processing data from the city directories and other sources must be acknowledged and explained. Neither the city directories, nor the office of the Dallas County Tax Assessor, nor the United States Census agree on the number of houses in Hamilton Park or in the control neighborhood of Spring Valley Park. Canvassers for the city directories appeared in Hamilton Park almost every year, however, and over time confusions and anomalies involving house numbers and residents were resolved. Therefore the number of houses listed in the city directories for Hamilton Park, 737, is accepted as correct. Computer-generated information derived from data entered from the city directories discovered 739 "valid" entries. No doubt the discrepancy is traceable to data-entry errors that could not be discovered and corrected. Thus 739, not 737, is the basis for calculations and computations from the directories. Variations in the number of households exist from census to census and between any census and a comparable city directory. The record of taxpaying property diverges from the city directories and the census.

The differences noted here are no barrier to drawing valid conclusions, because of the basic questions asked of the data and because of the unrefined numeration, including rounding. For example, 100 is 13.6 percent of 737; 13.5 percent of 739. In the scheme of things, the one-tenth of 1 percent is not a significant difference.

APPENDIX B

CENSUS AND TAX INFORMATION

The decennial United States census from 1940 through 1990 was invaluable for this study. Its essential information on population growth and racial residential succession comes from the census. Beginning in 1960, both Hamilton Park and the relevant section of Spring Valley Park were included in the block statistics. The block statistics allowed comparisons between Hamilton Park and its control neighborhood. Fortunately the census blocks in Spring Valley Park coincided with those from which the random sample of Spring Valley houses were drawn, except for the eighteen houses on the west side of Purple Sage Road. The census block statistics do not identify individual houses or households; therefore the 161 houses (minus 18) selected at random for examination through the city directories could not be isolated from the 280 in the census blocks.

The limitation of the published census is that few comparisons may be made between the block statistics and the personal data aggregated elsewhere in the census. The block statistics compile information principally about the level of housing in every block, using such measurements as the value of each property, its overall condition, the number of persons per room in each house, whether it is rented or owner-occupied, and so on. Most statistics concerning income, educational level, occupation, and similar categories are gathered at the tract level, from which many comparisons may be made by race, gender, age, and other human categories. The tracts including Hamilton Park were either too large or too diverse, or both, to permit their deductive use in comparisons involving Hamilton Park.

The tax valuation information at the Dallas County Tax Office was computerized for the 1990 tax year and, in isolated instances, for a few previous years. In a very small number of instances the tax information was not available for a street address listed in the city directories. The tax information listed the value of the property as a whole and, in a separate category, the value of the land. The tax records also listed the name and address of the person to whom the tax bill was sent, making it possible to determine whether that person lived at the assessed property, elsewhere within the subdivision, or outside the subdivision.

Property values in Spring Valley Park rose so far above those in Hamilton Park beyond the first three streets that no useful comparisons could be made. That situation and the occasional house not on the computerized tax roll meant that only forty-two of the randomly-selected houses could be taken from the roll.

APPENDIX C

THE OCCUPATIONAL SCALE

Ranking or rating occupations by their required level of education and skill, by their social contribution, by their prestige, or by some other category is a subject over which some ink has been spilled (Peter M. Blau and Otis Dudley Duncan, *The American Occupational Structure* [New York: Wiley, 1967]; Albert J. Reiss Jr., *Occupations and Social Status* [New York: Free Press, 1961]; and Olivier Zunz, "The Organization of the American City in the Late Nineteenth Century: Ethnic Structure and Spatial Arrangement in Detroit," *Journal of Urban History* 3 [August 1977]: 465–66). Although there is broad agreement among the students of occupational ranks, and their conclusions were of assistance in constructing a nine-level occupational scale, some departures from their consensus were necessary. Hamilton Park's existence as a black community means that its pioneer residents all suffered from the restraints of the dual labor market, which limited African-American job opportunity to the lower levels of the occupational pyramid, except for those few exceptionally fortunate, able, or ambitious enough to ascend to professional, proprietary, or service vocations, usually those with a black clientele.

Given the dual labor market, the prestige of some jobs was higher in blacks' eyes than whites'. For example, public-school teaching, a task requiring education and offering indoor work in professional attire, was highly regarded in Hamilton Park. A member of the clergy who ministered to a church able to pay a full salary was also highly regarded. So were most proprietary occupations, such as barber, service-station operator, independent trucker, or owner of a janitorial service. This is not to argue that such occupations were despised by majority citizens. Rather it should be taken to mean that almost any escape from the dual labor market into a highly skilled trade, a profession, or a proprietary setting was looked upon with favor.

The dual labor market restrictions, never entirely rigid, began to give way in the 1950s, and some residents of Hamilton Park were able to take advantage of the changing situation and move up in the occupational scale. In some cases the upward move coincided with a move out of Hamilton Park.

The occupational scale itself identifies the following categories, coded for computerization: Category 01, unskilled manual labor, including such occupations as porter, laborer, and cotton handler; 10, semiskilled, including service-station attendant, construction worker, sky cap, and machine operator; 20, domestic/food service, including maid, waiter, and chauffeur; 30, upper-level manual labor, including beautician and barber, plumber, electrician, machinist, and foreman; 40, public-safety and other service, including security guard, military (a too-low scaling perhaps, but the small number of military people, their transiency, and their enlisted rank, mitigate any error), firefighter, and police; 50, lower nonmanual, a category containing many occupations, including librarian, club musician, secretary, letter carrier, and purchasing agent; 60, proprietary, including trucking-firm owner, barbershop owner, owner of an animal hospital, caterer, and building contractor; 70, lower professional and managerial, including bookkeeper, draftsman, manager of a restaurant, and sales manager; and 80, upper professional and managerial, including teacher, principal, minister, physician, dentist, and engineer.

Any occupational rating has its difficulties. No such ranking states the worth of a human being, because a person's dignity, social worth, or value to the community is not necessarily determined by occupation. The owner of a trucking firm that consists of one truck and the owner of a multimillion dollar mail contracting company are both proprietors, but on a substantially different scale of operation. Householders' rankings on the occupational scale depend on the response that they gave to the city directory canvassers. Some probably inflated the importance of their jobs by investing themselves with more important titles than were justified. On the other hand, one interviewee always listed himself simply as an employee, which placed him in the 01 category, when in fact he moved up through the skilled ranks of his company until his retirement. Some, and by hearsay many, householders in Hamilton Park held down two jobs, but the city directory listed only one, and not necessarily the "highest." Others might describe themselves as a bookkeeper one year, an accountant the next, and a bookkeeper the third, descriptions that would move them up the occupational scale, then down, even though

The Occupational Scale

their tasks had not changed. Still others were students, retired, or listed no occupation. Moving Hamilton Park's occupational categories, based as they are on the African-American biases, to Spring Valley Park introduces some distortion.

Granted all of the difficulties with this or any other scale, it is a fair indicator of occupational trends in Hamilton Park. Transferring the scale to the random households in Spring Valley Park allows some comparison with a nearby neighborhood founded exclusively for whites.

APPENDIX D

THE INTERVIEWS

The fifty-three interviews with fifty-eight people stretched over four years beginning in the spring of 1987. They covered four distinct if overlapping areas: the experiences of pioneer residents in Hamilton Park; the experiences of those residents who grew up in the community or who moved there after its founding; circumstances surrounding the founding and early years of the community from the viewpoint of nonresidents; and the issues involved with the desegregation of the Hamilton Park School.

In the case of the pioneer interviews, the purpose was to interview community leaders as well as those citizens of Hamilton Park who made a home in the community but who were not highly visible in its activities. All the interviewees were contacted by a letter explaining the project and a follow-up telephone call. Those who agreed to an interview were then met, usually in their homes, where an additional explanation of the project took place. Following the second explanation, the interview began. Most interviews lasted about two or two and one-half hours, and required two sessions. A few were completed in a little more than one hour, while another few ran for some six hours spread over three recording sessions. The pioneer residents in most cases lived in Hamilton Park at the time of the interview; a few had moved to other parts of Dallas; in one instance, the move was out of the city.

All the interviews except the first four or five were obtained by asking interviewees for recommendations of others to interview. Some of those recommendations were, for various reasons, not pursued, but most of them were. A number of people refused requests to interview, offering several different reasons or no reason. They were, of course, entirely free to refuse. One couple, having agreed to interview, and having heard my explanation of the project, then refused to proceed, even as my fingers were on the record keys of the tape recorder; it was an amazing experience. One interview was begun but could not be completed. It is not listed below.

All the other interviews were held for the other purposes mentioned in the first paragraph of this appendix. A larger proportion of them were conducted in offices. A number of nonresidents were involved in the interviews concerning the founding of Hamilton Park and the concerns of the school and its desegregation.

Each interview except one was recorded and transcribed under a contract protecting the legal rights of the interviewee, as author, and the Oral History Collection at the University of North Texas, as custodian of the interview. All but three of the interviews are open to serious research. Those that were closed are noted; I was not given permission to use two of them. All the interviews were valuable, but some were used more heavily than others. Sometimes the extensive use or the relative lack of it had to do with whether the interview was transcribed sooner or later. A lack of funding delayed many transcriptions.

Citations to the interviews include only the date of the first interview session. The pagination of each interview is continuous. Those who wish to obtain information on the problems of oral history may read, among several good studies, Michael Frisch, *A Shared Authority: Essays on the Craft and Meaning of Oral and Public History* (Albany: State University of New York Press, 1990); Jaclyn Jeffrey and Glenace Edwall, *Memory and History: Essays on Recalling and Interpreting Experience* (Lanham, Md.: University Press of America, 1994); Donald A. Ritchie, *Doing Oral History* (New York: Twayne, 1995); and Valerie Raleigh Yow, *Recording Oral History: A Practical Guide for Social Scientists* (Thousand Oaks, Calif.: Sage, 1994).

Pioneer interviews: Freddie Allen and Ola Lee Allen, OH 1020; George Brewer, OH 894*; Cicero H. Bruton, OH 893; Myra L. Christian, OH 1033; Lapetta Collier, OH 1036; Barbara Darden, OH 916; Henry L. Davis III, OH 873; Pauline Dixon, OH 868; A. W. Dupree Jr., OH 842; Albertus Edley, OH 864; William J. Edmond Sr., OH 918; Lavonia Ephram, OH 844†; Freddie Ervine, OH 912; Le Verne Fields, OH 835; Mary E. Garnett, OH 958; Sadye Gee, OH 827; Zan W. Holmes, OH 921; Velma Jackson, OH 862; Willie B. Johnson, OH 819; Irene Mitchell and Marion Mitchell, OH 962; Freddie M. Nance, OH 895; Edward Newhouse Sr. and Mary A.

*Closed; opened with conditions.
†Closed; permission to use not granted.

Newhouse, OH 956; Mildred Patrick, OH 965; Robert E. Price, OH 963; Pearline Proctor, OH 981; Doris Robertson and Lincoln Robertson, OH 817; J. B. Simpson and Dorothy Simpson, OH 841; Charles E. Smith, OH 793; Curtis J. Smith, OH 826; Ona B. Smith, OH 1032; Willie F. Smith, OH 829; Vivian T. Starks, OH 1005; Laurice Stevenson, OH 875; Ocie Turner, OH 977; Ruby Watson and Streetman Watson, OH 825; Dr. Joseph R. Williams, OH 871.

Hamilton Park nonpioneer interviews: Sheila R. Allen, OH 1012; Charlotte Brewster, OH 1007; Richard Bonner, OH 924; Eiland Collins, OH 970; Donald Payton, OH 865; Thelma Self, OH 902*; Thelma Wells, OH 903.

Founding Hamilton Park interviews: Thomas J. Hayman, OH 807; Charles Inge†; Vincent Rohloff, OH 808.

Hamilton Park School interviews: Henry D. Akin Jr., OH 790; Robert Cook, OH 695; James O. Griffin, OH 715; John Roberts, OH 716; Doris Robertson, OH 697; Charles E. Smith, OH 724; Curtis J. Smith, OH 703.

*Closed; permission to use not granted.
†Telephone interview and other Inge materials not part of the Oral History Collection.

ABBREVIATIONS

CESP	Charles E. Smith Papers, copies in author's possession
CJSP	Curtis J. Smith Papers, copies in author's possession
CR	Records of the Dallas City Council, City Hall
DCIA	Dallas Citizens' Interracial Association Papers, University of North Texas Archives
DE	*Dallas Express*
DMN	*Dallas Morning News*
DNCC	Dallas Negro Chamber of Commerce Collection, MA 80.3, Texas and Dallas Archives, Dallas Public Library
DTH	*Dallas Times Herald*
FMNP	Freddie M. Nance Papers, copies in author's possession
HF	Archives of the Hoblitzelle Foundation, Dallas
HPCL	Hamilton Park Civic League and Hamilton Park Civic League Home Owners Association, copies of minutes in author's possession
HPDA	Hamilton Park Development Association, copies of material from the Sadye Gee Papers in author's possession
HPHSCSR	*Hamilton Park High School Community Study Report (A Summary)*
HPUMC	Archives of the Hamilton Park United Methodist Church, Dallas
JECC	John Oscar and Ethelyn M. Chisum Collection, M.A. 83-5, Texas and Dallas Archives, Dallas Public Library
NTA	University of North Texas Archives
PCD	City Directories (Polk), Texas and Dallas Archives, Dallas Public Library
OH	Oral History Collection, University of North Texas Archives
RDN	*Richardson Daily News*

RISD	Richardson Independent School District Archives, Richardson, Texas
RG207, NA	Record Group 207, Records of the Department of Housing and Urban Development, National Archives, Washington, D.C.
RMGP	Reuben M. Ginsberg Papers, Dallas
SGP	Sadye Gee Papers, copies in author's possession
TDG, DPL	Texas and Dallas Collection, Dallas Public Library

NOTES

Chapter 1: Community and the History of Hamilton Park

1. Darwin Payne, *Big D: Triumphs and Troubles of an American Supercity in the 20th Century* (Dallas: Three Forks Press, 1994), 172-74.

2. Arnold R. Hirsch, *Making the Second Ghetto: Race and Housing in Chicago, 1940-1960* (Cambridge: Cambridge University Press, 1983). In the north and far west there were some proposals for mixed-race housing; also some infill housing in African-American neighborhoods in all sections of the country. See George and Eunice Grier, *Equality and Beyond: Housing Segregation and the Goals of the Great Society* (Chicago: Quadrangle, 1966).

3. For scholarly use of the second ghetto, see Raymond A. Mohl, "Making the Second Ghetto in Metropolitan Miami, 1940-1960," *Journal of Urban History* 21 (March 1995): 397-404. For private housing, see 411-12. See also Christopher Silver and John V. Moeser, *The Separate City: Black Communities in the Urban South, 1940-1968* (Lexington: University Press of Kentucky, 1995), 133, 139-40.

4. For traditional African-American suburbs, see two articles by Andrew Wiese: "'Life on the Other Side of the Tracks': African Americans in a Domestic Service Suburb, Evanston, Illinois, 1916-1940," *Locus: An Historical Journal of Regional Perspectives on National Topics* 5 (spring 1993): 163-83; and "Places of Our Own: Suburban Black Towns Before 1960," *Journal of Urban History* 19 (May 1992): 30-54. For 1920s subdivisions, see Howard L. Preston, *Automobile Age Atlanta: The Making of a Southern Metropolis* (Athens: University of Georgia Press, 1979), 75-110; Timothy J. Crimmins, "Bungalow Suburbs: East and West," 83-94; Dana F. White, "The Black Sides of Atlanta: A Geography of Expansion and Containment, 1970-1870," 199-225, both in *Atlanta Historical Journal* 26 (summer-fall 1982); and Kenneth T. Jackson, *Crabgrass Frontier: The Suburbanization of the United States* (New York: Oxford University Press, 1985), 200.

5. Silver and Moeser, *Separate City,* 139-40.

6. William Julius Wilson, *The Declining Significance of Race: Blacks and Changing American Institutions,* 2d ed. (Chicago: University of Chicago Press, 1978, 1980). Quotations at 150; for Wilson's discussion of the middle class, see 126-29. Alan L. Keyes, *Masters of the Dream: The Strength and Betrayal of Black America* (New York: William Morrow, 1995), 41-105.

7. Ellis Cose, *The Rage of a Privileged Class* (New York: HarperCollins, 1993); bell hooks, *Killing Rage: Ending Racism* (New York: Henry Holt, 1995); Glenn C. Loury, *One by One from the Inside Out: Essays and Reviews on Race and Responsibility in America* (New York: Free Press, 1995); Robert C. Smith, *Racism in the Post-Civil Rights Era: Now You See It, Now You Don't* (Albany: State University of New York Press, 1995); and Shelby Steele, *The Content of Our Character: A New Vision of Race in America* (New York: Harper Perennial, 1991). For quotation, see Walt Harrington, *Crossings: A White Man's Journey into Black America* (New York: HarperCollins, 1992), 363.

8. David J. Russo, *Clio Confused: Troubling Aspects of Historical Study from the Perspective of U.S. History* (Westport, Conn.: Greenwood, 1995), 84-88.

9. See, for an example that also includes anthropologists, Russo, *Clio Confused*, 59, 96, and elsewhere. For the agreement among many sociologists see Larry Lyon, *The Community in Urban Society* (Philadelphia: Temple University Press, 1987), 95. Dissenters and those having significant qualifications about the "loss" of community include Albert Hunter, "The Loss of Community: An Empirical Test Through Replication," *American Sociological Review* 40 (October 1975): 537-52; Darrett B. Rutman, "Community Study," *Historical Methods* 13 (winter 1980): 29-41; John Clayton Thomas, *Between Citizen and City: Neighborhood Organizations and Urban Politics in Cincinnati* (Lawrence: University Press of Kansas, 1986); and Barry Wellman and Barry Leighton, "Networks, Neighborhoods, and Communities: Approaches to the Study of the Community Question," *Urban Affairs Quarterly* 14 (March 1979): 363-90.

10. Seymour J. Mandelbaum, *Community and Communications* (New York: W. W. Norton, 1972), for quotations in order, 27 and 26.

11. M. Scott Peck, *The Different Drum: Community Making and Peace* (New York: Simon & Schuster, 1987). For Peck's definition of community, see 86-106. For manipulation, see 118-35. For the limited number of examples, see 136-65. Quotations at 108, 118.

12. Howard Rheingold, *The Virtual Community: Homesteading on the Electronic Frontier* (Reading, Mass.: Addison-Wesley, 1993), 64 (quotation), 132, 145-75.

13. Albert S. Broussard, *Black San Francisco: The Struggle for Racial Equality in the West, 1900-1954* (Lawrence: University Press of Kansas, 1993); Silver and Moeser, *Separate City*; and a study that covers more than its subtitle suggests, Quintard Taylor, *The Forging of a Black Community: Seattle's Central District from 1870 through the Civil Rights Era* (Seattle: University of Washington Press, 1994). For black voting, see Robert C. Smith and Richard Seltzer, *Race, Class, and Culture: A Study in Afro-American Mass Opinion* (Albany: State University of New York Press, 1992), 122-23; and Kenneth L. Kusmer, "African Americans in the City Since World War II: From the Industrial to the Post-Industrial Era," *Journal of Urban History* 21 (May 1995): 471-74.

14. Thomas Bender, *Community and Social Change in America* (Baltimore: Johns Hopkins University Press, 1978), 149; and Rowland Berthoff, *An Unsettled People: Social Order and Disorder in American History* (New York: Harper & Row, 1971), 479. The arguments of Bender and Berthoff are similar to the "statist communitarian" position analyzed by political and social conservatives in "Symposium: Habits of

the New Communitarian Heart," *The Intercollegiate Review: A Journal of Scholarship & Opinion* 32 (spring 1997): 9-39. The analysis is less historical than it is philosophical and cultural, to the extent that those categories may be separated.

15. Zane L. Miller, *Suburb: Neighborhood and Community in Forest Park, Ohio, 1935-1976* (Knoxville: University of Tennessee Press, 1981), quotations at xxiv, xxv, 30, 94, 148, 176, and 197. For an analysis of the supposed decline of community and the potential for its restoration as they were posited by various thinkers, see Park Dixon Goist, *From Main Street to State Street: Town, City and Community in America* (Port Washington, N.Y.: Kennikat, 1977).

16. Robert E. Park and Ernest W. Burgess, *The City* (1925; reprint, with an introduction by Morris Janowitz, Chicago: University of Chicago Press, 1967), 114-19; 142-55; and Gerald D. Suttles, *The Social Construction of Communities* (Chicago: University of Chicago Press, 1972), 21-43.

Chapter 2: Searching for a Black Subdivision

1. William Neil Black, *Empire of Consensus: City Planning, Zoning, and Annexation in Dallas, 1900-1960* (Ann Arbor: University Microfilms International, 1982); Warren Leslie, *Dallas Public and Private: Aspects of an American City* (New York: Grossman Publishers, 1964), 76; and Jim Schutze, *The Accommodation: The Politics of Race in an American City* (Secaucus, N.J.: Citadel Press, 1986), 77-82 (quotation at 77). For an insightful critique of the "empire of consensus" thesis, see Patricia Evridge Hill, *Dallas: The Making of a Modern City* (Austin: University of Texas Press, 1996), xiii-xxix, 109-27.

2. For the growth of Dallas, see Hill, *Dallas,* xiii-xxix, 109-27; "Dallas by the Decade," *Legacies: A History Journal for Dallas and North Central Texas* 2 (fall 1991): 17-32; and Elizabeth York Enstam, "How Dallas Grew . . . and Why," ibid.: 33-38.

3. For black population figures, U.S. Department of Commerce, Bureau of the Census, *Sixteenth Census of the United States: 1940: Population, Characteristics of the Population* (Washington: GPO, 1943), hereafter cited as *Sixteenth Census, 1940,* 2, pt. 6: 1027. For other population figures, U.S. Department of Commerce, Bureau of the Census, *A Report on the Seventeenth Decennial Census of the United States: Census of Population, 1950* (Washington: GPO, 1952), hereafter cited as *Seventeenth Census, 1950,* 2, pt. 43, 43-11. For black neighborhoods, Harland Bartholomew and Associates, *Your Dallas of Tomorrow: Report Number Seven: A System of Parks and Schools* (Dallas: City Plan Commission, 1944), 6.

4. Robert B. Fairbanks, "From Consensus to Controversy: The Rise and Fall of Public Housing in Dallas," *Legacies* 1 (fall 1989): 37-38; and Schutze, *Accommodation,* 9.

5. Bartholomew, *Your Dallas of Tomorrow: Report Number Seven,* 6.

6. Ibid., *Report Number Ten: Housing* (Dallas, City Plan Commission, 1944), 37. For expansion areas, see ibid., *Report Number Seven,* 6.

7. Ibid., *Report Number Seven,* 6.

8. *Seventeenth Census, 1950,* 2, pt. 43, 43-119. The census number is for the "nonwhite" population, however the number of "nonwhites" other than blacks in the Dallas metropolitan area in 1950 was negligible.

9. Smith to F. A. Van Patten, 8 March 1948, Records of the Department of

Housing and Urban Development, Record Group 207, Program Files, Race Relations, Program 1946-1956, box 751, folder Dallas, Texas Racial Relations, National Archives, hereafter cited as RG 207, NA; *Dallas Morning News,* hereafter cited as *DMN,* 21 February 1948, sec. 2, p. 3; and *DMN,* 2 March 1948, sec. 2, p. 3. For the continuing relationship, see Dallas Negro Chamber of Commerce Collection, hereafter cited as DNCC, MA 80.3, box 1, folder 14, J. W. Rice Correspondence: 1950, Texas and Dallas Archives, Dallas Public Library. For earlier recognition of the problem, see *DMN,* 2 February 1945, p. 11; and Smith to Frank S. Horne, memorandum, 16 January 1947, RG 207, NA.

10. For the pattern, see Smith to Van Patten, n. 9. For an earlier meeting, *DMN,* 2 February 1945, sec. 1, p. 11. For Rice's statements, see *DMN,* 25 March 1948, sec. 2, p. 1.

11. *DMN,* 25 March 1948, sec. 2, p. 1.

12. *DMN,* 15 April 1948, sec. 2, p. 1.

13. *Dallas Times Herald,* hereafter cited as *DTH,* 11 April 1948, sec. 3, p. 1 (Johnson quotation); *DMN,* 12 April 1948, sec. 2, p. 1 ("officials" quotation).

14. *DMN,* 13 April 1948, sec. 2, p. 1. See also *DTH,* 11 April 1948, sec. 2, p. 1.

15. *DMN,* 15 April 1948, sec. 2, p. 1.

16. *DMN,* 23 May 1948, sec. 4, p. 1. For Shepherd's visit, see 19 May 1948, sec. 1, p. 4.

17. For previous Dicker statements, see *DTH,* 11 April 1948, sec. 3, p. 1; and *DMN,* 15 April 1948, sec. 2, p. 1. For his comments on Shepherd's decision, see *DTH,* 23 May 1948, pt. 3, p. 1; and *DMN,* 23 May 1948, sec. 4, p. 1. For Shepherd's opposition to lower standards, see *DMN,* 21 August 1948, sec. 2, p. 14; for his later comment, see *DTH,* 13 January 1950, sec. 1A, p. 1.

18. *DMN,* 13 July 1948, sec. 2, p. 1; and 15 July 1948, sec. 2, p. 1.

19. *DMN,* 16 July 1948, sec. 2, pp. 1, 20.

20. *DMN,* 15 July 1948, sec. 2, p. 1; and 21 July 1948, sec. 2, pp. 1, 20.

21. *DMN,* 27 August 1948, sec. 2, p. 1; and Donald McGregor to Franklin D. Richards, 27 July 1948, RG 207, NA.

22. For Shepherd and Stuart quotations, see *DMN,* 27 August 1948, sec. 2, p. 1; for mortgage-officer quotation, see McGregor to Richards, n. 21.

23. Martin to Harry S. Truman, 14 April 1950, RG 207, NA; and *DMN,* 19 February 1950, sec. 8, p. 1.

24. A. Maceo Smith to Frank S. Horne, 17 May 1950, RG 207, NA; Martin to Truman, n. 23; and, for contest, *Dallas Express,* hereafter cited as *DE,* 15 January 1949, p. 3.

25. Curtis J. Smith, interview by William H. Wilson, 22 February 1990, OH 826, 42, 43; and Henry L. Davis III, interview by Wilson, 23 May 1990, OH 873, 35, both in Oral History Collection, University of North Texas Archives, hereafter cited by number only. Martin to Sheppard [sic], 17 March 1949, RG 207, NA.

26. Martin to Truman, n. 23. For the syndicate, see *DMN,* 21 May 1950, pt. 4, 11.

27. Frank S. Horne, "College 'Housing Clinic' Aids in Meeting Housing Problem," *Journal of Housing* 5 (July 1948): 185-86; and *DMN,* 21 April 1948, sec. 1, 12.

28. Smith to Herbert C. Redman, 21 February 1949, RG 207, NA.

29. Smith to R. E. Shepherd, 1 August 1949, RG 207, NA.

30. *DMN,* 3 September 1949, sec. 2, p. 14; and 8 January 1950, sec. 3, pp. 1, 2.

31. *DMN,* 8 January 1950, sec. 3, p. 2.

32. For Hill's experience, see Irene Mitchell and Marion Mitchell interview by Wilson, 11 December 1990, OH 962, 48-50. For indirect quotations of Shepherd, see *DMN,* 12 January 1950, pt. 3, p. 2; and 13 July, 1948, sec. 2, p. 1. For Hill quotation, see *DMN,* 8 January 1950, sec. 2, p. 1. For "civic groups" quotation, see Charles Abrams, *Forbidden Neighbors: A Study of Prejudice in Housing* (New York: Harper, 1955), 242, which quotes the FHA directive on the same page.

33. *DMN,* 9 January 1950, pt. 3, p. 1.

34. *DTH,* 11 January 1950, sec. 2, pp. 1, 8; and *DMN,* 11 January 1950, pt. 3, pp. 1, 8.

35. *DMN,* 11 January 1950, pt. 3, p. 1.

36. Mitchell interview, OH 962, 48. For living in Trinity Valley, see 33-36, 46-48. See also *DMN,* 12 January 1950, pt. 3, p. 4; 14 January 1950, pt. 3, p. 1; and *DE,* 21 January 1950, p. 1.

37. Another Oak Cliff councilman tabled the motion, *DTH,* 11 January 1950, sec. 2, p. 1. For Pelt's resignation, see *DTH,* 16 April 1950, p. 1. For his election to the DCIA, see *DE,* 30 October 1954, p. 1.

38. *DTH,* 12 January 1950, sec. 2, pp. 1, 7; and *DMN,* 13 January 1950, pt. 3, p. 2.

39. *DTH,* 13 February 1950, sec. 1A, p. 1. For the related bombing and public-housing issues, see Fairbanks, "From Consensus to Controversy," 39; and Schutze, *Accommodation,* 13-26, 67-74; Davis interview, OH 873, 82-83.

40. *DMN,* 16 January 1950, pt. 3, p. 1; 26 January 1950, sec. 4, p. 1; and 9 May 1950, sec. 1, p. 1.

41. *DTH,* 15 July 1951, sec. 2, p. 1.

42. *DTH,* 16 February 1950, sec. 1, p. 9. For racially motivated bombings, arson, and riots in Dallas and other cities at about the same time, see Abrams, *Forbidden Neighbors,* 82-83, 86, 87, 89-90.

43. *DMN,* 21 November 1950, sec. 3, p. 2; and 22 November 1950, sec. 3, p. 2.

44. Transcript of meeting of the Dallas Interracial Committee, 5 September 1950, papers of the Dallas Citizens Interracial Association, hereafter cited as DCIA, unprocessed collection, University of North Texas Archives. For blacks' reluctance to move, see *DE,* 3 February 1951, pp. 1, 8.

45. Transcript, Dallas Interracial Committee meeting, 5 September 1950, DCIA.

46. Ibid.; and *DE,* 12 January 1951, p. 1. For the alleged connection between the violence and Moore, who is not named, see Schutze, *Accommodation,* 72-73.

47. Transcript, Dallas Interracial Committee meeting, 5 September 1950, DCIA.

48. *DTH,* 26 February 1950, sec. 1, pp. 1, 22; and *DMN,* 26 February 1950, sec. 4, p. 1.

49. *DMN,* 26 February 1950, sec. 4, p. 1, and for successful and unsuccessful housing developments, see *DMN,* 12 January 1950, pt. 3, p. 2. For Arlington Park, see "Dallas, Texas 1950 Negro Housing Data" Box 1, folder 4, DNCC.

50. For West Dallas, see Robert B. Fairbanks, "Dallas Leadership and the Black

Housing Crisis, 1940-1960," paper presented to the Southwestern Social Science Association annual meeting, 1987, 11; "From Consensus to Controversy," 39; and Schutze, *Accommodation,* 9-10. For Pelt quotation and development possibilities, see *DMN,* 26 February 1950, sec. 4, p. 1.

51. *DMN,* 1 March 1950, pt. 3, p. 1; and *DTH,* 1 March 1950, sec. 1, p. 1.

52. Smith to Herbert C. Redman, 7 March 1950, RG 207, NA.

53. For leader quotation, see *DMN,* 3 March 1950, pt. 3, p. 5. For clubwoman quotation, see *DE,* 18 March 1950, p. 1.

54. For clubwoman quotation, see *DE,* 18 March 1950, p. 1. For editorial, see *DE,* 1 April 1950, p. 19. H. S. Austin to J. W. Rice, 16 March 1950, box 1, folder 14, DNCC.

55. For editorial, see *DMN,* 2 March 1950, pt. 3, p. 2. For Irving Chamber of Commerce, see *DMN,* 3 March 1950, pt. 3, p. 1. For Carpenter's statement, see *DMN,* 7 March 1950, pt. 3, p. 1.

56. Smith to Redman, n. 52.

Chapter 3: Organizing for Hamilton Park

1. For the Carpenter quotation, see *DMN,* 7 March 1950, pt. 3, p. 1. For the chamber's commitment, see *Dallas* (magazine of the Dallas Chamber of Commerce) 28 (March 1949): 18-22; and 29 (March 1950): 30. See also "The President's Report," *Dallas* 29 (December 1950): 29.

2. The council's attitude had undergone a change, see *DTH,* 10 February 1950, sec. 1, p. 1, and the story including the "ultimatum" quotation, *DTH,* 7 March 1950, sec. 2, p. 1. For the 1,808 units, see *DMN,* 8 March 1950, pt. 3, p. 1. For more on the black housing problem, see *DMN,* 21 March 1950, pt. 3, p. 1. For the collapse of the coalition effort, see *DMN,* 15 March 1950, pt. 3, p. 1.

3. *DMN,* 11 March 1950, pt. 3, p. 1; and, for first quotation, *DMN,* 25 March 1950, pt. 2, p. 4. For second quotation, see "Report of Joint Committee of Dallas Chamber of Commerce and Dallas Citizens' Council on Negro Housing in Dallas County," RG 107, NA. *DTH,* 28 May 1950, reprinted the report, sec. 1, pp. 5, 18. It was also reprinted in the pamphlet *Toward Better Understanding,* issued by the Dallas Inter-Racial Committee, 24 January 1951, pp. 4-11.

4. *DMN,* 25 April 1950, pt. 3, p. 1.

5. All subsequent quotations are from the report. The report was not the first to note the problems of black housing. See, for example, Justin F. Kimball, *Our City—Dallas: A Community Civics* (Dallas: Kessler Plan Association, 1927), 195-99.

6. A. Maceo Smith to R. E. Shepherd, 18 August 1950, RG 207, NA. For studies, see *Toward Better Understanding,* 12-29.

7. For quotations, Smith to Shepherd, n. 6. See also *DTH,* 15 August 1951, sec. 2, p. 2.

8. Vincent Rohloff, interview by Wilson, 31 October 1989, OH 808, 2-4, 7, 9. For Crossman's obituaries, see *DMN,* 16 January 1970, p. 12A; and *DTH,* 16 January 1970, p. 21A.

9. For Crossman's adherence to traditional racial mores, see Dr. Joseph R. Williams, interview by Wilson, 24 August 1990, OH 871, 6-9, 65. For quotation, see *DMN,* 27 March 1952, pt. 1, p. 1.

10. Bartholomew, *Your Dallas of Tomorrow: Report Number Ten*, 37. For Smith's obituaries, see *DMN*, 20 December 1977; and *DTH*, 20 December 1977, clippings in Smith vertical file, Texas and Dallas Collection, DPL.

11. For quotation, Donald W. Wyatt, "Better Homes for Negro Families in the South," *Social Forces* 28 (March 1950): 301. See also "Orlando—a New Subdivision Created," *Journal of Housing* 12 (October 1955): 320-21.

12. For quotations, see Wyatt, "Better Homes for Negro Families in the South," 301.

13. Douglas Rosenblum to Raymond M. Foley, 6 May 1947, box 6, folder 650, Racial Relations 1947, RG 207, NA.

14. *DMN*, 9 August 1950, sec. 3, p. 1; and Smith to Frank S. Horne, 9 August 1950, RG 207, NA.

15. Smith to R. E. Shepherd, 18 August 1950, RG 207, NA; and transcript of meeting of the Dallas Interracial Committee, 5 September 1950, DCIA.

16. Quotations three and four in Smith to Frank S. Horne; Quotations one, two, and five in Smith to R. E. Shepherd, 18 August 1950; and quotation six in "Statement of Inter-Racial Committee," 14 November 1950, by M. J. Norrell, chairman, attached to Smith to James E. Hicks, 22 November 1950, all in RG 207, NA. See also Charles Inge, telephone interview by Wilson, 25 March 1991, and statement of property transactions in which Inge was involved, dated January 1988, courtesy of Mr. Inge, in the author's possession.

17. For quotations ending with *negligible*, see *DTH*, 19 July 1951, sec. 1, p. 1. For all other quotations, see *DTH*, 23 July 1951, sec. 2, p. 1.

18. *DMN*, 20 July 1951, sec. 3, p. 1; *DTH*, 22 July 1951, sec. 2, p. 3; *DTH*, 31 August 1951, sec. 2, p. 3; quotation in 2 October 1951, at sec. 2 , p. 2. For the charter, see *DTH*, 1 November 1951, sec. 1, p. 8; and Charter of the Dallas Citizens' Interracial Association, filed 29 October 1951, file 17-108361-1, D4RA, pp. 1-5, Office of the Secretary of State, State of Texas, Austin, Texas.

19. Charter and bylaws of the DCIA; lists of officers, directors, and advisory council; and minutes of the membership and board of directors meeting, 13 November 1951, DCIA.

20. Minutes of the meeting of the board of directors and advisory council, DCIA. Quotations in *DMN*, 27 March 1952, at pt. 1, p. 1.

21. Ibid.

22. Memorandum minutes 26 June 1952, DCIA. The acreage was thought to be 169 at the time, but surveyed at 172.96 acres. For simplicity's sake the original acreage will be referred to as 173. Quotations in "DCIA sites committee preliminary report," H. Leslie Hill, n.d., DCIA Minutes, DCIA. For background, see also the Inge interview and statement, n. 16.

23. Memorandum minutes 26 June 1952; quotations in "DCIA sites committee preliminary report," H. Leslie Hill, n.d., DCIA minutes, both DCIA.

24. Memorandum minutes, 3 July 1952; quotations in memorandum minutes 24 July 1952, DCIA.

25. Memorandum minutes, 24 July 1952, DCIA. For the median wage, see *Seventeenth Census, 1950*, 2, pt. 43, 43-591.

26. Memorandum minutes, 31 July 1952; and 26 August 1952; minutes of the

meeting of the steering committee, 16 October 1952; and minutes of the meeting of the board of directors, 1 June 1953, all in DCIA. See the warranty deed, 19 February 1953, copy, DCIA.

27. Robert B. Fairbanks, "A Clash of Priorities: The Federal Government and Dallas Airport Development, 1917-1964," in *American Cities and Towns: Historical Perspectives,* ed. Joseph F. Rishel (Pittsburgh: Duquesne University Press, 1992): 175, 179; *DMN,* 4 December 1952, sec. 3, p. 1; and Stanley Marcus, "Chamber Demands Adequate Air Service," *Dallas* 32 (May 1953): 12-13, 45.

28. Quotations from handwritten remarks about the 27 January 1953 bond issue, holograph probably prepared for one of Chisum's speeches, box 3, folder 2, John Oscar and Ethelyn M. Chisum Collection, hereafter cited as JECC, M.A. 83-5, DPL. See also, in general, box 3 of this collection.

29. The editorial is unsigned but the phrasing is Landrum's. *DMN,* 22 January 1953, in box 3, folder 8, JECC; quotation in *DTH,* 23 January 1953, at p. 17, and see also p. 1. For the bond-issue vote, see *DE,* 31 January 1953, p. 1. For interviews with North Park residents, see *DE,* 14 February 1953, p. 1; and 7 March 1953, pp. 1, 10 (quotations).

30. *DTH,* 7 June 1953, sec. D: 1-2, for Crossman's statement. For Chisum, see clipping attributed to the *Fort Worth Press,* 20 November 1954, box 3, folder 7, JECC.

31. *DTH,* 1 March 1953, in DCIA.

32. Minutes of the meeting of the board of trustees of the Hoblitzelle Foundation, 19 May 1949, Minute Book, 1: 5,6, Archives of the Hoblitzelle Foundation, hereafter cited as HF.

33. Minutes of the board of trustees, Hoblitzelle Foundation, 31 January 1950, Minute Book, 2: 3, HF. All amounts quoted in the text are rounded to the nearest dollar.

34. Hoblitzelle reported the transaction at the board of trustees meeting of 9 April 1953, Minute Book, 2: 7. The cost to the Hoblitzelle Foundation for 172.96 acres was $1,205.12 per acre, Van Alen Holloman to Hoblitzelle, 30 July 1953. To protect itself the foundation required a per-acre repayment slightly above its cost—see Crossman to John Adams, 16 November 1953. For a repayment see Partial Release, 5 April 1956. For an extension of the note, see J. E. Magouirk to Crossman, 4 March 1957. For forgiveness of interest, see John Q. Adams to Crossman, 14 March 1960. For cancellation of the note, see Release of Lien, 27 July 1960. All correspondence and releases are in folder Dallas Citizens' Interracial Association, HF.

35. For annexation, see the following in DCIA: unattributed article and editorial in support of the annexation, 16 August 1953; and clipping from *DMN,* 18 August 1953. For water line, see DCIA, contract between City of Dallas and DCIA, 1 August 1953, which also refers to electrical-service agreement of 23 December 1952. See also Crossman to the Commissioner of Internal Revenue, 30 April 1954, DCIA.

36. The Ben Wooten comment is reported in Vincent Rohloff interview, OH 808, 15. See also Ben H. Wooten, interview by E. Dale Odom, 27 October 1969, OH 29, 13-14. For second quotation, see minutes of the annual membership meeting

of the DCIA, 26 October 1953, DCIA. For FHA and VA loans, see *DMN* clipping, 19 July 1953; minutes of the meeting of the board of directors of the DCIA, 10 February 1953; and T. J. Hayman to Crossman, 5 August 1953, all in DCIA.

37. Thomas J. Hayman, interview by Wilson, 4 December 1989, OH 807, 10, 33-34, quotation at 34.

38. OH 807, quotation about Collins at 12, quotation about financing at 14. See also 10-12.

39. OH 807, 12. See also minutes of the board of directors of the DCIA, 1 June 1953, DCIA. Leonard Brewster Murphy, "A History of Negro Segregation Practices in Texas, 1865-1958" (master's thesis, Southern Methodist University, 1958), 31. Murphy used A. Maceo Smith's paper, "Housing of Minority Groups in Texas," presented at the Texas Methodist Conference, Huston-Tillotson College, Austin, 12-13 September 1957, now lost.

40. Statement of John W. Rice, secretary-manager, Dallas Negro Chamber of Commerce, 11 August 1953, RG 207, NA.

41. Hayman to Crossman, 5 August 1953, folder Dallas Citizens' Interracial Association, HF; quotation, Hayman interview, OH 807 at 32.

42. The most complete story on Crossman's announcement is *DTH*, 7 June 1953, clipping in DCIA papers. Quotation in Earle Cabell, interview by E. Dale Odom, 21 March 1974, OH 273 at 168. See also *DE*, 15 March 1952, p. 1; and for Schlitz, 22 March 1952, p. 1. For Hoskins, see Larry Bowman, "Breaking Barriers: David Hoskins and Integration of the Texas League," *Legacies* 3 (spring 1991): 14-19. For integration of rest rooms, see Edward L. Newhouse Sr. and Mary A. Newhouse, interview by Wilson, 6 December 1990, OH 956, 8-10, 30.

Chapter 4: A Transition in White and Black

1. Among the advance stories and reports of the dedication are *DE*, 3 October 1953, clipping, and unattributed clippings, probably the *Dallas Star Post* and *DMN*, DCIA. See also *DTH*, 5 October 1953, sec. 2, p. 6; and "Chamber Completes Negro Housing Plan," *Dallas* 32 (October 1953): 16-17.

2. For quotation, see "Chamber Completes Negro Housing Plan," 17.

3. Hayman interview, OH 807, 15. For other quotations, see *Dallas Star Post*, 10 October 1953, clipping in DCIA.

4. *Dallas Star Post*, 10 October 1953, clipping in DCIA. For other cities, see Wyatt, "Better Homes for Negro Families in the South," 300-302.

5. *DTH*, 5 October 1953, sec. 2, p. 6.

6. Ocie Turner, interview by Wilson, 14 September 1991, OH 977, 38. Other information comes from personal observation and remarks scattered through several interviews. The topography of the area is on U.S. Geological Survey Map, Carrollton Quadrangle, Texas, Scale 1:62,500, compiled 1962.

7. For Frank Dixon, see Pauline Dixon, interview by Wilson, 9 August 1990, OH 868, 71. For Sadye Gee, see Sadye Gee, interview by Wilson, 28 May 1990, OH 827, 32-33. For Freddie Allen, see Freddie and Ola Lee Allen, interview by Wilson, 24 February 1991, OH 1020, 10.

8. Richard Bonner, interview by Wilson, 29 September 1991, OH 924, 13-14, quotation at 20.

9. *DMN,* 5 February 1987, pp. 29A, 33A.

10. Sadye Gee, "Hamilton Park" pamphlet, Sadye Gee Papers, hereafter cited as SGP, copies in the author's possession.

11. SGP; and Gee interview, OH 827, 111. For Oberlin, see John Barnard, *From Evangelism to Progressivism at Oberlin College, 1866-1917* (Columbus: Ohio State University Press, 1969), 3.

12. Hayman interview, OH 807, 15. For white interest, see Mary E. Garnett, interview by Wilson, 21 June 1990, OH 958, 23; and Williams interview, OH 871, 55.

13. Hayman interview, OH 807, 11-12, quotations at 16, 17. For the companies, see also Crossman to John Q. Adams, 2 March 1960, folder Dallas Citizens' Interracial Association, HF. For the sales office, see also *DTH,* 5 October 1953, sec. 2, p. 6.

14. Hayman interview, OH 807, 17. For confirmation, see Velma Jackson, interview by Wilson, 18 October 1990, OH 862, 29; Doris Robertson, Lincoln Robertson, interview by Wilson, 7 January 1990, OH 817, 15; and Sadye Gee interview, OH 827, 22-23.

15. *DTH,* 23 April 1954, clipping; and *DMN,* 21 May 1954, clipping (number of houses sold); and quotation in *DMN* clipping, 2 May 1954, all in DCIA.

16. *DMN,* 3 May 1954, clipping, DCIA. Quotations by Adove, Thornton, and Florence in "Families Now Occupying Chamber Housing Units," *Dallas* 32 (May 1954): 13.

17. For the quotation, Rice to Crossman, 6 August 1954, box 1, folder 2, J. W. Rice Correspondence, 1954, DNCC; minutes of the annual membership meeting of the DCIA, 22 October 1954, DCIA; Rohloff interview, OH 808, 21; minutes of the meeting of the board of directors of the DCIA, 24 October 1955; and "Hamilton Park Addition," n.d. but c. February 1956, both in DCIA.

18. Quotations in Rice to Crossman, 6 August 1954. Crossman to Rice, 26 July 1954; and Rice to Crossman, 24 August 1954, box 1, folder 2, J. W. Rice Correspondence, 1954, DNCC.

19. Hayman interview, OH 807, 25-26.

20. For the school, see chapter 7. For the Baptist church, see *The Link,* 27 August-2 September 1986, 1-2. For the Methodist church, see *Church History,* compiled from Eloise S. Valley Hatchett, coordinator, *The History of Hamilton Park United Methodist Church, 1957-1981,* ed. Earnest Benson (Dallas, n.d.), Archives of the Hamilton Park United Methodist Church, hereafter cited as HPUMC. For the Civic League and the Interorganizational Committee (later the Interorganizational Council), see chapter 6. For the batching plant, see Rohloff interview, OH 808, 25; and Charles E. Smith, interview by Wilson, 24 August 1989, OH 793, 117-19.

21. Release of lien, 27 July 1960, folder Dallas Citizens' Interracial Association, HF; and, for school integration, three undated clippings, DCIA.

22. Rohloff interview, OH 808, 21, 33, 34.

23. Crossman to John E. Mitchell Jr., 12 October 1964; Crossman to Carr P. Collins, 22 February 1965; and Collins to Crossman, 1 March 1965—all DCIA. See also Crossman to Hoblitzelle, 2 February 1965, folder Dallas Citizens' Interracial Association, HF. For forfeiture, see Crawford C. Martin, 1 September 1965, reel

108361-1 D4, RA number 17 719-1700-711, 9, 10, 11, Office of the Secretary of State, State of Texas, Austin.

24. For McShann Road, see *DTH*, 29 July 1989, p. 1A. For Highland Hills, see *DMN*, 13 January 1995, p. 13A. For Bishop College, see *DMN*, 18 April 1963, clipping in the Bishop vertical file, TDC, DPL; and Dorothy Neville, *Carr P. Collins: Man on the Move* (Dallas: Park Press, 1963), 122-24. The census information is from U.S. Department of Commerce, Bureau of the Census, *1950 Population Census Report: Census Tract Statistics, Dallas, Texas, and Adjacent Area* (Washington: GPO, 1952) 3: ch. 14: map and 8-9; and *U.S. Census of Population and Housing, 1960: Final Report, Census Tracts, Dallas, Tex. Standard Metropolitan Statistical Area* (Washington: GPO, 1962), map and 17-18. The division of South Dallas into eight census tracts follows the practice of the 1950 census, which consolidated the population totals for tracts 27A and 27B and for tracts 39A and 39B, thereby counting them, in effect, as two tracts, not four.

25. Hoblitzelle quotation in *DMN*, 3 May 1954; for Landrum quotations, see *DMN*, 8 March 1954, clippings in DCIA.

26. For quotation, meeting of the board of directors, 24 October 1955, DCIA. For the additional land purchase, see Crossman to the board of directors and the advisory board of the DCIA, 8 August 1960, DCIA; and Rohloff interview, OH 808, 26.

27. Frank H. Malone to John Q. Adams, 23 March 1964 and 7 April 1964; Adams to Malone, 8 April 1964; for the sale, see Malone to Adams, 22 April 1964—all in folder Dallas Citizens' Interracial Association, HF. See also Charles Inge, January 1988 statement, in the author's possession.

28. *Concord Corporation v. Dallas Citizens' Interracial Association*—plaintiff's original petition, case 69161F, in 116th Judicial Court, n.d.; statement of Crossman and Hoblitzelle, 27 February 1961; amended petition, n.d.; and other papers, all in folder Dallas Citizens' Interracial Association, HF. The court records were destroyed before they could be examined—see *DMN*, 26 February 1995, pp. 35A, 36A.

29. Barbara Darden, interview by Wilson, 13 December 1990, OH 916, 34-37.

30. Willie F. Smith to Hoblitzelle Foundation and the Dallas Citizens' Interracial Association, 22 November 1971, folder Dallas Citizens' Interracial Association, HF.

31. Louis J. Hexter to Van Holloman, 15 December 1971; penciled note on copy of Smith letter, n. 30; and Van Alen Holloman to Willie F. Smith, 28 December 1971, folder Dallas Citizens' Interracial Association, HF.

32. First quotation in Crossman to Dear Members, 21 January 1955; for clippings, see *Kansas City Call*, 4 and 11 February 1955, and *Pittsburgh Courier*, 12 February 1955; second and third quotations in Crossman to board of directors and advisory board of the DCIA, 8 August 1960; fourth quotation in Crossman to John Q. Adams, 2 March 1960—all in DCIA.

Chapter 5: The Early Community and Beyond

1. For the 1949 median male wage, see *Seventeenth Census, 1950*, 2: pt. 43: 43-591. For the 1959 median wage, see U.S. Department of Commerce, Bureau of the

Census, *Eighteenth Decennial Census of the United States: Census of Population, 1960: Characteristics of the Population* (Washington: GPO, 1963)1: pt. 45: 45-100. For the range of typical prices, see Ocie Turner, interview by Wilson, 14 September 1991, OH 977, 23; and Allen interview, OH 1020, 20. Tax records are in the Tax Office, Dallas County Records Building, Dallas. For computation of monthly income, see n. 2.

2. Seventeen interviewees recalled their family income at the time of their move-in. Recollections ranged from $40,000 to $2,880. Five, including the interviewee earning the $40,000, claimed incomes in five figures. The dollar amounts are suspect in four cases, and the probability is that a reported income of $2,880 is too low. Excluding these figures produces an average family income for the remaining thirteen cases of $5,468, comfortably above the 1959 single-earner Dallas black income of $3,255.

3. Laurice Stevenson, interview by Wilson, 4 September 1990, OH 875, 13; Albertus Edley, interview by Wilson, 9 October 1990, OH 864, 8; Mitchell interview, OH 962, 53-54; Willie B. Johnson, interview by Wilson, 9 February 1990, OH 819, 68-69, quotation at 68; Freddie Ervine, interview by Wilson, 30 October 1990, OH 912, 25; Charles Smith interview, OH 793, 13-14; Le Verne Fields, interview by Wilson, 9 July 1990, OH 835, 53; and Mr. and Mrs. Streetman Watson, interview by Wilson, 14 March 1990, OH 825, 53.

4. Williams interview, OH 871, 63-64; Myra L. Christian, interview by Wilson, 3 April 1991, OH 1033, 20-21; Robertson interview, OH 817, 20; Gee interview, OH 827, 22, 23; and Stevenson interview, OH 875, quotations at 15, 16.

5. Johnson interview, OH 819, 69.

6. Robertson interview, OH 817, 32 for Mr. Robertson's job and quotations at 21.

7. Velma Jackson, interview by Wilson, 18 October 1990, OH 862, 29, 30.

8. Andrew Wiese, "Places of Our Own," 35.

9. Selections from the "underclass" literature include Douglas S. Massey and Nancy A. Denton, *American Apartheid: Segregation and the Making of the Underclass* (Cambridge, Mass.: Harvard University Press, 1993); and Andrew Hacker, *Two Nations: Black and White, Separate, Hostile, Unequal* (New York: Charles Scribner's Sons, 1992). These studies have forebears in Ken Auletta, *The Underclass* (New York: Random House, 1982) and William Julius Wilson, *The Truly Disadvantaged: The Inner City, the Underclass, and Public Policy* (Chicago: University of Chicago Press, 1987). Books in the other categories include David Levering Lewis, *When Harlem Was in Vogue* (New York: Alfred A. Knopf, 1981), Louis R. Harlan, *Booker T. Washington: The Making of a Black Leader* (New York: Oxford University Press, 1972) and *Booker T. Washington: The Wizard of Tuskegee, 1901-1905* (New York: Oxford University Press, 1983), Charles V. Hamilton, *The Black Preacher in America* (New York: William Morrow, 1972), John Edward Hasse, *Beyond Category: The Life and Genius of Duke Ellington* (New York: Simon & Schuster, 1993), David L. Lewis, *W. E. B. DuBois: Biography of a Race* (New York: Henry Holt, 1993), Kenneth R. Manning, *Black Apollo of Science: The Life of Earnest Everett Just* (New York Oxford University Press, 1983), Harvard Sitkoff, *The Struggle for Black Equality, 1954-1992* rev. ed.

(New York: Hill and Wang, 1993), and William H. Harris, *The Harder We Run: Black Workers Since the Civil War* (New York: Oxford University Press, 1982).

10. Vivian T. Starks, interview by Wilson, 23 April 1991, OH 1005, 11, with second quotation at 77, first and third quotations at 78.

11. Only those interviews open or open with conditions are included. For analyses of the emotional and intellectual support for the suburb, see Kenneth T. Jackson, *Crabgrass Frontier: The Suburbanization of the United States* (New York: Oxford University Press, 1985), 45-137; for the influence of the FHA, ibid., 203-18. Jackson's demonstration that the FHA program helped to undermine central cities, meanwhile helping minorities relatively little, is less important here than his general discussion of the program itself. See also Robert Fishman, *Bourgeois Utopias: The Rise and Fall of Suburbia* (New York: Basic Books, 1987), 3-154. Both authors develop the conception of a suburban ideal into the late nineteenth or early twentieth century, then veer off into discussions of post-World War II land development, broadly defined. Peter G. Rowe, however, links the earlier and later ideals in *Making a Middle Landscape* (Cambridge, Mass.: MIT Press, 1991), 35-63, 217-47.

12. Curtis J. Smith, interview by Wilson, 2 February 1990, OH 826, 38-39; and Gee interview, OH 827, first quotation at 21, second at 73, and see also 72. See also Mildred Patrick, interview by Wilson, 11 April 1991, OH 965, 37-39.

13. Mitchell interview, OH 962, 8-15, 20-23; J. B. and Dorothy Simpson, interview by Wilson, 17 July 1990, OH 841, 2-6. Fields interview, OH 835, 2, 3-4.

14. Fields interview, OH 835, 8; George Brewer, interview by Wilson, 23 August 1990, OH 894, 14-15; Jackson interview, OH 862, 3-4; and Alfred W. Dupree Jr., interview by Wilson, 23 July 1990, OH 842, 5.

15. Edley interview, OH 864, first quotation at 11, second at 8, and also see 7; Robertson interview, OH 817, 11; Dixon interview, OH 868, 73; and Freddie M. Nance, interview by Wilson, 1 September 1990, OH 895, 25.

16. Simpson interview, OH 841, 23; Dixon interview, OH 868, 26; Cicero H. Bruton, interview by Wilson, 15 September 1990, OH 893, 22; Darden interview, OH 916, 6, 9; Dupree interview, OH 842, 24; and Fields interview, OH 835, 18.

17. Ervine interview, OH 912, 49-50; Robertson interview, OH 817, 16; Williams interview, OH 817, 73; and Bruton interview, OH 893, 25.

18. Information is compiled and analyzed from the Polk city directories in the Texas and Dallas Archives, Dallas Public Library, 1955-1991 inclusive, hereafter cited as PCD. See appendix A.

19. Bruton interview, OH 893, second quotation at 9, first at 17-18; Johnson interview, OH 819, 80; and Smith interview, OH 793, 26-27.

20. Ervine interview, OH 912, 18-19, 29-33; Robinson interview, OH 817, quotation at 22, and see also 10, 15, 20.

21. Crossman to board of directors and advisory board of the DCIA, 8 August 1960, DCIA. For move-outs, see PCD. Dixon interview, OH 868, 19; Charles Smith interview, OH 793, 15; Watson interview, OH 825, 20-21; and Curtis Smith interview, OH 826, 39.

22. Williams interview, OH 871, 85; Stevenson interview, OH 875, 27; Gee

interview, OH 827, 76; Simpson interview, OH 841, 22; Dixon interview, OH 868, 32; and Brewer interview, OH 894, 80.

23. Simpson interview, OH 841, 23; Nance interview, OH 895, 23-24; Jackson interview, OH 862, 45; and Brewer interview, OH 894, 80.

24. Don [Donald] Payton, interview by Wilson, 9 July 1991, OH 865, 5; Dixon interview, OH 868, 33; Curtis Smith interview, OH 826, 41; Williams interview, OH 871, 88; and Zan W. Holmes, interview by Wilson, 19 September 1991, OH 921, 38. For Holmes's career, see *DMN*, 9 August 1987, sec. E. pp. 1-3. Sheila R. Allen, interview by Wilson, 21 June 1991, OH 1012, 55.

25. Dixon interview, OH 868, 46; Payton interview, OH 865, 5.

26. Nance interview, OH 895, 26; Watson interview, OH 825, 64; Darden interview, OH 916, 25; Payton interview, OH 865, first quotation at 5, second at 21.

27. Jackson interview, OH 862, 48. For black motorists' inquiries, see Jackson interview, 49; and Dixon interview, OH 868, 36. Willie F. Smith, interview by Wilson, 31 May 1990, OH 829, 15, 16.

28. Holmes interview, OH 921, 13; Smith interview, OH 829, 14.

29. Brewer interview, OH 894, quotations, in order, at 102, 84, 85, and 82.

30. Dixon interview, OH 868, 77, first quotation at 88, third at 78. Nance interview, OH 895, 15.

31. Petition, n.d., and J. W. Rice to Crossman, 26 July 1954, box 2, folder 1, J. W. Rice correspondence, 1954, DNCC. Simpson interview, OH 841, 29, quotation at 28. Bruton interview, OH 893, 28, quotation at 29. See also Charles Smith interview, OH 793, 15-16, 56-59.

32. Dixon interview, OH 868, 44, 76; and Robertson interview, OH 817, 12-13.

33. Gee interview, OH 827, 24-25.

34. Starks interview, OH 1005, 7, 8.

35. Johnson interview, OH 819, 45-47, 122; and Ervine interview, OH 912, 23.

36. Ervine interview, OH 912, 30-33; Nance interview, OH 895, 21; Simpson interview, OH 841, 28.

37. Darden interview, OH 916, 3-5; Johnson interview, OH 819, 5-6, 15-16; Smith interview, OH 793, 16.

38. Christian interview, OH 1033, first quotation at 10, second at 31, and see 32, 37-44.

39. Johnson interview, OH 819, 13. See also 7-16, 27.

40. Robertson interview, OH 817, 25-30, 70-72.

41. Ibid., 27, 28-31, 68-70, quotation at 27.

42. Simpson interview, OH 841, 12-14; William J. Edmond Sr., interview by Wilson, 17 December 1990, OH 918, 3-4, quotation at 4; Turner interview, OH 977, 6-9, quotation at 9; Smith interview, OH 826, 16-19.

43. Dupree interview, OH 842, 9-16, quotations at 14, 15. For the Ninety-ninth and its local relationships, see Stanley Sandler, *Segregated Skies: All-Black Combat Squadrons of WW II* (Washington, D.C.: Smithsonian Institution Press, 1992), 29-30.

44. *Sixteenth Census, 1940,* 1: 1042; and 2: 1027. *Seventeenth Census, 1950,* 2: pt. 43: 11, 121. U.S. Department of Commerce, Bureau of the Census, *The Eighteenth Decennial Census of the United States, Census of Population, 1960* (Washington,

GPO, 1963), hereafter cited as *Eighteenth Census, 1960,* 1: pt. 45: 56, 360, and 366.

45. For a discussion of Truman's order in its context, see Richard M. Dalfiume, *Desegregation of the U.S. Armed Forces: Fighting on Two Fronts, 1939–1953* (Columbia: University of Missouri Press, 1969). Davis interview, OH 873, 27, 28, 29, 30-31.

46. Williams interview, OH 817, 74-75.

47. PCD.

48. Ibid.

49. Ibid.

50. Allen interview, OH 1020, 5; and Smith interview, OH 793, 10-11, quotation at 11.

51. Mitchell interview, OH 962, 37-40, 43-46, 59-60, 84, 118-19. First quotation at 59, 60, second quotation at 39. The problems of black entrepreneurs such as Mitchell are explained in Ivan Light and Carlyn Rosenstein, *Race, Ethnicity, and Entrepreneurship in Urban America* (New York: Aldine de Gruyter, 1995).

52. Smith interview, OH 826, 20-36. Quotations at 28, 29, 20.

53. Smith interview, OH 824, first quotation at 65, second quotation at 5. For Smith's title-work experiences, see 8-10, 65-67. Work-related quotations at 8, 9.

54. For Smith's surviving the layoff, see OH 824, 66; for the Southland and church episodes, see 88-95, first quotation at 95, second at 91. The church policy forbidding the elevation of blacks to the priesthood changed in 1978. For discussion of the issue from different perspectives, see Leonard J. Arrington and Davis Bitton, *The Mormon Experience: A History of the Latter-Day Saints,* 2d. ed. (Urbana: University of Illinois Press, 1992), 321-25, and Klaus J. Hansen, *Mormonism and the American Experience* (Chicago: University of Chicago Press, 1981), 183-204.

Chapter 6: Organizing in Hamilton Park

1. "Hamilton Park Civic League Constitution and By-laws" (1977 revision), pamphlet, Charles E. Smith Papers, copies in author's possession, hereafter cited as CESP. "Constitution of the Interorganizational Council," mimeograph, Curtis J. Smith Papers, copies in author's possession, hereafter cited as CJSP. See also Charles Smith interview, OH 826, 65-66, 106-7; and Holmes interview, OH 921, 21, 22.

2. For the Methodist church, see *Church History,* HPUMC. For the Baptist church, see *The Link,* 27 August-2 September 1986, 1-2, in Freddie M. Nance Papers, copies in author's possession, hereafter cited as FMNP. For the Church of Christ church, see Edward L. Newhouse Sr. and Mary A. Newhouse, interview by Wilson, 6 December 1990, OH 956, 28. For the other clubs, see Robertson interview, OH 817, 59-62.

3. Letter and petition to Rice, n.d. but July 1954, box 2, folder 1, J. W. Rice Correspondence, 1954, DNCC.

4. Ibid.

5. Crossman to Rice, 27 July 1954, box 2, folder 1, J. W. Rice Correspondence, 1954. For other civic leagues, see J. W. Rice memorandum, "Report of Activities of the Dallas Negro Chamber of Commerce," prepared for annual meeting, 21 December 1950, box 3, folder 27, Annual Meetings, 1950. For first quotation, see Rice to Crossman, 26 July 1954, box 2, folder 1. For the groundwork, Rice to

Crossman, 6 August 1954, box 2, folder 1. For second quotation, Rice to Crossman, 24 August 1954, box 2, folder 1. All in DNCC.

6. "Constitution and By-Laws," quoted on 22, 3, and 12, CESP.

7. For league developments, see *Hamilton Park High School Community Study Report (A Summary)* (Dallas: Hamilton Park High School, 1966), hereafter cited as *HPHSCSR*, 66, copy in Sadye Gee Papers, copies in author's possession, hereafter cited as SGP; and Davis interview, OH 873, 73.

8. For youth problems, see, for example, Holmes interview, OH 921, 28-29, 41-42. For first quotation, see *HPHSCSR*, 691. Johnson interview, OH 819, 119.

9. Dixon interview, OH 868, 44-45; *HPHSCSR*, 63; and Johnson interview, OH 819, 112-13.

10. Holmes interview, OH 921, 29. See also 39-40. Dixon interview, OH 868, 45. Richard Bonner, interview by Wilson, 29 September 1991, OH 924, 21.

11. *HPHSCSR*, 63, 64, 69-70. Dixon interview, OH 868, 49-50.

12. Holmes interview, OH 921, 34-38, quotation at 28.

13. Payton interview, OH 865, 6. See also Darden interview, OH 916, 21-22.

14. Brewer interview, OH 894, quotations at 92-95.

15. *HPHSCSR*, 68-71.

16. Gee interview, OH 827, 88-89; for quotations, Holmes interview, OH 921, 40-41.

17. Holmes interview, OH 921, the robbery quotation at 29 and other quotations at 40-41.

18. Ibid., 38.

19. Watson interview, OH 825, 65; and Brewer interview, OH 894, 111.

20. *HPHSCSR*, 66, 76, 77. Brewer interview, OH 894, 110-14, quotation at 113.

21. For lack of lighting, Darden interview, OH 916, 17. For improvements, see *HPHSCSR*, 62-63, 66-67 and Charles Smith interview, OH 793, 52-53.

22. Charles Smith interview, OH 793, 86-87. For quotation, see Smith to Roland Tucker, 29 June 1982, CESP.

23. Robertson interview, OH 817, 54; Christian interview, OH 1033, 51.

24. Christian interview, OH 1033, 54; Robertson interview, OH 817, 54-55.

25. Charles Smith interview, OH 793, 82; Edley interview, OH 864, 13-14.

26. Davis interview, OH 873, 63-65.

27. Ibid., first two quotations at 65, 66; Davis to Hoblitzelle, 12 September 1960 (quotations); Hoblitzelle to Davis, 5 October 1960, and 23 December 1960; L. B. Houston to Lynn Harris, 19 September 1961, folder Hamilton Park: *Park Club House*, HF.

28. *HPHSCSR*, 74-75, 77; and Charles Smith interview, OH 793, 59-61. For mail boxes, see Willie Smith interview, OH 829, 76. For the bus service, see Charles Smith interview, OH 793, 56-59, Willie Smith interview, OH 829, 19-20, and Simpson interview, OH 841, 28-29.

29. Charles Smith interview, OH 793, 98-100, quotation at 98; Willie Smith interview, OH 829, 59. The analysis of the reciprocity between the apartments and the community is taken from PCD. The percentage of Hispanic families is the number of Hispanic-surnamed families divided by the total of occupied units. In 1986, thirty-three of eighty-one occupied units, or 40.7 percent, were Hispanic-

occupied. Twelve units were listed as vacant; forty-three were listed "no return." In 1991, only fifteen units were occupied, twelve by Hispanics. Ninety units were listed as vacant, with one "no return." For the 1961 suit, see Darden interview, OH 916, 34–37 and Willie Smith interview, OH 829, 61.

30. Rohloff interview, OH 808, 25. See also *HPHSCSR*, 76–77, Charles Smith interview, OH 793, 117–19, and Simpson interview, OH 841, 44–46.

31. For an exhortation to maintain property, see *HPHSCSR*, 73. A copy of the deed restrictions, 13 October 1953, signed by Crossman and Hoblitzelle, is in folder DCIA, Covenant Violations. The situation in late 1971, with quotations, is described in Willie Smith to the HF and the DCIA, 22 November 1971. Both are in HF.

32. Smith interview, OH 829, quotations at 68, 32; Bruton interview, OH 893, 61; Van Alen Holloman to Smith, 28 December 1971, folder DCIA, Covenant Violations, HF.

33. Smith interview, OH 829, 69–70.

34. Ibid., quotations, in order, at 32, 27.

35. For tract 89, see *Eighteenth Census, 1960: Census Tracts* (Washington: GPO, 1962), 22; also 18–27 and tract map. For the 1970 tracts, see U.S. Department of Commerce, Social and Economic Statistics Administration, Bureau of the Census, *1970 Census of Population and Housing: Census Tracts* (Washington: GPO, 1972), 5–16, and tract map. For 1959 income, see *Eighteenth Census, 1960;* 1: pt. 45: 444. For 1970 income, see *1970 Census of Population* (Washington: GPO, 1973) 1: 45, 635. The consumer price index is based on constant 1967 dollars. See U.S. Department of Commerce, Bureau of the Census, *Pocket Data Book, USA 1973* (Washington: GPO, 1973), 207, table 301.

36. Smith interview, OH 829, 32–33.

37. Thelma Wells, interview by Wilson, 19 October 1990, OH 903, 7, 41. Mrs. Wells's presidency followed that of Willie Smith, whose terms ended in 1971, Smith interview, OH 829, 23. 1977 PCD, street listings, 2: 1166.

38. Edmund interview, OH 918, quotations at 29, 30.

39. Smith interview, OH 829, 22 (beer parlor); 23 (cars); 28 (trucks). For the beer parlor, see also Christian interview, OH 1032, 56.

40. Dupree interview, OH 842, 78–80. Smith interview, OH 820, 23.

41. Smith interview, OH 826, 66.

42. Holmes interview, OH 921, 21–22 and, for church support, 27. Curtis Smith interview, OH 826, 71, 72, and IOC constitution, CJSP. For the IOC as a community council, a cooperative and coordinating group, and a clearing house, see Brewer interview, OH 894, 97–100.

43. Holmes interview, OH 921, 22–23. For the turnout, see Willie Smith interview, OH 829, 37, Simpson interview, OH 841, 62, Brewer interview, OH 894, 102, and Charles Smith interview, OH 793, 39.

44. Curtis Smith interview, OH 826, 70 ("litigation" quotation); and 86 ("said yes," quotation). For the rest of the IOC-TI relationship, see Ernest Randall to Curtis J. Smith, 28 July 1967, enclosing "Summary of Texas Instruments Presentation to Hamilton Park Group," and Smith to Randall, 24 August 1967, CJSP.

45. Smith interview, OH 826, 86.

46. For Connally's career, see James Reston Jr., *The Lone Star: The Life of John*

Connally (New York: Harper & Row, 1989); and for Mattox, *DTH,* 14 August 1983, K1, K6, clipping in Mattox vertical file, Texas and Dallas Archives. See also Curtis Smith interview, OH 826, 108, and Mitchell interview, OH 962, 136-39.

47. For the education building, see *Church History,* HPUMC. Smith interview, OH 826, first quotation at 74, others at 109-10.

48. Smith interview, OH 826, 75, quotations at 78, 77; Dixon interview, OH 868, 99.

49. Surveys of the Truman Administration and civil rights developments include Donald R. McCoy, *The Presidency of Harry S. Truman* (Lawrence: University Press of Kansas, 1984), 106-9, 153-62 (1948 election), 167-71, 182-83, and 254-56, William E. Pemberton, *Harry S. Truman: Fair Dealer and Cold Warrior* (Boston: Twayne, 1989), 112-16, 122-25 (1948 election), 145-48, and Gary W. Reichard, *Politics as Usual: The Age of Truman and Eisenhower* (Arlington Heights, Ill.: Harlan Davidson, 1988), 29-32, 32-45 (1948 election), 47-48. For the Texas scene, see William H. Wilson, "Desegregation of the Hamilton Park School, 1955-1975," *Southwestern Historical Quarterly* 95 (July 1991): 45-46.

50. For Kennedy's civil rights activity, see James N. Giglio, *The Presidency of John F. Kennedy* (Lawrence: University Press of Kansas, 1991), 159-87. For Johnson's activity, see Vaughn Davis Bornet, *The Presidency of Lyndon B. Johnson* (Lawrence: University Press of Kansas, 1983), especially 94-96, 98-100, 129, 228-33.

51. Chester J. Patch Jr. and Elmo Richardson, *The Presidency of Dwight D. Eisenhower* (Lawrence: University Press of Kansas, 1991), 139-49. See also Robert Frederick Burk, *The Eisenhower Administration and Black Civil Rights* (Knoxville: University of Tennessee Press, 1984).

52. Smith interview, OH 826, for quotations, in order, see 109, 78, 75, and 78. Other information is on 73 and 79. See also Dixon interview, OH 868, 101-2.

53. Smith interview, OH 826, 79, for mailings; quotation, ibid., 106-7. Interviews concerning the IOC recommendations are, in the order quoted, Williams interview, OH 871, 117; Edley interview, OH 864, 44; Stevenson interview, OH 875, 50; Jackson interview, OH 862, 64, 65; Patrick interview, OH 965, 50; and Pearline Proctor, interview by Wilson, 6 May 1991, OH 981, 32.

54. For the vote totals, see *DMN,* 4 November 1964, p. 18; 9 November 1972, p. 42A; 9 November 1988, p. 3K. Ascertaining the Hamilton Park vote presents problems: voting records, including the numbers assigned to precincts, are destroyed within a few months of every election. For most of the period surveyed here, the newspapers only erratically reported election results at the precinct level, sometimes omitting locations and giving only the precinct numbers. The Hamilton Park precinct, established about 1962, originally embraced the community only, but later was extended to include a larger area. The extension appears to have affected neither the Democratic predilection nor the wide margin of votes for Democratic candidates.

55. For the league's activities, see *HPHSCSR,* 70, Charles Smith interview, OH 793, 50-51, and flyer announcing the annual picnic, 24 August 1985, CESP.

56. Robertson interview, OH 817, 60-62.

57. Ibid., 62-63.

58. Curtis Smith interview, OH 826, 67-69; Jackson interview, OH 862, 49-50, quotation at 50; Edley interview, OH 864, 17.

59. Willie Smith interview, OH 829, 80; Dupree interview, OH 842, 70-71, quotation at 65.

60. David M. Tucker, *Black Pastors and Leaders: Memphis, 1819-1972* (Memphis: Memphis State University Press, 1975), brings out the human values of the black church in a setting similar to that of Dallas.

61. For the first services, *Church History,* HPUMC. Holmes interview, OH 921, 31-33, quotation at 33; for financial support, Hatchett and Benson, *History of Hamilton Park United Methodist Church,* 8, HPUMC.

62. Quotation in Holmes interview, OH 921, at 9. *Church History,* HPUMC. For Holmes, see *DMN,* 9 August 1987, pp. 1E-3E; 9 December 1990, pp. 1J-8J; and 2 July 1991, pp. 1A, 6A. For the church school, see Hatchett and Benson, *History of Hamilton Park United Methodist Church,* 1, HPUMC. Davis interview, OH 873, 100.

63. Hatchett and Benson, *History of Hamilton Park United Methodist Church,* 15-16.

64. *The Link,* 27 August-2 September 1986, 1-2, in FMNP.

65. For active participation, Newhouse interview, OH 956, 28. Freddie M. Nance, a Roman Catholic, did not change her faith, Nance interview, OH 895, 32. Dixon interview, OH 868, 38-39. Smith interview, OH 829, 12, 81-82, quotation at 82. Edmond interview, OH 918, 32.

66. Robertson interview, OH 817, 39-62. Newhouse interview, OH 956, 49-108 (all activities) and 105-6 (satisfaction with Hamilton Park).

Chapter 7: School and Community

1. *Seventeenth Census, 1950* 2: pt. 43: 43-159. Minutes of the Board of Trustees of the Richardson Independent School District, hereafter cited as RISD Board Minutes, in the archives of the Richardson Independent School District, archives hereafter cited as RISD, v. 2, 4 January 1954, 2. The relationships within the school and between school and community are strikingly similar to those found by Vanessa Siddle Walker and others, although they examine mostly rural and small-town schools. See Walker's *Their Highest Potential: An African American School Community in the Segregated South* (Chapel Hill: University of North Carolina Press, 1996).

2. RISD Board Minutes, v. 2, 7 June 1954, 9. For increase in property values and quotations, see the minutes, v. 2, 5 July 1954, 10. For approval of the plans for the school, see the minutes, v. 2, 6 September 1954, and, for naming the school, see the minutes, v. 2, 2 May 1955, 29. All in RISD.

3. *Brown v. Board of Education of Topeka,* 17 May 1954, *Supreme Court Reporter* (St. Paul: West Publishing, 1954), 74: 686-93, and *Brown v. Board of Education of Topeka* [*Brown* II], 31 May 1955, ibid. (1955), 78: 753-57.

4. On Crossman's relation to the school, see Rohloff interview, OH 808, 19-20.

5. For attitudes toward the school, see *HPHSCSR,* 78-79 and the following interviews by Wilson: Robert F. Cook, 2 May 1987, OH 695; Doris A. Robertson, 7 June 1987, OH 697; Charles E. Smith, 29 March 1988, OH 724; Curtis J. Smith,

8 September 1987, OH 703. Material on the proposed integration is from a confidential source.

6. Payton interview, OH 865, 22. Theresa Patrick, interview by Wilson, 10 June 1991, OH 925, 15; and Bonner interview, OH 924, quotations at 5, 6, 7.

7. Bonner interview, OH 924, 4, 5-6, *HPHSCSR,* 18, 37; Starks interview, OH 1005, 10, 11, 68-73; Garnett interview, OH 958, 11-14, 17-18, 34.

8. Bonner interview, OH 924, 8 (poverty quotations); and 11, 12 (football team quotations).

9. Allen interview, OH 1012, quotations at 4, 7; Patrick interview, OH 925, quotations at 3, 8; and Payton interview, OH 865, 17.

10. Starks interview, OH 1005, 70; and Garnett interview, OH 958, 37, 38.

11. Starks interview, OH 1005, quotation at 74 and see also 73. Garnett interview, OH 958, quotations at 37 and 39.

12. Allen interview, OH 1020, 61-63, quotation at 61; Jackson interview, OH 862, 76-80; Ervine interview, OH 912, 65; Newhouse interview, OH 956, 70-71; Patrick interview, OH 925, 27-28; Robert E. Price, interview by Wilson, 22 April 1991, OH 963, 31-32 and quotation at 71.

13. Price interview, OH 963, 71-77. For quotations, in order, see 73, 74, 76. For Pearce's obituary, see *DMN,* 11 September 1995, pp. 13A, 16A.

14. *HPHSCSR,* 40-41.

15. Ibid., 13-17. Quotations at 16, 17. See also Garnett interview, OH 865, 34-36.

16. Hamilton Park student records are no longer retained by the RISD—telephone conversation with Gene Gumm, the RISD official in charge of records, in 1988. Most of the information is from a memorandum, "Information Concerning Hamilton Park School," folder H.E.W.-1965-68, RISD. Some percentage information is from a confidential source.

17. For first quotation, Willie Smith interview, OH 829, 44. Bruton interview, OH 893, 71.

18. Edley interview, OH 864, 38; Simpson interview, OH 841, 63; Starks interview, OH 1005, 91; Garnett interview, OH 958, 40.

19. For Lockhart's career, see excerpt from *Texas Black High School Sports,* Vertical File, Texas and Dallas Archives; and Robert S. La Forte and Richard L. Himmel, *Down the Corridor of Years: A Centennial History of the University of North Texas in Photographs, 1890-1990* (Denton: University of North Texas Press, 1987), 229. Mitchell interview, OH 962, 74-80, 107-10, quotations at 109. See also James O. Griffin, interview by Wilson, 19 November 1987, OH 715, 4.

20. Charlotte Brewster, interview by Wilson, 3 March 1991, OH 1007, quotations at 19, 26 and see also 9, 29. Bonner interview, OH 924, 13-15. For quotations see 17, 18.

21. For Walls, see *DMN,* 23 October 1988, pp. 1B, 20B and 24 June 1990, p. 34A; and *DTH,* 12 September 1990, p. 1C. Patrick interview, OH 925, 5; Griffin interview, OH 715, 4-5.

22. Payton interview, OH 865, 29; Mitchell interview, OH 962, 113; Willie Smith interview, OH 829, 79; Charles Smith interview, OH 793, 46; Allen interview, OH 1020, 29.

23. *HPHSCSR*, quotations at 9, 12. Calculations from the 1960 census show that, in 1960, 8.8 percent of nonwhite males aged thirty-five through forty-four in the Dallas Standard Metropolitan Statistical Area had completed four years of college; 8.2 percent had completed eight years of primary school; 25 percent had completed four years of high school. Among women in the same age group, 38 percent completed four years of high school, 5.4 percent completed one year of college, and 6 percent completed four years of college. See *Eighteenth Census, 1960*, 1: pt. 45: 45-720. Calculations from a sample in the 1970 census show that, in 1970, 2 percent of black men aged forty through forty-four had completed four years of college; 20.5 percent had completed four years of high school. Among women in the same age group, 25.7 percent had completed four years of high school and 4.1 percent had completed four years of college. See *1970 Census of Population: General Population Characteristics, Texas* (Washington: GPO, 1971) 1: Pt. 45, sec. 2: 45-1373. For national comparisons revealing the relatively high level of educational attainment in Hamilton Park, see Gerald David Jaynes and Robin M. Williams Jr., eds., *A Common Destiny: Blacks and American Society* (Washington: National Academy Press, 1989), 332-38. This analysis assumes that most Hamilton Park fathers and mothers surveyed in 1965 were born in the 1920s and that, therefore, the age cohorts in the 1960 and 1970 censuses would provide the best comparable data.

24. Ibid., 41, 51-52; Robertson interview, OH 817, 44-51, quotation at 45-46.

25. Robertson interview, OH 817, 45; and *HPHSCSR*, 41.

26. *HPHSCSR*, quotations at 56, 57; third and fourth quotations in Willie Smith interview, OH 829 at 41, 44. The PTA and the Dads Club coordinated their carnivals to avoid conflict, OH 829, 73-74.

27. *HPHSCSR*, 53-55; Mitchell interview, OH 962, 87.

28. For cooperation, see Willie Smith interview, OH 829, 41. For grade-school growth, see *HPHSCSR*, 38. High-school growth is from a confidential source. For improvements, see Attachment No. 9, Motion for Supplemental Relief, 23 May 1974, *United States v. Texas Education Agency*, et al. [RISD], CA-3-4101-C, Office of the Clerk, United States District Court for the Northern Division of Texas, hereafter cited as *U.S. v. RISD*. For periodic overcrowding, see Cook interview, OH 695, 6.

29. Smith interview, OH 724, 3; Turner interview, OH 977, quotations at 48, 49, and see also 50.

30. Watson interview, OH 825, 34-35; Cook interview, OH 695, 5-6.

31. Williams interview, OH 871, quotations, in order, on 55, 57, 109, and 57; and Garnett interview, OH 958, 42-43, quotation at 43.

32. Smith interview, OH 724, 7; Gee interview, OH 827, 43; Griffin interview, OH 715, 32, 33. See also John Roberts, interview by Wilson, 15 December 1987, OH 716, 11, 15-17.

33. Williams interview, OH 871, 64-65. Information concerning CALL is from a confidential source.

34. Stevenson interview, OH 875, 56, 60, 63-64, 65-66, quotation at 69. Information on the CALL visit is from a confidential source.

35. The record of the CALL meetings is from a confidential source. Starks interview, OH 1005, 96; for confrontation, 82. Garnett interview, OH 958, 48. Wells interview, OH 903, 19, 18. The quotation "he ... man" is on 29 and the quotation

"completely ... wife" is on 44 of the Garnett interview, OH 958. For protocol, see Garnett interview, OH 958, 44-45, and Starks interview, OH 1005, 96.

36. For the meeting, see Garnett interview, OH 958, 47-48. For Goss's response to the letter and the loss of his principalship, see Garnett interview, OH 958, 48-49, and Starks interview, OH 1005, 83-84. For denials, see Starks interview, OH 1005, 85, and Stevenson interview, OH 875, 62-63. Other information, including the Goss quotation, is from a confidential source.

37. *HPHSCSR*, 7. Goss wrote the report, see Griffin interview, OH 715, 31-32. Holmes interview, OH 921, 43.

38. The 40 percent is an educated guess based on all the related documents and interviews, especially Charles Smith interview, OH 793, 49, and *HPHSCSR*, 9. See Griffin interview, OH 715, 33 (education and parent-participation quotations), and 35 (quotations on fund-raising and contrast with other RISD schools).

39. For the income figures, see, in order, U.S. Department of Commerce, Bureau of the Census, *U.S. Census of Population and Housing, 1960: Census Tracts, Dallas, Texas* (Washington: GPO, 1962) pt. 34, 21; *U.S. Census of Population, 1960: General Social and Economic Characteristics, Texas* (Washington: GPO, 1962) 45C: 45-427; *1970 Census of Population: General Social and Economic Characteristics, Texas* (Washington: GPO, 1972) pt. 45: 45-801; and *1970 Census of Population: Census Tracts, Dallas, Texas* (Washington: GPO, 1972), P-112. The Hamilton Park family incomes are necessarily speculative. The census tracts that included Hamilton Park took in white housing that was more expensive than almost all the homes in the subdivision; therefore, the family income is listed as being below the tract median of $6,518 in 1959 and the tract mean of $10,500 in 1969. Griffin interview, OH 715, 33, 34-35.

40. Griffin interview, OH 715, 38; and *HPHSCSR*, 31. For dropouts, see memorandum, undated but probably 1966, indicating a high dropout rate, folder Health Education Welfare no. 1, RISD. Starks interview, OH 1005, 81.

41. For RISD concern with the Civil Rights Act, see folder Federal Funds, RISD. For doubts about equality, see Stevenson interview, OH 875, 57; Curtis Smith interview, OH 703, 14-16; and Cook interview, OH 695, 18. All other information is from a confidential source.

42. Brewer interview, OH 894, 95; Cook interview, OH 695, 35; Griffin interview, OH 715, 46-47.

Chapter 8: The School Transformed

1. Desegregation studies abound. Four books presenting the issue from various points of view are Frank T. Read and Lucy S. McGough, *Let Them Be Judged: The Judicial Integration of the Deep South* (Metuchen, N.J.: Scarecrow Press, 1978); Walter G. Stephan and Joe Feagin, eds., *School Desegregation: Past, Present, and Future* (New York: Plenum Press, 1980); J. Harvie Wilkinson III, *From Brown to Bakke: The Supreme Court and School Integration, 1954-1978* (New York: Oxford University Press, 1979); and Raymond Wolters, *The Burden of Brown: Thirty Years of School Desegregation* (Knoxville: University of Tennessee Press, 1984). Lino A. Graglia, *Disaster by Decree: The Supreme Court Decisions on Race and the Schools* (Ithaca: Cornell University Press, 1976), presents searching analyses of federal court deci-

sions from a legalistic, conservative vantage point. Jack Bass, *Unlikely Heroes: The Dramatic Story of the Southern Judges of the Fifth Circuit Who Translated the Supreme Court's Brown Decision into a Revolution for Equality* (New York: Simon and Schuster, 1981), presenting the great range of problems and issues confronting the fifth circuit, applauds the court's desegregation decisions and lauds the judges who wrote them. George R. Metcalf, *From Little Rock to Boston: The History of School Desegregation* (Westport, Conn: Greenwood Press, 1983), deals with many of the political difficulties of desegregation from a liberal perspective. Robert A. Pratt, *The Color of Their Skin: Education and Race in Richmond, Virginia, 1954-89* (Charlottesville: University Press of Virginia, 1992), weaves national and state issues into the Richmond situation, criticizing white attitudes toward desegregation. A fine, legal-constitutional study rich in local drama is Davison M. Douglas, *Reading, Writing, and Race: The Desegregation of the Charlotte Schools* (Chapel Hill: University of North Carolina Press, 1995). Julianne Lewis Adams and Thomas A. DeBlack, *Civil Obedience: An Oral History of School Desegregation in Fayetteville, Arkansas, 1954-1965* (Fayetteville: University of Arkansas Press, 1994), concerns a Southern district that desegregated early and with little fanfare. Although the words *integration* and *desegregation* have distinct meanings, they are used interchangeably here.

2. Public Law 88-352, 2 July 1964, *United States Statutes at Large, 1964* (Washington: GPO, 1965), 78: 246-49, 252-53. The quotation is from a confidential source. For the RISD's determination to comply with the law, see Henry D. Akin Jr., interview by Wilson, 22 February 1989, OH 790, 4-5, 10-11. Akin served as the attorney for the RISD during the desegregation era. The quotation is from a confidential source.

3. "General Statement of Policies Under Title VI of the Civil Rights Act of 1964 Respecting Desegregation of Elementary and Secondary Schools," appendix to *Price v. Denison Independent School District Board of Education*, 2 July 1965, *Federal Reporter* (St. Paul: West Publishing, 1966): 2d ser., v. 348, fourth and fifth quotations at 1015, first, second, and third quotations at 1016, 1017, and 1018-20. RISD Board Minutes, v. 11, 28 June 1965, 28-28A, RISD. J. J. Pearce to Francis Keppel, 30 June 1965, and Keppel to Pearce, 23 August 1965, folder Desegregation Plan 1964-65, RISD.

4. Public Law 88-352, *United States Statutes at Large, 1964*, 248; "Statement of Policies for School Desegregation Plans under Title VI of the Civil Rights Act of 1964," *Federal Register*, 9 April 1966, 30: 5623-25 (quotation at 5626), 5627-34. For enrollment figures, see compliance information form, folder Desegregation Plan 1964-65, RISD. An excellent summary of national developments in relation to educational problems is Diane Ravitch, *The Troubled Crusade: American Education, 1945-1980* (New York: Basic Books, 1983), 129, 132-34, 142-48, 166-68.

5. For the strategy, see James A. Knox to J. J. Pearce, 20 April 1966. For the Holmes-Pearce conference, see memorandum, 19 May 1966, both in folder Health Education Welfare No. 1, RISD.

6. The December 1966 suggestion of the HEW official is from a confidential source. For the later conference, see "Minutes of Meeting Between Officials of H.E.W. and R.I.S.D. and Counsel, 16 January 1967," folder H.E.W.—1965-67, RISD.

7. The memorandum is from a confidential source.

8. The memorandum is from a confidential source.

9. For the first quotation, see Henry D. Akin Jr. to Jack W. Evans, 20 April 1966, folder Health, Education, Welfare No. 1 (copies), RISD. For second quotation, see Akin interview, OH 790, 14. The steps to the HEW-RISD agreement may be recapitulated from the RISD archives. Key material includes James A. Knox to J. J. Pearce, 20 April 1966, folder Health, Education, Welfare No. 1; Akin to Evans, cited above; clipping, *DTH,* 6 October 1966, folder Federal Funds; minutes cited in n. 6; Albert T. Hamlin to Akin, 27 March 1968, untitled green folder; and "Plan for Improving the Educational Program of the Senior High Students at Hamilton Park, Approved by RISD Board of Trustees April 8, 1968," folder Court Orders (RISD Desegregation Cases). For Congressional opposition, see Beryl A. Radin, *Implementation, Change, and the Federal Bureaucracy: School Desegregation Policy in H.E.W., 1964-1968* (New York: Teachers College Press, 1977), 65-68, 111-14.

10. Watson interview, OH 825, quotations at 36, 37; Patrick interview, OH 925, quotations at 10, 35; Allen interview, OH 1012, 11.

11. See the plan, cited in n. 9. For careful planning, see also Griffin interview, OH 715, 26-29. Information on CALL is from a confidential source. Davis interview, OH 873, 93-98.

12. The generalizations about the reconciliation of residents to the loss of their school and minimal difficulties with transfers come from a reading of all the interviews and represent a consensus, not unanimity. For the problem of the mingling of all age groups, see Willie F. Smith to State Commissioner of Education, 16 January 1968, and Leon R. Graham to Smith, 30 January 1968, folder H.E.W.— 1965-68, RISD. Cook interview, OH 695, 7-8.

13. The quotation is from a confidential source. The IOC was then named the Hamilton Park Interorganization Committee. For rumors about closing, see Charles Smith interview, OH 724, 13. No evidence survives in the RISD archives, nor is there any indication in the board minutes that the RISD intended to close the school. See also Roberts interview, OH 716, 36-37.

14. The Smith-McCarley correspondence is from a confidential source.

15. CALL information is from a confidential source.

16. CALL information is from a confidential source.

17. RISD Board Minutes, v. 12, 25 November 1968, 34, and meeting of 2 December 1968, 36-37.

18. Ibid., 2 December 1968, 36-37.

19. Akin interview, OH 790, 26-27; and Roberts interview, OH 716, quotations at 18, 19.

20. *Green v. County School Board of New Kent County, Virginia,* 27 May 1968, *Supreme Court Reporter* (St. Paul: West Publishing, 1969), hereafter cited as *Green v. County School Board,* 88A: 1689-93, 1694 (quotations), 1695-96. See also Reed and McGough, *Let Them Be Judged,* 479-91. For quotations from the 28 July 1970 meeting, see undated memorandum, untitled green folder, RISD.

21. Transcript of proceedings, 20, 24 August 1970; and Order, W. M. Taylor Jr., 20 August 1970, *U.S. v. RISD.* The majority-to-minority transfer allowed any student to transfer from a school in which he or she was a member of the majority race to one in the same district having the student's race in the minority.

22. Transcript, 24 August 1970, 134, 136; and Order, W. M. Taylor Jr., 10 September 1970, *U.S. v. RISD*. For the command, see *Green v. County School Board, Supreme Court Reporter*, 88A: 1693. For alternatives to closing, see "Hamilton Park Evaluation Committee, April 22-23, 1969," folder H.E.W—1965-68, RISD. For the parents' organizations, see Willie Smith interview, OH 829, 41, and Robertson interview, OH 817, 66. For the advantages of the compromise, see Akin interview, OH 790, 39-40.

23. Allen interview, OH 1012, 25, 31-32, the "made no effort" quotation at 32.

24. Allen interview, OH 1012, four quotations ("the cultures" and "we black," "the white girls," and "talk back") at 15. See also 16. For the other quotations, see 31.

25. Allen interview, OH 1012; for buses, see 25; for "would come" quotation, see 20; for the account of the fight on the basketball court and quotations, see 26-27; for walkouts, see 25; and for black aggression, see 29. For "boiling point" quotation, see 24.

26. Allen interview, OH 1012; for "we were" quotation, 25; for the bus and walking home incident, and quotations, see 22-23. Freddie and Ola Lee Allen interview, OH 1020, 45-46.

27. Allen interview, OH 1012, quotation at 38; for Allen's later career, see 37-48, 66.

28. *Swann v. Charlotte-Mecklenburg Board of Education*, 20 April 1971, *Supreme Court Reporter* (St. Paul: West Publishing, 1972), 91A: 1267-84. The discarding of the Civil Rights Act while quoting from it is on 1276-77; acceptance of busing is on 1282-83. The monograph on the background and decision process of *Swann* is Bernard Schwartz, *Swann's Way: The School Busing Case and the Supreme Court* (New York: Oxford University Press, 1986). For reactions to *Swann*, see Schwartz's work and the sources listed in n. 1; also Judith F. Buncher, ed., *The School Busing Controversy: 1970-75* (New York: Facts on File, 1975). For quotations, see Public Law 88-352, *United States Statutes at Large, 1964*, 248. Metcalf, in *From Little Rock to Boston*, argues that President Nixon seriously impeded desegregation. That Nixon slowed the pace is probable, but he failed to thwart it, especially in districts such as the RISD in which by 1971 it was already well advanced.

29. Akin interview, OH 790, quotations at 39, 40-41; and Roberts interview, OH 716, 15.

30. Motion for Supplemental Relief (quotation) and Memorandum in Support of Motion for Supplemental Relief, both 23 May 1974; and Closing Statements of Counsel, 2 August 1974, 23, *U.S. v. RISD*.

31. Akin interview, OH 790, 41-43, quotation at 43. For the courtroom arguments, see Memorandum in Support of Motion for Supplemental Relief, 11; Defendant RISD's Reply to Plaintiff's Motion for Supplemental Relief and Memorandum in Support Thereof, 2 August 1974 (quotations), and Closing Statements of Counsel, 2 August 1974, 33, *U.S. v. RISD*.

32. Akin interview, OH 790, 46. Closing Statements of Counsel, 2 August 1974, 42-47, quotations at 48, 49.

33. For Akin quotations, see Akin interview, OH 790, 53. Order, W. M. Taylor Jr., 2 August 1974, *U.S. v. RISD; United States v. The Texas Education Agency,*

22 April 1975, *Federal Reporter* (St. Paul: West Publishing, 1975) 2d ser.: 512: 898 (Fifth Circuit Court quotation); and *Richardson Daily News,* hereafter cited as *RDN,* 17 June 1975, p. 1.

34. Akin interview, OH 790, 53. Petition, 28 June 1974, folder Richardson Ind. School District School System Summary Report, *U.S. v. RISD* for quotations from petition. See also *RDN,* 20 May 1975, p. 1; and Robertson interview, OH 817, 2-3.

35. Brief for the United States, 3 November 1974, *United States v. Richardson Independent School District,* 74-3686, Fifth Circuit Court, folder Court Orders, RISD; Motion to Intervene by Clifford E. Abrams, 7 July 1975; and Report to the Court by Samuel W. Webster Jr., 7 July 1975, *U.S. v. RISD.*

36. Roberts interview, OH 716, first quotation at 27. For the marathon sessions naming the program, see Akin interview, OH 790, 55, 61. For other quotations, see Proposed Arrangements, RISD, 20 June 1975, *U.S. v. RISD.*

37. Proposed Arrangements, RISD, 20 June 1975, 3, *U.S. v. RISD.*

38. For lack of enthusiasm, see Roberts interview, OH 716, 25-26. Akin interview, OH 790, 58. Proposed Arrangements, RISD, 20 June 1975; Response of the United States, 7 July 1975, *U.S. v. RISD.*

39. Letters to Taylor, folder Justice Department 1975 Pacesetter Information, RISD; Abrams and Webster statements, n. 35; and *RDN,* 11 July 1975, p. 1; 13 July 1975, pp. 1, 3.

40. Proceedings, Remarks of the Court [15 July 1975], quotation at 6; and Order, W. M. Taylor Jr., 16 July 1975, folder Current File, RISD. Akin interview, OH 790, 56.

41. *RDN,* 17 July 1975, p. 1; 18 July 1975, p. 1; 27 July 1975, p. 1; and 1 August 1975, p. 1; exhibit seven, Report to the Court, Henry D. Akin Jr., 1 August 1975, *U.S. v. RISD;* and Roberts interview, OH 716, 30-34.

42. *RDN,* 27 August 1975, p. 1. Griffin interview, OH 715, 25, quotations, in order, at 25, 24, 23, 23-24, 24.

43. For the daughters, see Robertson interview, OH 697, 25-26; and Akin interview, OH 790, 49-50. For the enthusiasm of grandparents, see Darden interview, OH 916, 29-30; and Lapetta Collier, interview by Wilson, 25 January 1991, OH 1036, 37-38. For PTA open-house quotations, see *RDN,* 20 August 1975, p. 1. For the supply store quotations, see Robertson interview, OH 817, 49. For Mrs. Robertson's volunteer work, see Robertson interview, OH 697, 23-24. For Mrs. Nance's volunteer work, see *The Link,* September 1974, 1: 1-9, FMNP; and Nance interview, OH 895, 37-39.

44. *RDN,* 16 September 1975, clipping, folder Pacesetter—Correspondence and Background Information, Public Information Office; and news release, 24 January 1976, folder Hamilton Park Elementary, Public Information Office, RISD. *RDN,* 7 October 1975, p. 1; 30 January 1977, quotations at p. 1; and 9 November 1986, pp. 1A, 8A. For the renovation, see *DMN,* 20 January 1992, p. 17A.

45. Williams interview, OH 871, quotations at 101, 102.

46. Roberts interview, OH 716, quotations at 26, 28, 28-29.

47. Griffin interview, OH 715, 13 (enrollment quotations); and 21 (teacher-limit quotation). For the prebirth enrollment, see Starks interview, OH 1005, 99. Cook interview, OH 695, 38.

48. For special-education classes, *DMN*, 9 May 1991, pp. 1A, 24A. No black principal or coprincipal was named by the end of 1991—see *DMN*, 20 January 1992, p. 17A. For blacks' concerns about the lack of African-American principals and administrators in the RISD generally, see Dixon interview, OH 868, 82-85; and Mitchell interview, OH 962, 99-100.

49. Patrick interview, OH 925, 13. For the several proposed pairing and clustering plans, see *RDN*, 11 July 1975, p. 1; and PTA petition and letter to Taylor, 28 June 1974, folder Richardson Ind. School District School System Summary Report, *U.S. v. RISD*.

50. The quotation is from a confidential source.

51. For previous suggestions, see "Minutes of Meeting Between Officials of H.E.W. and R.I.S.D. and Counsel, 16 January 1967," folder H.E.W.—1965-68, RISD; Betty X. Davis to Taylor, 29 July 1974 (quotation). Roberts did not know of the previous suggestions, Roberts interview, OH 716, 34-36, but he stated that many of the Pacesetter program's elements were in the minds of people in the RISD, 29-30.

Chapter 9: Another Transition and the Buyout

1. *DMN*, 24 May 1985, p. 25A.

2. Address counts are from the city directories of the named years. The count includes one for each building and one for each address within a building. The completion date and traffic counts are from the library of District 18 of the Texas Department of Transportation, Dallas.

3. The completion date and traffic counts are from the traffic count source in n. 2.

4. The population figures are in U.S. Department of Commerce, Bureau of the Census, *Dallas, Texas, by Census Tracts and Blocks: 1960, Dallas, Texas, four of eight; U.S. Census of Housing, 1960: City Blocks* 3: ser. HC (3) No. 377 (Washington: GPO, 1961); Geography Division, *Dallas-Fort Worth Area Map Sheet M-23, Sheet No. 8* [1970]; *Census of Housing: 1970 Block Statistics*, final report HC (3)-229, Dallas, Texas Urbanized Area (Washington: GPO, 1971), 62-63; *1980 Block Statistics: Characteristics of Population and Housing Units by Blocks, Dallas County, Texas:* filmed 3 June 1982, table 2, Tex.-86; Eighteenth Census, 1960: Census Tracts, map and 21; and *1980 Census of Population and Housing, Census Tracts: Dallas-Fort Worth, Tex. Standard Metropolitan Statistical Area*, sec. 1 (Washington: GPO, 1983), map and x, P-298-99.

5. Charles E. Smith to Robert S. Folsom, 27 June 1977, CESP. For the apartments, see Charles Smith interview, OH 793, quotations at 98, 99. For speeding, see Smith interview, OH 793, 86-87; and Smith to Roland [*sic*] Tucker, 29 June 1982, CESP. For opposition to the rezoning, see Smith to Dear Neighbors, 26 October 1976, CESP, and Smith interview, OH 793, 106. An office building was later built on the site, use for which the property was zoned. The apartments would have required a "backzone" or "downzone" for their construction.

6. Charles E. Smith to J. D. Hall, 7 June 1978, CESP.

7. Charles E. Smith to Editor, *DTH*, 23 January 1979; draft letter, n.d.; petition form; Smith to Earnest Haywood, and to Calvin Person, 12 March 1979, CESP. Quotations in Smith interview, OH 793, at 110, 112; see also 111.

8. Hamilton Park Civic League to the Homeowners of Hamilton Park, n.d., CESP. For the turnout, see Smith interview, OH 793, quotation at 111; and Nance interview, OH 895, 36, 56–57. For the purchase, see Starks interview, OH 1005, 59–60.

9. Charles E. Smith to Roland [sic] Tucker, et al., 18 October 1982; and to Executive Director, Texas Air Control Board, 29 October 1982; Bill Stewart to Smith, 12 January 1983; and copy, Stewart to Herbert J. Belknap, 12 January 1983, CESP. Smith interview, OH 793, 123–24. Hamilton Park Civic League, manuscript minutes of meetings, 15 March 1983–26 November 1987, meeting of 17 January 1984, minutes books in the possession of Le Verne Fields, copies in author's possession, hereafter cited as HPCL Minutes.

10. For odor, see Charles E. Smith to Jim Houlditch, 7 September 1984, CESP; and Smith interview, OH 793, second and third quotations at 125. For the helistop, see Smith interview, OH 793, 127–29, quotation, at 127; and HPCL Minutes, 20 January 1987.

11. Smith interview, OH 793, 76.

12. For Forest Lane, see Thelma L. Wells to Dallas Negro Chamber of Commerce, 4 January 1972; David E. Pickett to Richard Smith, 19 May 1976, copy, CESP; and Smith interview, OH 793, 79–80. For the Shepherd Road–Floyd Road problem, including the quotation, see Wells to Dallas Negro Chamber of Commerce, 4 January 1972; and Rolan G. Tucker to Smith, 29 August 1980, CESP. See also Smith interview, OH 793, 82–86.

13. On the park, see, for example, Charles E. Smith to Fretz Park Recreation Advisory Committee, 11 February 1977; J. R. Carmichael to Smith, 18 February 1977; and Smith to Roland [sic] Tucker, 29 January 1982, CESP; Smith interview, OH 793, 130–35; and Dallas City Council Records, Office of the City Secretary, hereafter cited as CR, approved 22 April 1987, No. 87-1266.

14. Thelma Wells to Mike Morgan Jr., 23 February 1972, CESP; and Wells interview, OH 903, 43.

15. First quotation in Smith to Tyrone D. Tyler, 28 September 1976, second in Smith to J. A. Gunn III, 21 March 1977, CESP; Smith interview, OH 793, 65–66 (third quotation at 66); Smith to Dave Andres, 9 February 1981 (fourth quotation), CESP; Smith interview, OH 793, 69–70, for trash barrels; Christian interview, OH 1033, 56–64; HPCL Minutes, 21 April 1987; and Eiland Collins, interview by Wilson, 18 January 1991, OH 970, 47–48, quotation at 48.

16. PCD.

17. Ibid.

18. Ibid. All occupational categories are expressed in percentages because of wide decadal and half-decadal variations in the number of gainfully employed household heads. The steady growth in the number of household heads reporting no occupation or reporting retirement, and the fluctuating numbers of houses listed as vacant or "no return," affected the number of household heads reporting gainful employment.

19. Ibid. Evidence of Spring Valley Park's beachhead status is revealed in the persistence in 1990 of but 18 pioneer household heads and an equal number of

second-occupant heads of household. Only 22 third-occupant heads of household and 11 fourth-occupant household heads remained. To put the situation another way, only 69 of 161 houses, or less than 43 percent, were lived in by people who were likely to have any emotional or intellectual investment in the historical legacy of Spring Valley Park. In contrast, 647 household heads in Hamilton Park were first, second, third, or fourth residents, or more than 87 percent of the total. Conversely, 23 head residents of Spring Valley, or more than 14 percent, were the tenth through fourteenth occupants of their houses. Only 3 Hamilton Park householders were the tenth occupants, a minuscule 0.4 percent. No house in Hamilton Park was home to more than 10 heads of household.

20. Ibid. The 1980 and 1985 percentages for categories not in the text are: semiskilled manual labor, 16.2 and 17.1; domestic and food service, 5.9 and 5.4; upper-level manual labor, 6.2 and 4.4; public-safety and other service, 1.3 and 1.8; lower-nonmanual, 13.5 and 10.8; and proprietary, 7.2 and 8.8.

21. Brewer interview, OH 894, 119, 131-32, 138-40; Smith interview, OH 829, 84-86, quotation at 84.

22. Christian interview, OH 1033, 83-84, 94; Wells interview, OH 903, 63-64.

23. Holmes interview, OH 921, 17.

24. Edmond interview, OH 918, 32; Bruton interview, OH 893, 23; Newhouse interview, OH 956, 30-31; Collier interview, OH 1036, 18-19; and Fields interview, OH 835, 37.

25. Patrick interview, OH 965, 13; and Christian interview, OH 1033, 48-49.

26. Newsletter, n.d. (quotations); Officers of the Hamilton Park Civic League, "Greetings," n.d.; and Smith to Members and Residents, 22 June 1975, CESP. For membership, Smith interview, OH 793, 49; and HPCL Minutes, 18 October 1983.

27. For automobiles, see Charles E. Smith to Harold Prince, 7 September 1976, CESP; and Smith interview, OH 793, 64, 65. Smith to Hugh Snodgress, 21 March 1977; and to W. H. Sinclair, 13 May 1977 (quotation), CESP. For the council member's reply, see Richard Smith to Charles Smith, 15 November 1977, CESP. The "until" quotation in Smith interview, OH 793, at 68.

28. Charles Smith interview, OH 793, quotations at 74, 73.

29. Ibid., first and last quotations at 70; and Watson interview, OH 825, 67.

30. Notice of neighborhood-watch meeting, 15 March 1983, CESP. HPCL Minutes, 14 May 1984; and 16 June 1986. Smith interview, OH 793, 93-95, quotation at 94.

31. For the rumors, see Starks interview, OH 1005, 49; Proctor interview, OH 981, 49; and Mitchell interview, OH 962, 142. For the TI program, see HPCL Minutes, 20 January 1987.

32. For the block party, see Sheila Allen interview, OH 1012, 62-66; and Freddie and Ola Lee Allen interview, OH 1020, 65-66. For Smith's interview with the real-estate agent, and quotations, including the quotation concluding this paragraph, see Smith interview, OH 793, 143-44. For the "insult" quotation, see HPCL Minutes, 21 January 1985. Johnson quotation in *DTH*, 4 February 1985, at p. 14A.

33. Legal Counsel Committee to Reuben M. Ginsberg, 11 October 1984,

Reuben M. Ginsberg Papers, in the possession of Mr. Ginsberg, hereafter cited as RMGP. For Smith's and the committee's actions, see Smith interview, OH 793, 144, 147–48; Dixon interview, OH 868, 57; Williams interview, OH 871, 121–22.

34. For the Home Owners Association, see HPCL Minutes, 17 November 1987; Dixon interview, OH 868, 58–60; and Smith interview, OH 793, quotation at 147.

35. Minutes of meeting of Hamilton Park Civic League Home Owners Association, 21 January 1985, hereafter cited as HPCL Minutes. The circular from which the quotations are taken is to the Hamilton Park Home Owners, 15 October 1984, CESP. The final quotation in the paragraph is from Smith interview, OH 793, 149.

36. HPCL Minutes, 19 February 1986.

37. *DTH*, 4 February 1986, p. 14A; and HPCL Minutes, 19 February 1986.

38. HPCL Minutes, 19 February 1986. For some potential problems involved in moving, see Robertson interview, OH 817, 74–78, and Dixon interview, OH 868, 64–65.

39. For the city policy, see *Dallas/Fort Worth Business Journal*, 10 February 1985: 28; and *DMN*, 23 May 1985, p. 25A. Proctor interview, OH 981, 50; Edmond interview, OH 918, 44; and Edley interview, OH 864, 23.

40. Copies of the letter, 26 February 1985, are in folder Hamilton Park Developers, RMGP.

41. Ibid., and Ginsberg to Mrs. Self and Charles Smith, 27 February 1985, folder Hamilton Park Developers, RMGP. First quotation in HPCL Minutes, 16 April 1985, second in Smith interview, OH 793, at 144–45.

42. At one time, Hamilton appeared to have made a minimum offer of $262,500, but that apparent offer later was dropped from the negotiations (see n. 43). Hamilton had moved from Dallas by the time the author attempted to discuss the Buyout with him by letter of 3 June 1992. For Ginsberg's activities, see his letter to Smith, 29 May 1985; the quotation is in letter to Hamilton, 29 April 1985. Both are in folder Hamilton Park 4/25/85 offer—Acceptances Hamilton Financial Group, Inc. offer, RMGP.

43. For Hamilton's statements, see *DTH*, 24 May 1985, p. 25A. See also *DTH*, 24 May 1985, pp. 1, 18. There are no minutes of this meeting in HPCL Minutes. For the increasing number of owners willing to sell, see Charles Smith to Hamilton Park Property Owners, 4 August 1986, CESP; HPCL Minutes, 28 January 1986; and HPCL Minutes, 26 November 1987. For the City of Dallas "hot spot" policy, see CR, No. 84-3646. Significant developments may be followed in *RDN*, 11 June 1985, p. 1 and 6 September 1985, p. 3A.

44. The purchaser was required to place 5 percent of the total sale price in escrow as earnest money at least ninety days in advance of the closing. See Earnest Money Contract, C 5762; see also Exhibit A, Occupancy Agreement and Option to Purchase, both in box 213, Ginsberg archives in storage, RMGP.

45. For an example of revisions, see the folder Hamilton Park—Acceptance of June 13, 1985, Letter of Intent of Hamilton Park Financial Group, RMGP. HPCL Minutes, 19 February 1985 (quotations); and 20 March 1985.

46. First quotation in Jackson interview, OH 862, at 103. For Smith's warning, see HPCL Minutes, 16 April 1985. Second quotation in Smith interview, OH 793,

at 150-51. Ona Smith interview, OH 1032, quotations on emotionalism and pressure at 80; houses quotation at 81.

47. "How To Seminars" announcement; Thelma Self Realtors, *Monthly Newsletter*, May 1985; *The Sign Post*, v. 6, n.d.; and ABCO Industries flyer, n.d., all in SGP. For contingent sale tie-ins, see Gee interview, OH 827, 97. For Mrs. Self's statement, see HPCL Minutes, 19 February 1985.

48. First quotation in Gee interview, OH 827, at 101; other quotations at 102.

49. Quotations in Nance interview, OH 895, at 50, 51; Smith interview, OH 826, 97; Starks interview, OH 1005, 50.

50. Stevenson interview, OH 875, 95, 96-98; Gee interview, OH 827, quotations at 102, 107; and Collier interview, OH 1036, 51, quotation at 50; and Allen interview, OH 1020, 63-69.

51. Gee interview, OH 827, 98; Mitchell interview, OH 962, 142-43.

52. Collier interview, OH 1036, 50; Gee interview, OH 827, the "And even" quotation at 96, the "it fizzled" quotation at 103-4; and Edley interview, OH 864, quotations at 25, 28. For the Hamilton Park Development Association, hereafter cited as HPDA, see minutes of HPDA meeting, 16 October 1985; HPDA agenda meeting, 12 November 1985, "HPDA: Articles of Agreement," and other materials in SGP.

53. Mildred Patrick interview, OH 965, 52-53; Smith interview, OH 1032, 81; and Gee interview, OH 827, 97. For the agent with the business cards, see *DTH*, 24 May 1985, p. 18. For the letter, see Larry Jagours to Dear Residents, n.d., SGP.

54. HPCL Minutes, 18 June 1985; Earnest Money Contract, C 5762, box 213, Ginsberg archives in storage, RMGP; W. E. Hamilton to Cleophus Gee, 15 January 1986, SGP; HPCL Minutes, 28 January 1986; 18 February 1986; and 18 March 1986.

55. For both sides of the revelation issue, see Mitchell interview, OH 962, 152-55; and Proctor interview, OH 981, 51.

56. Bonner interview, OH 924, 30. For TI, see Bruton interview, OH 893, 55. Among those who believed that Hamilton was representing no one but himself were A. W. Dupree Jr. and Laurice Stevenson. See Dupree interview, OH 842, 71-72, and Stevenson interview, OH 875, 95.

57. For quotation, see *Dallas/Fort Worth Business Journal*, 10 February 1986: 1. For skepticism about buying at $35 per foot, ibid.: 28. For speculation on the collapse of the Buyout, see two undated letters from Patrick Beeby to homeowners, SGP.

58. For an example of Ginsberg's responses, see HPCL Minutes, 16 July 1985. For the ovation, see HPCL Minutes, 18 March 1986.

59. Proctor interview, OH 981, 53-54; Turner interview, OH 977, 70. For decline, see Mildred Patrick interview, OH 965, 53. Bonner interview, OH 924, 26.

Chapter 10: A Mature Community and Its Meaning

1. C. J. Smith to Whom It May Concern, n.d., but 1980, CJSP. For endorsements, see IOC to Dear Voter, n.d., but 1984, CJSP. For the Hamilton Park vote, see *DMN*, 8 November 1984, p. 35A.

2. For the Strauss victory, see *DMN,* 19 April 1987, pp. 1A, 17A; and for Richards's, *DMN,* 8 November 1990, p. 26A.

3. Smith interview, OH 793, 40.

4. Smith to Tom Anderson, 30 September 1980, CESP.

5. For adding to the bond provision, 14 October 1981, and the council's accepting the low bid, 16 March 1983, see CR, No. 81-2978. See also *DTH,* 14 April 1983, p. 1C.

6. Sample petition, SGP. Nomination statement, ARCO Oil and Gas Company 1981 Outstanding Volunteer Awards Program, CESP. Johnson interview, OH 819, quotations at 62-63, 64. Smith interview, OH 793, quotations at 135, 137.

7. For Mrs. Gee quotation, see "News: Ground-Breaking Ceremony Held," SGP. See also *RDN,* 3 December 1984, p. 1A. For the steps in naming the center, see Charles Smith to Jack Robinson, 27 March 1984; Robinson to Smith, 19 April 1984; and Oscar McGaskey Jr. to Smith, 10 September 1984, CESP; and CR, Approval of No. 84-3411, 24 October 1984.

8. Charles Smith to Laura V. White, 16 November 1985, CESP; Charles Smith interview, OH 793, 53, 140-43; and *DMN,* 20 June 1987, p. 33A.

9. Collins interview, OH 970, 41-42; for league activities, OH 970, 17-24, 48-50. For the reception, see notice, CESP; Charles Smith interview, OH 793, 50-52; and reception program, 1 October 1988, FMNP.

10. For the Baptist church, see *The Link,* 27 August-2 September 1986, 1-2, FMNP. For the Church of Christ church, see Mildred Patrick interview, OH 965, 42-43.

11. General information on the Methodist church is from *Church History* and from Hatchett and Benson, *History of Hamilton Park United Methodist Church,* 18-28, quotation at 32. For the day-care center, see folder on day-care center. For membership, see Membership Roster, 20 June 1991. Another eleven members either had no address or were listed as having post office boxes. All of the above materials are in HPUMC. For the Helping Hand Committee, see Curtis Smith interview, OH 826, 62-64, 110-14.

12. See *1960 City Blocks,* 61, 99; *1970 Block Statistics,* 62-63, 114; *1960 Block Statistics,* 147-48, 298-99; and U.S. Department of Commerce, Bureau of the Census, *1990 Census of Population and Housing: Block Statistics* (Washington: 1992). The 1990 census for the West South Central Division (Arkansas, Louisiana, Oklahoma, and Texas) is stored on diskette CD 90-1.B-9. The 1970 census figures are for female-headed households and almost certainly overstate the number of single-parent households. The 1980 and 1990 figures omit the census tract containing the apartments in the northwest corner of Hamilton Park, which also eliminates the households on the west side of Rialto Drive. The relevant maps are, for Hamilton Park, P.W. 94-171 County Block Map (1990) Parent Sheet 11, and for Spring Valley Park, the same map, Parent Sheet 4.

13. PCD.

14. For the contingent offer, see Robinson interview, OH 817, 79-80. For Mrs. Self's request, see Turner interview, OH 977, 63-64.

15. See 1990 tax rolls, Dallas County Tax Assessor's Office.

16. Charles Smith to Herschel G. Brown and Dallas City Planning Commis-

sion, 31 October 1977, and other letters in CESP; and Charles Smith interview, OH 793, 106-9.

17. CR, No. 85-1109, Official Action of the Dallas City Council, 28 August 1985 and other documents; and also No. 86-3856, unadopted, 10 December 1986, for the size of the park land that was involved. See also Charles Smith interview, OH 793, 106-9.

18. For community problems, none of which could be linked to TI, see Mitchell interview, OH 962, 130-33; Mildred Patrick interview, OH 965, 48-49; and Nance interview, OH 845, 55. See Charles Smith interview, OH 793, for Floyd Road at 84-85, and for the office tower at 103-4. For the informal entrance and the fence, see Freddie and Ola Lee Allen interview, OH 1020, 57-59.

19. In order to protect the sources, sources for critical quotations are not cited here. For the rental situation, see *1960 City Blocks*, 61; *1970 Block Statistics*, 62-63; *1980 Block Statistics*, 298-99; and *1990 Block Statistics*.

20. For the sweeps, see Smith interview, OH 793, 74-75. See also first sentence, n. 19.

21. See first sentence, n. 19.

22. See first sentence, n. 19.

23. See first sentence, n. 19.

24. First, second, and fourth quotations in *DMN*, 12 November 1989, p. 42A; Collins interview, OH 970, 25-27, 30-31, quotations at 25, 31.

25. HPCL Minutes, 15 April 1986; and 15 July 1986. The 1964 voting-age population is determined by computing the population over age eighteen from the 1970 census percentages for each block, then adjusting for the fact that only persons twenty-one years or older could vote in 1964. The computed over-eighteen population is used for the 1972 vote. See *1970 Block Statistics*, 62-63. The 1988 over-eighteen population is taken from the 1990 census, *1990 Block Statistics*. For the vote totals, see *DMN*, 4 November 1964, p. 18; 9 November 1972, p. 42A, and 9 November 1988, p. 3K.

26. See first sentence, n. 19. *1960 City Blocks*, 61; *1970 Block Statistics*, 62-63; and *1990 Block Statistics*.

27. See first sentence, n. 19.

28. *HPHSCSR*, 67, 69, quotation at 74. For the first two quotations, see first sentence, n. 19.

29. Smith interview, OH 1032, 85-86.

30. Among many analyses and biographies of Saul Alinsky and the community-organization revolution are Harry C. Boyte, *Community Is Possible: Repairing America's Roots* (New York: Harper & Row, 1984); P. David Finks, *The Radical Vision of Saul Alinsky* (New York: Paulist Press, 1984); and Robert A. Slayton, *Back of the Yards: The Making of a Local Democracy* (Chicago: University of Chicago Press, 1986).

31. Robert Fisher, *Let the People Decide: Neighborhood Organizing in America* (Boston: Twayne Publishers, 1984), quotation at 73. For Marxist interpretations, see Joseph M. Kling and Prudence S. Posner, eds., *Dilemmas of Activism: Class, Community, and the Politics of Local Mobilization* (Philadelphia: Temple University Press, 1990).

32. Darden interview, OH 916, 45.

33. Bruton interview, OH 893, 77; Price interview, OH 983, 92.

34. For the defended neighborhood, see Suttles, *Social Construction of Communities,* 21-43. Two interviewees who lived in Hamilton Park as children have returned there—see Sheila Allen interview, OH 1012, 73; see also Donald Payton interview, OH 865, which was held in part in a house that Payton was rehabilitating. Many houses and lots, however, appear to offer little opportunity for restorations that both accommodate later ideas of adequate living space, bedrooms, and bathrooms and at the same time retain the appearance of the original structure.

35. Hayman interview, OH 807, 35-36; Collier interview, OH 1036, 62.

36. For the community of limited liability, see Suttles, *Social Construction of Communities,* 44-81.

37. Miller, *Suburb,* 30-31.

38. Dupree interview, OH 842, 54-55; Price interview, OH 963, 50; Johnson interview, OH 819, 73-74; Smith interview, OH 1032, 42; Turner interview, OH 977, 59-60.

INDEX

Adams, Nathan, 43
Adoue, James B., 59
African-American middle class. *See* black middle class
Akin, Henry D., 142; and Pacesetter program, 154–57; and RISD legal matters, 146–47, 148, 152; and *Swann* decision, 151
Akin, Mary, 157
Alinsky, Saul, 196–97
Allen, Freddie, 56; and Buyout, 182; employment experience of, 88
Allen, Ola Lee, 123, 127, 150
Allen, Sheila R., 78, 122, 143, 149–50
American Association of Retired Persons (AARP), 188, 199
American Friends Service Committee (AFSC), 84
Amigos, 116
Anderson Bonner School, 93, 116, 119–20
Anderson family, 56
Arcadia Park, 21
Arlington Heights, 35
Arlington Park, 18, 22, 29, 67
Associated Construction, Inc., 51, 52, 58, 59, 194
Aston, James, 26–27, 33, 45
Aston-Mitchell report, 34–37
Atlanta, Georgia, 13, 55

B. F. Darrell Elementary School, 57
Bartholomew, Harland, 11–12
Bel Aire Estates, 19–20, 35
Belafonte, Harry, 57
Bellafonte Drive, 57, 77, 100
Bender, Thomas, and community, 8
Berkner High School, 126

Berthoff, Rowland, and community, 8
Bishop College, 61, 62, 63, 104
black housing alliance, 12–14
black middle class, 3–4, 12
black subdivisions, 2, 12–13; attempts for in Dallas, 16–24
Bonner, Richard, 57; and Buyout, 183, 184–85; and schools, 120–21, 126
Bonner family, 56
Booker T. Washington High School, 57, 72, 119
Booty, Lee J., 116
Braniff Airlines, 88, 89
Brewer, George, 72, 99; and Boy Scouts, 97; and remembrances of Hamilton Park, 77, 79–80; and school deficiencies, 136
Brewster, Charlotte, 126
Brewster, Leroy, 126
Broussard, Albert S., 7
Brown decisions, 65, 91, 119
Brownell, Herbert, 111
Bruton, Cicero: and Bobcat games, 125; budgeting for, 75; and buses, 81; and covenant, 104; reasons for buying in Hamilton Park, 73, 198
Bryan, Texas, 121
Buckner, Hal F., 15
Buckner Orphans Home, 15
Bunche, Ralph, 57
Bunche Drive, 56, 57, 102, 179, 190
Bunkley, C. B., Jr., 44, 54, 55
Bush, George, 186
Bush-Dukakis contest, 194
Buyout, 180; background of, 162–63, 174; and block party, 174; collapse of, 183–84; decline in upkeep as reason for, 179–80;

Buyout (*continued*)
and Hamilton Park Civic League Home Owners Association, 175; and Hamilton Park Development Association, 182; homeowners' response to, 177; and land price, 176–78, 183; reverberations of, 189–90; TI interest in, 174

Cabell Dairy, 52
Cadillac Fairview, 177
CALL, 116; infiltrated by Richardson police informants, 145; petition of, to RISD board, 145–47; school committee activities of, 145–47; visit of, to Hamilton Park grade school, 131, 132
Campanella, Roy, 57
Campanella Drive, 57, 79, 101, 191
Carpenter, John W., 32, 43
Carter, Jimmy, 186
Cedar Crest (Dallas neighborhood), 17
Cedar Crest–Skyline Improvement League, 17
Cheyenne, Wyoming, 82
Chicago School (of sociologists), and community, 9
Chisum, John O., 46–47, 75
Christian, Myra: and credit screening, 68; and flooding of Schroeder Road, 101; and move from Hamilton Park, 170; occupations of, 83
Christian Action Layman's League. *See* CALL
Church of Jesus Christ of Latter Day Saints, 90
Churchill Way, 190
Civic League, 92–93, 163–64; alley paving, 99; and apartments, 163; and Buyout, 174–75; and community standards, 106, 172, 194; and concrete batching plant, 61, 103; and continuing community involvement, 188–89; and Crime Watch program, 173; efforts of, to maintain community, 172–73; and IOC, 102; lawn-of-the-week contest, 100; and lumber yard, 163–65; RISD school bus transportation, 93–94; and shopping center, 167–68; and street lighting, 99–100; and TI, 165–66; and violations of covenants, 103–4, 105–6; and Willie B. Johnson Recreation Center, 187–88; and Willowdell Park, 97–98, 187–88; and youth programs, 99

civil rights, national legislation, 138–39
Cockrell Hill, 21, 22
Coit Road, 93, 116; site, 41–42
Cole, Albert, 51
Collier, Lapetta, and U. J., and Buyout, 181–82
Collins, Carr P., 46, 50–52; and Associated Construction, Inc., 51; and FHA guarantees, 51
Collins, Eiland, 168, 194
Collins Radio, 131
Colonial Baptist Church, 26
community, definition of, 4–9
Concord Missionary Baptist Church, 116
concrete batching plant, 61, 103
Connally, John, 108–9
Cook, Robert, 159; and high school closing, 144; and school deficiencies, 130, 136
Corsicana, Texas, 72, 121
Cose, Ellis, 4
Cottonwood Creek, 56; flooding of, 97, 100–101, 188
credit screening, 68; and Doris and Lincoln Robertson, 69; and Laurice Stevenson, 68; and Sadye and Cleophus Gee, 68; and Velma and Norman Jackson, 69; and Willie B. Johnson, 68–69
Critchlow, Matthew, 58, 69
Crossman, Jerome, 38–39, 41, 43, 63–66; analysis of 1951 bombings, 42; and decline of DCIA, 61, 63–66; and formal opening of Hamilton Park, 59; and Hamilton Park Civic League, 93–94; as housing committee president, 43, 44–45; and Love Field expansion, 46–47; and RISD, 119–20; and VA and FHA loan offices, 59–60
Crossman Plan, 38

Dallas: and Bel Aire Estates, 19–20; black housing in, 10, 104–5; business elite, 10; Highland Park area, 74; population increase of, 10, 12, 85, 162–63; Preston Hollow area, 75; residential bombings in, 25–26, 42; —Crossman analysis of, 42; —effect of, on housing subcommittee, 42–44; racial demonstrations in, 15, 17, 25–26; residential succession in, 11, 26, 36–37; State-Thomas area, 74; University Park area, 75

Index

Dallas Black Chamber of Commerce, 164. *See also* DNCC
Dallas Chamber of Commerce, 10, 33
Dallas Citizens' Council (DCC), 10, 33; and Aston-Mitchell report, 34-37; and bus tour, 34; five-man committee of, 33-34
Dallas Citizens' Interracial Association. *See* DCIA
Dallas City Council, 21, 24, 31
Dallas Cowboys, 127
Dallas Express, 28
Dallas Home Builders Association (DHBA), 14, 43
Dallas Housing Authority (DHA), 11
Dallas Independent School District. *See* DISD
Dallas Interracial Committee, 37-38; and Coit Road site, 41-42; housing subcommittee of, 41; as recommendation of Aston-Mitchell report, 37
Dallas Morning News, 13, 32, 59, 147
Dallas Negro Chamber of Commerce. *See* DNCC
Dallas Star Post, 58
Dallas Transit Company, 102
Dandridge, Dorothy, 57
Dandridge Drive, 57
Darden, Barbara, 78; and changes in Hamilton Park, 197; occupation of, 82
Darden, Barbara, and Robert C., 73-74
Davis, Henry L., III, 25, 195; and alley paving, 99; and Bel Aire Estates, 20; and Civic League, 94; and Hamilton Park Methodist Church, 115; and U.S. Army Reserve, 85-86; and Willowdell Park restrooms, 101-2
Davis, Mable, and Willowdell Park restrooms, 101-2
Davis, Sammy, Jr., 82
DCIA, 43; decline of, 61-62; and Hamilton Park School, 119; and land-use disputes, 63-65; and Roland Pelt, 24-25, 28-29; and site selection, 44-48; and utilities extensions, 49
Declining Significance of Race (William J. Wilson), 3
Department of Education, U.S., 157
Department of Justice. *See* DOJ
DHA: applications to, for public housing units, 35; Roseland Homes, 11
Diamond Hill, 21-24, 35; approval of, by Dallas City Plan Commission, 23; and Aston-Mitchell Report, 35, 36; opposition to, 12-24; support for, 21-22, 23
Dicker, Edward T., 14-15, 16-17
Different Drum, The: Community Making and Peace (M. Scott Peck), 6
DISD, 93
"Dixiecrat" party, 110
Dixon, Frank, 56, 86, 118
Dixon, Pauline, 73, 76, 77, 78, 82, 86, 118; and Civic League, 95-96, 175
DNCC, 13, 57; and Hamilton Park street names, 57; support of, for Crossman Plan, 42. *See also* Dallas Black Chamber of Commerce
Dobie School, 152
Doggett, Lloyd, 186
DOJ, and Hamilton Park School desegregation suit, 151-52
Dr. Pepper Bottling Company, 50
dual labor market, 70, 82, 85
Dupree, A. W., 73, 74, 106; social life of, 114; World War II experience of, 85

East Dallas Chamber of Commerce, 15-16
Ebony, 57
Ebony Drive, 57, 106
Edley, Albertus, 73; and Arlington Park, 67, 70; and Bobcat games, 125; and Buyout, 177, 182
Edmond, William, 85, 116; and Buyout, 177; and covenant violators, 105; and Red Ball Express, 85
Eisenhower, Dwight D., and his administration, 110, 111
Elm Thicket (North Park), 29, 46, 47, 68
Ervine, Freddie: and Hamilton Park construction, 74; and Hamilton Park School, 123; housing areas considered, 68, 70; occupations of, 75, 82
Estell, Ernest C., 54, 55

Fair Park (Redman Circle), 74
Federal Aviation Administration (FAA), 165
Federal Housing Administration (FHA), 13, 16, 19
Ferraro, Geraldine, 186
Fidelity Union Life Insurance Company, 46, 50, 51

Fields, Le Verne, 68, 72; as Civic League secretary, 175
Fields, Le Verne, and Willis, 74
Fields family, 56, 57, 190
First Baptist Church of Richardson, 188
First National Bank, 50
Fisher, Robert, 197
Florence, Fred, 1, 48, 54, 59
Floyd Road, 108
Foley, Raymond M., 41
Folsom Investments, 177
Ford, Charles C., 44
Forest Lane, 44, 56, 93, 166, 176, 181, 187
Forest Park, Ohio, 7
Foster, Rev. J. L., 118

Gaines, Claudia, 93
Galva Drive, 75, 78, 100
Garnett, Mary, 82; and Hamilton Park School, 121, 122-23, 126, 131, 132-33
Garrison, B. C., 26
Garza-Little Elm (Lake Lewisville), 29
Gee, Cleophus, and Sadye, qualifying for Hamilton Park, 68, 71-72
Gee, Sadye, 56, 71, 76, 82, 187; and Buyout, 180-81, 182; and school deficiencies, 131; and shopping, 81
Gemini Twin Theater, 166
Ginsberg, Reuben M., attorney, 174, 176-78, 183-84
Goss, Emmanuel V.: and desegregation of school, 144, 145; Hamilton Park High School principal, 131, 132-34
Gramm, Phil, 186
Grapevine (Lake), 29
Green decision, by Supreme Court, 147
Greensboro, North Carolina, 110
Griffin, James O., Hamilton Park School principal, 122, 131, 136, 158-59
Gurwin, Steven H., DOJ lead attorney, 151-52, 155

Hallum, Mary E., 57
Hallum Street, 57, 101, 191
Hamilton, Dr. Richard T., 57
Hamilton, William E., 178-79, 183
Hamilton Financial Group. *See* Hamilton, William E.
Hamilton Park, 197-99; alternate routes to, 101; apartments in, 66; Band Parents, 93, 129, 148; bus service to, 80-81; Buyout (*see* Buyout); and community history, 195, 198-99; covenant violations in, 64, 103-4, 172-73; Dad's Club, 93, 128-29, 172-73; demographic changes in, 162-63, 168-70, 189-92, 194-95; description of, 55, 98-102; desirability of, to pioneers, 70-74; development plans for, 190; drug problem in, 191, 194; economic comparison with Spring Valley Park, 87-88; educational level in, 127-28; expansion of, 63; and family values, 71-73, 98; financing for, 60; formal opening of, 54-55, 59; Gold Cup Garden Club, 93, 113; Hamilton Park Civic League (*see* Civic League); Hamilton Park Residents Relocation Program, 180; Hamiltonettes, 93, 114; Hamiltonians, 93, 113-14; Hamonites, 93, 114; house prices in, 67; improvement of houses in, 171; income levels in, 67, 134; interest in, 57-58; and lumber yard, 163-64; marriage within community, 127; payment for, 75-76; pioneers: —background of, 71-73, 74-75; —former areas of, 74-75; —occupations of, 75-76, 87, 127-28; —persistence of, 196; property values in, 190; publicity for, 54, 60; reasons for leaving, 104-5, 169, 170-71; remoteness of, 76, 79, 81; safety in, 191-93; sales of houses in, 58-60; scouting in, 96-97, 124; as second ghetto, 1; shift to community control, 60-65, 103; shopping in, 81, 167-68; as showcase, 78-79; site selection of, 44-45; —Hexter, 45; —Majors, 45; streets of, 57; and TI, 190-91; utilities extensions in, 49-50; voting record of, 110-12, 186, 194; yard planting and maintenance in, 77, 100, 191; YMCA in, 96
Hamilton Park Apartments, 102, 163
Hamilton Park Church of Christ, 92, 114, 116, 188
Hamilton Park First Baptist Church, 92, 114, 118, 188
Hamilton Park (United) Methodist Church, 114; Altar and Flower Guild of, 115-16; day care center, 118; expansion of, 190; Harambee House, 189; Helping Hand Committee, 189; Methodist Men, 115-16; as mission church, 115
Hamilton Park School, 60-61, 118, 121; at-

Index

tendance zone of, 140, 141, 144; Bobcats, 125; closing of high school, and PTA, 141, 142–43; and clustering and pairing, 154; Cub Scouts in, 124; desegregation suit, 140–41; discipline in, 124, 131; enrollment rise in, 129; expectations for children in, 122–23; extracurricular activities in, 124; facilities and expansion of, 129; junior high closing, 149; Junior Red Cross in, 124; occupations of graduates of, 127; parent commitment to education, 123; parent dissatisfaction with, 130; parent involvement in, 133, 134–35; Parent-Teachers Association (PTA), 93, 128–29, 153; and sports, 125; staff of, 121; and symbiosis with community, 129–30; transportation to, 93; vandalism and other behavior in, 141–42

Harris, Esther Lee, 186
Hawkins, Texas, 72
Hayman, Thomas, 50–51, 55, 58, 60, 198
Health, Education, and Welfare, Department of. *See* HEW
Hendry & Associates, 180
HEW: "HEW Guidelines" (1965), 139–43; and 1970 desegregation plan, 147–48
Hexter, Louis J., 45
High Point Circle, 74
Highland Hills subdivision, 62
Highland Park Methodist Church, 54; as sponsor of mission church, 115
Hill, H. Leslie, 43, 44
Hill, J. Hub, 21
Hirsch, Arnold R., 1–2
Hoblitzelle, Karl, 43, 48–49, 62
Hoblitzelle Drive, 77
Hoblitzelle Foundation: early housing plans, 48; land-use disputes, 63–64; loan to DCIA, 48–49; Willowdell Park restroom, 101–2
Holmes, Zan W., 78, 79, 98–99, 115, 171; and community involvement, 95–96; and Crusaders, 96; and Hamilton Park schools, 133–34; and IOC, 107; and Methodist Church, 115
hooks, bell, 4
Hoskins, David, 52
Hot Springs, Arkansas, 96
Houston & Texas Central Railway, 56, 63
Hudson, Samuel W., Jr., 37, 43

Huey and Philip, 52
Hughes, Sara T., 48

Inge, Charles, 63
Inge-Hayman Construction Company, 50
Interstate 635 (Lyndon Baines Johnson Freeway), 150; addresses on, 162; traffic counts on, 162
Interstate Theaters, 48
IOC, 61, 92, 107–8; candidate endorsement list, 108–9, 110, 111; and candidate forums, 108–9; and Democratic Party, 110–11, 186; functions of, 107, 112; and new precinct, 102; recommendation of, for integration of Hamilton Park School, 144–45; and TI, 107–8; and voter registration, 107
Italy Colored School, 72
Iwo Jima, 85

Jackson, Velma: childhood of, 72–73; occupations of, 83; and school discipline, 123
Jackson, Velma, and Norman, 69, 77, 80
Johnson, Bailey, 15, 16
Johnson, Lyndon B., and civil rights, 110
Johnson, Willie B.: and community involvement, 188–89, 199; and licensed vocational nursing, 82; and Parkland Hospital, 82–83; and payment for home, 75; recreation center (*see* Willie B. Johnson Recreation Center); and South Dallas, 68, 70; and youth programs, 95
Jones, Felix L., principal of Hamilton Park School, 129, 131
Juneteenth celebration, 188

Kennedy, John F., 109, 110
Keys, Alan L., 3
King, Martin Luther, Jr., 110
Korean conflict, 89

Lake Highlands High School, 127
Landrum, Lynn, *Dallas Morning News* columnist, 13–14; on Dallas Interracial Committee housing subcommittee, 41; 1954 support of black housing, 62–63; response of, to Chisum's criticisms, 47
Lee, Umphrey, 48
Lincoln Property Company, 177
Lively, Tom, 17, 18

Lively-Rupley project, 17
Lockhart, Carl "Spider," 126
Lodi, Texas, 121
Loop 12 (Northwest Highway), 76
Loud, Rev. Ira B., 115
Love Field, 12, 47, 63, 75
Lowry, Glenn C., 4

Magnolia Building (downtown Dallas), 76
Majors, B. "Hick," 41, 45
Majors site, 41, 45–46
Malakoff, Texas, 121
Mandelbaum, Seymour J., and community, 5–6
Marcus, Stanley, 43
Martin, Joseph B., and Bel Aire Estates, 19–20
Mattox, Jim, 109
McCarley, Ben, 145
McShann Road, 62, 67
Memphis, Tennessee, 13, 55
Mercantile National Bank, 50
Mesquite, Texas, 15–16; Chamber of Commerce, 15; Lions Club, 15; Negro School, 16; Women's Club, 15
Miami, Florida, 55
Mill Creek (Dallas neighborhood), 34
Miller, Henry S., 42
Miller, W. L. (councilman), 55
Miller, Zane L., and community, 7
Mitchell, Irene, 126
Mitchell, Irene, and Marion, 67, 127, 182
Mitchell, John E., Jr., 42, 46
Mitchell, Marion, 24, 72; employment experience of, 88–89
Moeser, John V., 7
Mondale, Walter, 186
Monterrey, Mexico, 96
Montgomery, Alabama, 65
Moore, Rev. John G., 26–28, 41

Nance, Easter, and Freddie, 77, 82, 127
Nance, Freddie, 73; and Buyout, 181; and early Hamilton Park experience, 78
National Association for the Advancement of Colored People (NAACP), 116, 199
New Deal, 110
New Orleans, Louisiana, 19
New York Giants, 127
Newhouse, Edward, 52, 117

Newhouse, Mary, 117, 123
Nixon-McGovern campaign, 194
Norrell, M. J., 37, 43, 44
North Central Expressway, 76, 93; address on, 162; traffic counts on, 162
North Park. *See* Elm Thicket
North Texas State University, 125, 126
Northwood Estates, 170

Oak Cliff, 23, 104–5
Oberlin College, 57
Oberlin Drive, 56, 57, 78, 99
Oklahoma City, Oklahoma, 55
Olin, Levi, 52
Orlando, Florida, as model for Crossman Plan, 39–40
Owens, George, 23–24

Pacesetter, Hamilton Park School program, 135, 154–57, 160
Parkland Hospital, 83
Patrick, Mildred, 123
Patrick, Theresa, 120, 122, 127, 143
Payton, Donald, 77, 78, 120, 122, 127
Peachtree Road (Dallas area), 15
Pearce, Joseph Jones, 93, 124, 156
Peck, M. Scott, 6
Pelt, Roland, 24–25, 28
Pelt Plan, 28–32
Perot, H. Ross, 177
Philips Petroleum, 90
Pinkston, Dr. L. G., 59
Pizza Hut, 90
Plessy v. Ferguson decision, 119
Prairie View Agricultural and Mechanical College, 20–21, 126
Price, Dolores, 123
Price, Dolores, and Robert E., 123–24, 198
Proctor, Pearline, and Buyout, 177
public housing, 11
Public Works Administration, 11

Radburn, New Jersey, 12
Reagan, Ronald, 186
Red Ball Express, 84–85
Republic National Bank, 50
Republic National Life, 51
Rettig, Mrs. Wilhelmina, 97

Index

Rheingold, Howard, 7
Rice, John W., 42, 51–52; and Civic League, 93, 94; and DHBA, 14; and housing statistics, 13–14; and Pelt Plan, 30–31
Richardson (Dallas suburb), 118
Richardson Daily News, 156
Richardson Independent School District. *See* RISD
Richardson Junior High School, 143, 149–50
Richardson Police Department, 145, 150
Richmond, Virginia, 40–41
RISD, 135–36; and Hamilton Park High School, 93–94, 118–19, 140, 141; and Hamilton Park High School desegregation, 143–44; and Hamilton Park Junior High School desegregation, 138, 141; and Hamilton Park School inadequacies, 144; and "HEW Guidelines," 139, 140; initiatives of, 119–20; and Pacesetter enrichment program, 156–57; and turn away from segregation, 139–40, 153
Roberts, John, 147, 151, 158
Robertson, Doris, 81, 117; and budgeting, 75–76; and flooding on Schroeder Road, 100–101; and Gold Cup Garden Club, 113; occupations of, 83–84; and PTA petition, 153
Robertson, Doris, and Lincoln, 69; reasons for buying in Hamilton Park, 73–74
Robertson, Wendy, 157
Rohloff, Vincent, 61, 103
Roseland Homes, 11, 73, 74
Rosenblum, Douglas, 40–41
Rupley, Ira L., 17–18
Ryan Consolidated Petroleum Corporation, 38

St. John Baptist Church, 55
St. Mark's United Methodist Church (Lockhart, Texas), 170
St. Paul Hospital, 86–87
St. Paul Methodist Church, 115
Salt Lake City, Utah, 90
Schroeder Road, 56, 100–101; flooding problems, 100–101; and traffic congestion, 166, 190
Scyene Road (Dallas area), 15
second migration, 1–2
segregated education, 120–22

Self, Melroe, and Thelma, 105
Self, Thelma, and Buyout, 176, 180, 189
7-Eleven, 90, 179
Shelley v. Kraemer, 27
Shelton, Robert, 25–26
Shepherd, R. E., FHA Regional Director, 16–19, 35; and Diamond Hill, 21, 23
Shepherd Road, 166
Shivers, Alan, 110
Silver, Christopher, 7
Simpson, Dorothy, 76–77, 82
Simpson, J. B., 72, 73, 81; and Bobcats, 125; and Red Ball Express, 83–84; and yard work, 76–77
Smith, A. Maceo: and Aston-Mitchell report, 34; and black housing, 13, 21; and Crossman Plan, 39, 41, 42; and Prairie View conference, 21
Smith, Charles E.: and apartments, 163; and Buyout, 174, 179–80; and Civic League clearinghouse function, 172–73; and distance of Hamilton Park from town, 76, 127, 167, 194; and early Buyout rumors, 174; and Elm Thicket, 68; and Hamilton Park School instruction, 130–31; and lumber yard, 163–65; occupations of, 75–88; and payment for home, 75; and shopping center, 167–68
Smith, Curtis J., 71, 73, 76, 78; and Bel Aire Estates, 20; and Braniff Airlines, 89; and Buyout, 181; and Hamilton Park School, 145; as IOC president, 109–10; and RISD, 145; and TI hiring, 108
Smith, Jessie, 79
Smith, Kelsey, 71
Smith, Ona, 199
Smith, Ona, and Roscoe, and Buyout, 180
Smith, Pearline, 83
Smith, Robert C., 4
Smith, Willie F., 79, 99, 116, 127; and covenant violations, 103–4; and Korean conflict, 89; and Lawyer's Title Insurance Company, 89–90
South Dallas, 12, 32; and bus tour, 34; opposition to black housing in, 25–26; property owners association of, 26; Regular Fellows in, 113; and residential bombings in, 25–26, 30–31
Southern Pacific (railroad), 101

Southern Terrace Apartments, 71
Southland Corporation, 90, 179
Southwestern Life Insurance Company, 51
Spring Valley Park: demographic changes in, 168, 192, 189; 1990 property values in, 190; occupations in, 87-88
Spring Valley School, 152
Starks, Vivian T., 71, 82; and Buyout, 181-83; and Hamilton Park School, 121, 122-23, 132-33; and USO, 82
State Fair of Texas, 33, 80, 188
Steak & Ale, 90
Steel, Dr. Marshall T., 54, 115
Steele, Shelby, 4
Stevenson, Laurice, 67, 70, 76; and Buyout, 181; and maintenance of school building, 131-32; and qualifying for Hamilton Park, 68
Stevenson, Margaret, 180
Strauss, Annette, mayor of Dallas, 165
Stuart, John J., 18-19
Stults Road School, 148, 154
Subers family, 56
Swann decision, by Supreme Court (1971), 151

Taylor, Quintard, 7
Taylor, William M., and RISD desegregation case, 147-48, 152-53, 155
Texas Air Control Board, 165
Texas & Pacific Railroad, 5
Texas Instruments (TI): and Buyout, 174; and Hamilton Park concerns, 107-8, 165-66, 191
Texas League, 52
Texas Western Lumber Company, 163-64
Thornton, Robert L., 1, 50, 59
TI. *See* Texas Instruments
Tobian, Louis, 43
Tobian Street, 57
Towns, Jerry W., 57
Towns Street, 56, 57
Trammel Crow Company, 177
Trinity River, 12, 18
Trinity Valley, 67

Truman, Harry S., 110
Turner, Lovell, 26
Turner, Ocie, 56, 130; and Buyout, 184; and U.S. Marine Corps, 85
Tuskegee Army Air Field, 85

United Service Organization (USO), 82
upper White Rock, 56, 140, 162

Valley, Eloise, 115
Vantage Companies, 177
Vickery (Dallas area), 56
Virtual Community: Homesteading on the Electronic Frontier (Howard Rheingold), 7

Wall Street Journal, 183
Walls, Everson, 126-27
Washington Shores (Orlando, Florida), 11, 39-40
Watson, Ruby: and Hamilton Park School, 130; and housing for blacks, 68; and loudspeaker on Galva Drive, 173; and remoteness of Hamilton Park, 76
Watson, Streetman, 78, 143
Wells, George, and Thelma, 105
Wells, Thelma, 132, 166, 167, 170
West Dallas, 12, 29, 68
Wheatley subdivision (South Dallas), 68
White Rock Creek, 12
White Rock Lake, 19
Wiese, Andrew, 69-70
Williams, Joseph, M.D., 68, 74, 76, 78; comments of, on Pacesetter, 157-58; and St. Paul Hospital, 86; and school deficiencies, 130-31
Willie B. Johnson Recreation Center, 186-88
Willowdell Drive, 56
Willowdell Park, 61-62; improvements to, 97-98, 186-88; restroom in, 102
Wilson, William J., 3
Wooten, Ben H., 50, 54

Your Dallas of Tomorrow, 11

Zion Hill Baptist Church, 118

ABOUT THE AUTHOR

William H. Wilson was born in 1935 in St. Joseph, Missouri, and was raised there. After receiving his B.J., M.A., and Ph.D. from the University of Missouri, he taught at the University of South Dakota and the University of Alaska before joining the faculty of the University of North Texas in 1968. It was there, in 1990, that he became a Regents' Professor of History. He is the author of *The City Beautiful Movement in Kansas City* (1964), *Coming of Age: Urban America, 1915-1945* (1974), and *Railroad in the Clouds: The Alaska Railroad in the Age of Steam, 1914-1945* (1977). His *The City Beautiful Movement* (1989) received the Lewis Mumford Prize of the Society for American City and Regional Planning History for the best book on American planning history and the Outstanding Book of the Year award in the category of architecture and urban planning from the Association of American Publishers. Wilson is also coauthor of *Carl F. Gould: A Life in Architecture and the Arts* (1995).

Library of Congress Cataloging-in-Publication Data

Wilson, William H. (William Henry), 1935–

Hamilton Park : a planned Black community in Dallas / William H. Wilson. — 1st ed.

p. cm. — (Creating the North American landscape)

Includes bibliographical references and index.

ISBN 0-8018-5766-X (alk. paper)

1. Hamilton Park (Dallas, Tex.)—History. 2. Dallas (Tex.)—History. 3. Afro-Americans—Texas—Dallas—History—20th century. 4. Afro-Americans—Texas—Dallas—Social conditions. I. Title. II. Series.

F394.D216H369 1998

976.4'2812—dc21   97-33379 CIP

WHITMAN COLLEGE LIBRARY

WITHDRAWN